# Home
# Soups,
# Stews
## & more

TASTE OF HOME BOOKS ● RDA ENTHUSIAST BRANDS, LLC ● MILWAUKEE, WI

© 2021 RDA Enthusiast Brands, LLC.
1610 N. 2nd St., Suite 102, Milwaukee, WI 53212-3906
All rights reserved. Taste of Home is a registered trademark of
RDA Enthusiast Brands, LLC.

Visit us at **tasteofhome.com** for other Taste of Home
books and products.

**International Standard Book Number:**
**Retail:** 978-1-61765-954-6
**DTC:** 978-1-62145-701-5
**Component Number:**115800533S.00.75
**LOCC:** 2020940119

**Executive Editor:** Mark Hagen
**Senior Art Director:** Raeann Thompson
**Editor:** Hazel Wheaton
**Assistant Art Director:** Courtney Lovetere
**Designer:** Jazmin Delgado
**Deputy Editor, Copy Desk:** Dulcie Shoener
**Copy Editor:** Sara Strauss

**Cover:**
**Photographer:** Dan Roberts
**Set Stylist:** Stacey Genaw
**Food Stylist:** Josh Rink

**Pictured on front cover:**
Spinach & Tortellini Soup, p. 169; Tex-Mex Chili, p. 85;
Broccoli Beer Cheese Soup, p. 67

**Pictured on spine:**
Autumn Pumpkin Chili, p. 98

**Pictured on back cover:**
Creamy Chicken Gnocchi Soup, p. 207; Maryland-Style Crab
Soup, p. 145; Apple Chicken Stew, p. 190; Arborio Rice & White Bean
Soup, p. 42; English Pub Split Pea Soup, p. 117; Steak & Beer Chili, p. 95

**Pictured on title page:**
Slow-Cooker Quinoa Chili, p. 97

INSTANT POT is a trademark of Double Insight Inc. This publication
has not been authorized, sponsored or otherwise approved by
Double Insight Inc.

Printed in China
3 5 7 9 10 8 6 4

# Table of Contents

I t's time to indulge in the comfort of a warm bowl of soup. Nothing brightens cloudy days, delivers goodness and warms hearts quicker than a savory broth featuring herbs, vegetables, beans or pasta.

The editors of *Taste of Home* searched through thousands of recipes and selected their favorite soups for *Soups, Stews & More*, a must-have cookbook that today's family cooks have been wanting. Inside you'll find 290 sensational delights that you can depend on when the temperature drops. From Mom's best chicken soup and Dad's five-alarm chili to impressive chowders and decadent bisques, the ideal dish is always at your fingertips with this new collection.

For the ultimate stick-to-your-ribs specialties, see the Cheesy & Creamy chapter, or turn to the Heartiest Stews section for fantastic meal-in-one options. Page to the Chilis area when the gang is headed over to watch the big game, or check out the recipes in the Healthy & Light chapter when you want to trim down. Not sure what to make for dinner? Revisit a staple with the All-Time Classics section or see Cook It Fast or Slow for recipes that can be made in either a slow cooker or an Instant Pot. You choose!

**You'll also enjoy...**

- A no-fuss guide to making homemade broth and stock

- Dozens of tips, hints and secrets throughout the book to speed dinner prep

- Vegetarian and meatless recipes, as well as seafood greats

- A complete set of nutrition facts with every dish

Find prep/cook times with each recipe, step-by-step directions, more than 150 photos, and diabetic exchanges where applicable. Simply flip through this lovely book and see how easy it'd be to ladle out bowls of joy tonight. With *Soups, Stews & More*, homemade comfort is always the special of the day.

# Look for These Icons:

### FAST FIX
Done in 30 minutes or less

### SLOW COOKER
Set it and forget it

### 5 INGREDIENTS
Made with five ingredients or fewer (not counting water, salt & pepper, oil and optional items)

### FREEZE IT
Make now, eat later

### INSTANT POT®
Recipes to make in your electric pressure cooker

More ways to connect with us:

SHOPTASTEOFHOME.COM

# Stock Up!

Making your own broth from scratch is easier than you think, and it's the simplest way to take your soups and stews to the next level. Simmer these three staples to start your stash.

**1 cup:** 148 cal., 6g fat (1g sat. fat), 0 chol., 521mg sod., 22g carb. (9g sugars, 5g fiber), 4g pro.

**TIP**

Avoid seasoning your broth with herbs and spices. The long simmer time extracts a lot of flavor from the herbs, which might overpower the finished broth. You'll add herbs and spices when you use the broth in a recipe.

## HOW TO MAKE
### VEGETABLE BROTH

Use this homemade broth in any recipe that calls for vegetable broth. It's an easy alternative to store-bought versions, and it'll be lower in sodium as well. Cover and refrigerate the broth up to three days or freeze up to six months.

**Prep:** 45 min. • **Cook:** 1¾ hours • **Makes:** 5½ cups

- 2 Tbsp. olive oil
- 2 medium onions, cut into wedges
- 2 celery ribs, cut into 1-in. pieces
- 1 whole garlic bulb, separated into cloves and peeled
- 3 medium leeks, white and light green parts only, cleaned and cut into 1-in. pieces
- 3 medium carrots, cut into 1-in. pieces
- 8 cups water
- ½ lb. fresh mushrooms, quartered
- 1 cup packed fresh parsley sprigs
- 4 sprigs fresh thyme
- 1 tsp. salt
- ½ tsp. whole peppercorns
- 1 bay leaf

**1.** Heat oil in a stockpot or a Dutch oven over medium heat. Add onions, celery and garlic. Cook and stir 5 minutes or until the vegetables are tender. Add the leeks and carrots; cook and stir 5 minutes longer.

**2.** Add water, mushrooms, parsley, thyme, salt, peppercorns and bay leaf; bring to a boil. Reduce heat; simmer, uncovered, 1 hour.

**3.** Remove from heat. Strain through a cheesecloth-lined colander; discard vegetables. If using immediately, skim fat. Or refrigerate 8 hours or overnight; remove fat from surface before using.

## HOW TO MAKE CHICKEN BROTH

Collagen-rich and laced with veggies and herbs, homemade broth is healthier than commercial versions, which can be laden with preservatives and salt. This broth will keep in the fridge, tightly covered, for four to five days. Or seal it tightly in a freezer-safe container and freeze it for up to a year.

**Prep:** 10 min. • **Cook:** 3¼ hours + chilling • **Makes:** about 6 cups

- 2½ lbs. bony chicken pieces (legs, wings, necks or back bones)
- 2 celery ribs with leaves, cut into chunks
- 2 medium carrots, cut into chunks
- 2 medium onions, quartered
- 2 bay leaves
- ½ tsp. dried rosemary, crushed
- ½ tsp. dried thyme
- 8 to 10 whole peppercorns
- 2 qt. cold water

**1 cup:** 245 cal., 14g fat (4g sat. fat), 61mg chol., 80mg sod., 8g carb. (4g sugars, 2g fiber), 21g pro.

**1.** Place all ingredients in a stockpot or Dutch oven. Slowly bring to a boil; reduce heat until the mixture is at just a simmer.

**2.** Simmer, uncovered, for 3-4 hours, skimming foam as necessary. Remove chicken.

**3.** Set chicken aside until cool enough to handle. Remove meat from bones. Discard bones; save meat for another use. Strain broth, discarding vegetables and seasonings.

**4.** Refrigerate for 8 hours or overnight. Skim fat from surface before using.

**1 cup:** 30 cal., 0 fat (0 sat. fat), 0 chol., 75mg sod., 0 carb. (0 sugars, 0 fiber), 6g pro.

## *HOW TO MAKE*
## BONE BROTH

Whether you're adding it to soups or sipping it straight, this rich stock is well worth the effort. You'll want to simmer it for 8-24 hours, so we recommend making this a weekend project. Measure some into your favorite soup recipe, then freeze the rest for up to six months.

**Prep:** 1½ hours • **Cook:** 8-24 hours
**Makes:** about 2½ qt.

- 4 lbs. meaty beef soup bones (beef shanks or short ribs)
- 2 medium onions, quartered
- 3 chopped medium carrots, optional
- ½ cup warm water (110° to 115°)
- 3 bay leaves
- 3 garlic cloves
- 8 to 10 whole peppercorns
  Cold water

**1.** Place the bones in a large stockpot or Dutch oven; add enough water to cover. Bring to a boil over medium-high heat; reduce heat and simmer 15 minutes. Drain, discarding liquid. Rinse bones; drain.

**2.** In a large roasting pan, roast boiled bones, uncovered, at 450° for 30 minutes. Add the onions and, if desired, carrots. Roast until the bones and vegetables are dark brown, 30-45 minutes longer; drain fat.

**3.** Transfer the bones and the vegetables to a large stockpot or Dutch oven.

**4.** Add ½ cup warm water to the roasting pan; stir to loosen browned bits. Transfer pan juices to pot. Add seasonings and enough cold water just to cover. Slowly bring to a boil, about 30 minutes. Reduce the heat; simmer, covered with the lid slightly ajar, 8-24 hours, skimming foam. If necessary, add water as needed to keep ingredients covered.

**5.** Remove beef bones; cool. Strain the broth through a cheesecloth-lined colander, discarding the vegetables and seasonings.

**6.** If using immediately, skim the fat. Or refrigerate the broth 8 hours or overnight; remove the fat from the surface before using.

 **TIP**

The longer you simmer the broth, the more collagen will be extracted from the bones—it's collagen that gives the final broth a silky, smooth texture and body. Don't worry if the bones start to fall apart or crumble. This is a sign you've extracted as much as you can from them.

## SOUP-FREEZING TIPS

**Keep this expert advice in mind so your soup tastes just as good as it did the day you made it.**

**1. Avoid freezing soups with pasta, rice or chunks of potato.** Starches soak up liquid and get soggy when reheated. (Pureed potatoes, though, hold up well.) If freezing one of these soups, hold pasta, rice or potato pieces. Add them after you've thawed the soup.

**2. Omit the dairy, too.** A freezer does odd things to milk's texture, and the soup will be grainy when it thaws. Add milk and other dairy products when you're reheating thawed soup.

**3. Never freeze hot soup.** Hot soup put directly in the freezer will develop large ice crystals and freeze unevenly, resulting in mushy soup when thawed. For the best results, first cool your soup to at least room temperature (but, preferably, to below 40° in the refrigerator).

**4. Watch portion size.** Freezing your soup in one- or two-person portions makes for easy meal planning and helps the soup freeze faster.

**5. Opt for freezer-safe containers and leave about 1½ inches of headspace.** Soup expands as it freezes, and you don't want your container to crack or break. When you're ready to eat, run cold water over the outside of the container to loosen the soup. It will pop out right into your pot.

THE ULTIMATE CHICKEN
NOODLE SOUP, P. 23

# All-Time Classics

Soup and stew lovers keep going back to these traditional, time-honored favorites.

FENNEL CARROT SOUP, P. 18

POTATO &
LEEK SOUP

## Potato & Leek Soup

Loaded with veggies and bacon plus a little tanginess from sour cream, a bowl of this comforting soup tastes just as terrific with a sandwich as it does with crackers.
—*Melanie Wooden, Reno, NV*

**Prep:** 20 min. • **Cook:** 8 hours
**Makes:** 8 servings

- 4 cups chicken broth
- 3 medium potatoes, peeled and cubed
- 1½ cups chopped cabbage
- 2 medium carrots, chopped
- 1 medium leek (white portion only), chopped
- 1 medium onion, chopped
- ¼ cup minced fresh parsley
- ½ tsp. salt
- ½ tsp. caraway seeds
- ½ tsp. pepper
- 1 bay leaf
- ½ cup sour cream
- 1 lb. bacon strips, cooked and crumbled

**1.** Combine the first 11 ingredients in a 4- or 5-qt. slow cooker. Cover and cook on low until vegetables are tender, 8-10 hours.
**2.** Before serving, combine sour cream with 1 cup of the soup; return all to the slow cooker. Stir in bacon and discard bay leaf.
**1 cup:** 209 cal., 11g fat (4g sat. fat), 27mg chol., 1023mg sod., 18g carb. (4g sugars, 2g fiber), 10g pro.

THE BEST EVER
TOMATO SOUP

## The Best Ever Tomato Soup

Creamy, rich and bursting with brightness, this soup is the ultimate sidekick to a grilled cheese sandwich.
—*Josh Rink, Milwaukee, WI*

**Prep:** 20 minutes, • **Cook:** 30 minutes
**Makes:** 16 servings

- 3 Tbsp. olive oil
- 3 Tbsp. butter
- ¼ to ½ tsp. crushed red pepper flakes
- 3 large carrots, peeled and chopped
- 1 large onion, chopped
- 2 garlic cloves, minced
- 2 tsp. dried basil
- 3 cans (28 oz. each) whole peeled tomatoes
- 1 container (32 oz.) chicken stock
- 2 Tbsp. tomato paste
- 3 tsp. sugar
- 1 tsp. salt
- ½ tsp. pepper
- 1 cup heavy whipping cream, optional

Fresh basil leaves, thinly sliced, optional

**1.** In a 6-qt. stockpot or Dutch oven, heat oil, butter and pepper flakes over medium heat until butter is melted. Add the carrots and onion; cook, uncovered, over medium heat, stirring frequently, until vegetables are softened, 8-10 minutes. Add garlic and dried basil; cook and stir 1 minute longer. Stir in tomatoes, chicken stock, tomato paste, sugar, salt and pepper; mix well. Bring to a boil. Reduce heat; simmer, uncovered, to let flavors blend, 20-25 minutes.
**2.** Remove pan from heat. Using a blender, puree soup in batches until smooth. If desired, slowly stir in the heavy cream, stirring continuously to incorporate; return pan to stove to heat through. If desired, top with fresh basil.
**1 cup:** 104 cal., 5g fat (2g sat. fat), 6mg chol., 572mg sod., 15g carb. (10g sugars, 2g fiber), 3g pro.
**Diabetic exchanges:** 1 starch, 1 fat.

## Egg Drop Soup

We start many stir-fry meals with this classic and easy soup, which cooks in minutes. We like to add cornstarch to thicken the soup and give it a rich, golden color. I got the recipe from my grandma's old cookbook.
—Amy Beth Corlew-Sherlock, Lapeer, MI

- - - - - - - - - - - - - - - - - - - - - - -

**Takes:** 15 min.
**Makes:** 4 servings

3 cups chicken broth
1 Tbsp. cornstarch
2 Tbsp. cold water
1 large egg, lightly beaten
1 green onion, sliced

**1.** In a large saucepan, bring broth to a boil over medium heat. Combine cornstarch and water until smooth; gradually stir into broth. Bring to a boil; cook and stir for 2 minutes or until thickened.
**2.** Reduce heat. Drizzle beaten egg into hot broth, stirring constantly. Remove from the heat; stir in onion.
**¾ cup:** 39 cal., 2g fat (0 sat. fat), 53mg chol., 714mg sod., 3g carb. (1g sugars, 0 fiber), 3g pro.

## Pasta Fagioli Soup

My husband enjoys my version of this soup so much that he's stopped ordering it at restaurants. He'd rather savor the version we can have at home. It's so easy to make, yet hearty enough to be a full dinner. You can cut the spinach into fine shreds or larger chunks, whatever your preference.
—Brenda Thomas, Springfield, MO

- - - - - - - - - - - - - - - - - - - - - - -

**Takes:** 30 min.
**Makes:** 5 servings

½ lb. Italian turkey sausage links, casings removed, crumbled
1 small onion, chopped
1½ tsp. canola oil
1 garlic clove, minced
2 cups water
1 can (15½ oz.) great northern beans, rinsed and drained
1 can (14½ oz.) diced tomatoes, undrained
1 can (14½ oz.) reduced-sodium chicken broth
¾ cup uncooked elbow macaroni
¼ tsp. pepper
1 cup fresh spinach leaves, cut as desired
5 tsp. shredded Parmesan cheese

**1.** In a large saucepan, cook sausage over medium heat until no longer pink; drain, remove from pan and set aside. In the same pan, saute onion in oil until tender. Add garlic; saute 1 minute longer.
**2.** Add the water, beans, tomatoes, broth, macaroni and pepper; bring to a boil. Cook, uncovered, until the macaroni is tender, 8-10 minutes.
**3.** Reduce heat to low; stir in the sausage and spinach. Cook until spinach is wilted, 2-3 minutes. Garnish with cheese.
**1⅓ cups:** 228 cal., 7g fat (1g sat. fat), 29mg chol., 841mg sod., 27g carb. (4g sugars, 6g fiber), 16g pro.
**Diabetic exchanges:** 1½ starch, 1 lean meat, 1 vegetable, ½ fat.

PASTA FAGIOLI SOUP

HEARTY
VEGETABLE SOUP

## Golden Cheese Soup

This is my own adaptation of a recipe served at a popular local restaurant. The generous serving size comes in handy when I'm cooking for large family gatherings and church socials.
—*Marilyn Hillam, Brigham City, UT*

**Prep:** 30 min. • **Cook:** 10 min.
**Makes:** 50 servings

- 2½ cups chopped onion
- 1¼ cups butter, cubed
- 1¼ cups all-purpose flour
- 1¼ cups cornstarch
- 2½ tsp. paprika
- 5 tsp. salt
- 2½ tsp. pepper
- 5 qt. chicken broth
- 5 qt. milk
- 5 cups chopped carrots, cooked
- 5 cups chopped celery, cooked
- 10 cups (2½ lbs.) shredded sharp cheddar cheese
- 2½ cups chopped fresh parsley

In a large Dutch oven over medium heat, saute onion in butter until tender. Combine flour, cornstarch, paprika, salt and pepper; stir into pan until a smooth paste forms. Gradually add broth, stirring constantly. Bring to a boil; cook and stir for 2 minutes or until thickened. Gradually add milk, stirring constantly. Add carrots, celery and cheese. Cook and stir over low heat until cheese is melted and soup is heated through. Add parsley just before serving.
**1 cup:** 222 cal., 15g fat (10g sat. fat), 50mg chol., 855mg sod., 14g carb. (6g sugars, 1g fiber), 10g pro.

## Hearty Vegetable Soup

A friend gave me the idea to use V8 juice in soup because it provides more flavor. This soup is perfect to make on a crisp autumn afternoon.
—*Janice Steinmetz, Somers, CT*

**Prep:** 25 min. • **Cook:** 1 hour 20 min.
**Makes:** 16 servings

- 1 Tbsp. olive oil
- 8 medium carrots, sliced
- 2 large onions, chopped
- 4 celery ribs, chopped
- 1 large green pepper, seeded and chopped
- 1 garlic clove, minced
- 2 cups chopped cabbage
- 2 cups frozen cut green beans (about 8 oz.)
- 2 cups frozen peas (about 8 oz.)
- 1 cup frozen corn (about 5 oz.)
- 1 can (15 oz.) garbanzo beans or chickpeas, rinsed and drained
- 1 bay leaf
- 2 tsp. chicken bouillon granules
- 1½ tsp. dried parsley flakes
- 1 tsp. salt
- 1 tsp. dried marjoram
- 1 tsp. dried thyme
- ½ tsp. dried basil
- ¼ tsp. pepper
- 4 cups water
- 1 can (28 oz.) diced tomatoes, undrained
- 2 cups V8 juice

**1.** In a stockpot, heat the oil over medium-high heat; saute carrots, onions, celery and green pepper until crisp-tender. Add garlic; cook and stir 1 minute. Stir in remaining ingredients; bring to a boil.
**2.** Reduce heat; simmer, covered, until the vegetables are tender, 1-1½ hours. Remove bay leaf.
**1 cup:** 105 cal., 2g fat (0 sat. fat), 0 chol., 488mg sod., 20g carb. (9g sugars, 5g fiber), 4g pro.
**Diabetic exchanges:** 1 starch.

HEARTY NAVY
BEAN SOUP

# Hearty Navy Bean Soup

Use economical dried beans and a ham hock to create this comfort-food classic. Bean soup is a family favorite that I make often.

—*Mildred Lewis, Temple, TX*

**Prep:** 30 min. + soaking
**Cook:** 1¾ hours
**Makes:** 10 servings

- 3  **cups (1½ lbs.) dried navy beans**
- 1  **can (14½ oz.) diced tomatoes, undrained**
- 1  **large onion, chopped**
- 1  **meaty ham hock or 1 cup diced cooked ham**
- 2  **cups chicken broth**
- 2½ **cups water**
   **Salt and pepper to taste**
   **Minced fresh parsley**

**1.** Rinse and sort the beans; soak according to package directions.

**2.** Drain and rinse beans, discarding liquid. Place in a Dutch oven. Add the tomatoes with juice, onion, ham hock, broth, water, salt and pepper. Bring to a boil. Reduce heat; cover and simmer until beans are tender, about 1½ hours.

**3.** Add more water if necessary. Remove ham hock and let it stand until cool enough to handle. Remove meat from bone; discard bone. Cut meat into bite-sized pieces. (For a thicker soup, let soup cool slightly, then puree about half the beans in a food processor or blender and return to pan.) Return ham to soup and heat through. Garnish with parsley.

**1 cup:** 245 cal., 2g fat (0 sat. fat), 8mg chol., 352mg sod., 42g carb. (5g sugars, 16g fiber), 18g pro.
**Diabetic exchanges:** 3 starch, 2 lean meat.

## Easy Butternut Squash Soup

When the weather turns cold, get cozy with a bowl of this soup. The cream adds richness, but if you're looking to cut calories, it can be omitted.
—Taste of Home *Test Kitchen*

**Takes:** 30 min. • **Makes:** 9 servings

- 1 Tbsp. olive oil
- 1 large onion, chopped
- 3 garlic cloves, minced
- 1 medium butternut squash (3 lbs.), peeled and cubed
- 4 cups vegetable broth
- ¾ tsp. salt
- ¼ tsp. pepper
- ½ cup heavy whipping cream
  Optional: Additional heavy whipping cream and crispy sage leaves

**1.** In a large saucepan, heat oil over medium heat. Add onion; cook and stir until tender. Add garlic; cook 1 minute longer.

**2.** Stir in squash, broth, salt and pepper; bring to a boil. Reduce heat; simmer, covered, 10-15 minutes or until the squash is tender. Puree soup using an immersion blender. Or cool slightly and puree soup in batches in a blender; return to pan. Add cream; cook and stir until heated through. If desired, garnish with additional heavy whipping cream and crispy sage.

**1 cup:** 157 cal., 7g fat (4g sat. fat), 17mg chol., 483mg sod., 23g carb. (6g sugars, 6g fiber), 3g pro.

EASY BUTTERNUT SQUASH SOUP

## Creamy Chicken Rice Soup

I came up with this flavorful soup while making some adjustments to a favorite stovetop chicken casserole. It's perfect for lunch with a crisp roll.
—*Janice Mitchell, Aurora, CO*

**Takes:** 30 min.
**Makes:** 4 servings

- 1 Tbsp. canola oil
- 1 medium carrot, chopped
- 1 celery rib, chopped
- ½ cup chopped onion
- ½ tsp. minced garlic
- ⅓ cup uncooked long grain rice
- ¾ tsp. dried basil
- ¼ tsp. pepper
- 2 cans (14½ oz. each) reduced-sodium chicken broth
- 3 Tbsp. all-purpose flour
- 1 can (5 oz.) evaporated milk
- 2 cups cubed cooked chicken breast

**1.** In a large saucepan, heat oil over medium-high heat; saute carrot, celery and onion until tender. Add garlic; cook and stir 1 minute. Stir in rice, seasonings and broth; bring to a boil. Reduce heat; simmer, covered, until rice is tender, about 15 minutes.
**2.** Mix flour and milk until smooth; stir into soup. Bring to a boil; cook and stir until thickened, about 2 minutes. Stir in chicken; heat through.
**1¼ cups:** 312 cal., 9g fat (3g sat. fat), 71mg chol., 699mg sod., 26g carb. (6g sugars, 1g fiber), 29g pro.
**Diabetic exchanges:** 3 lean meat, 2 starch, 1 fat.

BEEF VEGETABLE SOUP

## Beef Vegetable Soup

On busy days, I like the convenience of doing the prep work in the morning and letting the soup simmer all day.
—*Jean Hutzell, Dubuque, IA*

**Prep:** 20 min. • **Cook:** 9 hours
**Makes:** 7 servings

- 1 lb. lean ground beef (90% lean)
- 1 medium onion, chopped
- ½ tsp. salt
- ¼ tsp. pepper
- 3 cups water
- 3 medium potatoes, peeled and cut into ¾-in. cubes
- 1 can (14½ oz.) Italian diced tomatoes, undrained
- 1 can (11½ oz.) V8 juice
- 1 cup chopped celery
- 1 cup sliced carrots
- 2 Tbsp. sugar
- 1 Tbsp. dried parsley flakes
- 2 tsp. dried basil
- 1 bay leaf

**1.** In a nonstick skillet, cook beef and onion over medium heat until meat is no longer pink, breaking meat into crumbles; drain. Stir in salt and pepper.
**2.** Transfer to a 5-qt. slow cooker. Add the remaining ingredients. Cover and cook on low for 9-11 hours or until vegetables are tender. Discard bay leaf before serving.
**1⅓ cups:** 217 cal., 6g fat (2g sat. fat), 40mg chol., 536mg sod., 27g carb. (11g sugars, 3g fiber), 15g pro.
**Diabetic exchanges:** 2 lean meat, 2 vegetable, 1 starch.

CREAMY CHICKEN
RICE SOUP

## Cream of Turkey & Wild Rice Soup

A dear friend brought me some of this soup when I was ill. I asked her for the recipe, and I've made it several times since. Now I like to take it to friends when they're not feeling well. It's filling and really warms you up on a chilly day!

—Doris Cox, New Freedom, PA

**Prep:** 15 min. • **Cook:** 20 min.
**Makes:** 6 servings

- 1   medium onion, chopped
- 1   can (4 oz.) sliced mushrooms, drained
- 2   Tbsp. butter
- 3   cups water
- 2   cups chicken broth
- 1   pkg. (6 oz.) long grain and wild rice mix
- 2   cups diced cooked turkey
- 1   cup heavy whipping cream
      Minced fresh parsley

In a large saucepan, saute onion and mushrooms in butter until onion is tender. Add water, broth and rice mix with seasoning; bring to a boil. Reduce heat; simmer 20-25 minutes or until the rice is tender. Stir in turkey and cream; heat through. Sprinkle with parsley.

**1 cup:** 364 cal., 21g fat (12g sat. fat), 100mg chol., 857mg sod., 25g carb. (3g sugars, 1g fiber), 19g pro.

FENNEL CARROT SOUP

## Fennel Carrot Soup

This smooth, richly colored soup makes a wonderful first course for Christmas dinner. The fennel seed and curry complement the carrots, apple and sweet potato.

—Marlene Bursey, Waverly, NS

**Prep:** 10 min. • **Cook:** 45 min.
**Makes:** 8 servings

- 1   Tbsp. butter
- ½   tsp. fennel seed
- 1½  lbs. carrots, sliced
- 1   medium sweet potato, peeled and cubed
- 1   medium apple, peeled and cubed
- 3   cans (14½ oz. each) vegetable broth
- 2   Tbsp. uncooked long grain rice
- 1   bay leaf
- ¼   tsp. curry powder
- 1   Tbsp. lemon juice
- ½   tsp. salt
- ¼   tsp. white pepper
- 2   Tbsp. minced fresh parsley

**1.** In a large saucepan, melt butter over medium-high heat. Add fennel; cook and stir 2-3 minutes or until lightly toasted. Add carrots, sweet potato and apple; cook and stir 5 minutes longer.

**2.** Stir in broth, rice, bay leaf and curry powder; bring to a boil. Reduce heat; simmer, covered, 30 minutes or until vegetables and rice are soft.

**3.** Remove from heat; cool slightly. Discard bay leaf. Process in batches in a blender until smooth; return to pan. Stir in lemon juice, salt and pepper. Cook over medium heat 5 minutes or until heated through, stirring occasionally. Sprinkle with parsley.

**1 cup:** 117 cal., 2g fat (1g sat. fat), 4mg chol., 989mg sod., 23g carb. (0 sugars, 3g fiber), 3g pro. **Diabetic exchanges:** 2 vegetable, 1 starch.

# Lauren's Bouillabaisse

This golden-colored soup is brimming with an assortment of seafood and is paired with savory and colorful sourdough toast with spread.
—*Lauren Covas, New Brunswick, NJ*

**Prep:** 30 min. • **Cook:** 20 min.
**Makes:** 12 servings

- ⅔ cup chopped roasted sweet red pepper, drained
- ¼ cup reduced-fat mayonnaise

**TOASTS**
- 6 slices sourdough bread
- 1 garlic clove, halved

**BOUILLABAISSE**
- 1 medium onion, chopped
- 1 Tbsp. olive oil
- 2 garlic cloves, minced
- 2 plum tomatoes, chopped
- ½ tsp. saffron threads or 2 tsp. ground turmeric
- 3½ cups cubed red potatoes
- 2½ cups thinly sliced fennel bulb
- 1 carton (32 oz.) reduced-sodium chicken broth
- 3 cups clam juice
- 2 tsp. dried tarragon
- 24 fresh littleneck clams
- 24 fresh mussels, scrubbed and beards removed
- 1 lb. red snapper fillet, cut into 2-in. pieces
- ¾ lb. uncooked large shrimp, peeled and deveined
- ¼ cup minced fresh parsley

**1.** Place red pepper and mayonnaise in a food processor; cover and process until smooth. Refrigerate until serving.

**2.** For toasts, rub 1 side of each bread slice with garlic; discard garlic. Cut bread slices in half. Place on an ungreased baking sheet. Bake at 400° for 4-5 minutes on each side or until lightly browned.

**3.** In a stockpot, saute the onion in oil until tender. Add the garlic; cook 1 minute longer. Reduce heat; stir in the tomatoes and saffron. Add the potatoes, fennel, broth, clam juice and tarragon. Bring to a boil. Reduce heat; simmer, uncovered, for 10-12 minutes or until the potatoes are almost tender.

**4.** Add clams, mussels, snapper and shrimp. Cook, stirring occasionally, for 10-15 minutes or until the clams and mussels open and the fish flakes easily with a fork. Discard unopened clams or mussels. Spoon into bowls; sprinkle with parsley. Spread the pepper mayo over toasts; serve with bouillabaisse.

**1⅔ cups with 2 tsp. spread on ½ slice of bread:** 239 cal., 5g fat (1g sat. fat), 70mg chol., 684mg sod., 23g carb. (3g sugars, 2g fiber), 24g pro. **Diabetic exchanges:** 3 lean meat, 1½ starch, ½ fat.

### TIP

When using clams and mussels, first clean them under running water, using a scrub brush to remove any debris. Check to make sure the shells either are tightly closed or close when you tap on the top shell. If you find one that stays open, discard it. Also discard any that float. If there's a hairy "beard" sticking out from the shell, remove it by pinching it and pulling it out gently.

LAUREN'S BOUILLABAISSE

# Weeknight Goulash

With this recipe, you can put in a full day's work, run some errands and still get dinner on the table in hardly any time. Make it extra-special by serving the meat sauce over spaetzle.
—*Cyndy Gerken, Naples, FL*

- - - - - - - - - - - - - - - - - - - - - - -

**Prep:** 25 min. • **Cook:** 8½ hours
**Makes:** 2 servings

- 1  **lb. beef stew meat**
- 1  **Tbsp. olive oil**
- 1  **cup beef broth**
- 1  **small onion, chopped**
- ¼  **cup ketchup**
- 1  **Tbsp. Worcestershire sauce**
- 1½  **tsp. brown sugar**
- 1½  **tsp. paprika**
- ¼  **tsp. ground mustard**
- 1  **Tbsp. all-purpose flour**
- 2  **Tbsp. water**
   **Hot cooked egg noodles or spaetzle**

**1.** In a large skillet, brown beef in oil; drain. Transfer to a 1½-qt. slow cooker. Combine the broth, onion, ketchup, Worcestershire sauce, brown sugar, paprika and mustard. Pour over beef. Cover and cook on low until meat is tender, 8-10 hours.

**2.** In a small bowl, combine flour and water until smooth. Gradually stir into the beef mixture. Cover and cook on high until thickened, about 30 minutes longer. Serve with noodles.

**1 cup:** 478 cal., 23g fat (7g sat. fat), 141mg chol., 1005mg sod., 20g carb. (14g sugars, 1g fiber), 45g pro.

WEEKNIGHT
GOULASH

AMISH CHICKEN
CORN SOUP

## Amish Chicken Corn Soup

Creamed corn and butter make my chicken noodle soup homey and rich. This recipe makes a big batch, but the soup freezes well for future meals.
—*Beverly Hoffman, Sandy Lake, PA*

**Prep:** 15 min. • **Cook:** 50 min.
**Makes:** 12 servings

- 1   medium onion, chopped
- 2   celery ribs, chopped
- 1   cup shredded carrots
- 2   lbs. boneless skinless chicken breasts, cubed
- 3   chicken bouillon cubes
- 1   tsp. salt
- ¼   tsp. pepper
- 12  cups water
- 2   cups uncooked egg noodles
- 2   cans (14¾ oz. each) cream-style corn
- ¼   cup butter

**1.** Place the first 8 ingredients in a Dutch oven; bring slowly to a boil. Reduce heat; simmer, uncovered, until the chicken is no longer pink and vegetables are tender, about 30 minutes.

**2.** Stir in noodles, corn and butter. Cook, uncovered, until the noodles are tender, about 10 minutes, stirring occasionally.

**1⅓ cups:** 201 cal., 6g fat (3g sat. fat), 57mg chol., 697mg sod., 19g carb. (3g sugars, 2g fiber), 18g pro.
**Diabetic exchanges:** 2 lean meat, 1 starch, 1 fat.

BEET BORSCHT

## Beet Borscht

My mother used to make this hearty soup from her garden's bountiful crop of beets and other vegetables.
—*Ruth Andrewson, Leavenworth, WA*

**Prep:** 15 min. • **Cook:** 35 min.
**Makes:** 8 servings

- 2 cups shredded fresh beets
- 1 cup shredded carrots
- 1 cup chopped onion
- 2 cups water
- ½ tsp. salt
- 2 cans (14½ oz. each) beef broth
- 1 cup shredded cabbage
- 1 Tbsp. butter
- 1 Tbsp. lemon juice
  Optional: Sour cream and chopped chives or fresh dill sprigs

THE ULTIMATE
CHICKEN NOODLE SOUP

In a saucepan, bring the beets, carrots, onion, water and salt to a boil. Reduce heat; cover and simmer for 20 minutes. Add broth, cabbage and butter; simmer, uncovered, for 15 minutes. Just before serving, stir in lemon juice. If desired, top each serving with sour cream and chives or dill.

**1 cup:** 48 cal., 2g fat (1g sat. fat), 4mg chol., 375mg sod., 7g carb. (5g sugars, 2g fiber), 1g pro.
**Diabetic exchanges:** 1 vegetable, ½ fat.

## The Ultimate Chicken Noodle Soup

My first Wisconsin winter was so cold, all I wanted to eat was soup. This recipe is in heavy rotation at our house from November to April.
—*Gina Nistico, Denver, CO*

**Prep:** 15 min.
**Cook:** 45 min. + standing
**Makes:** 10 servings

- 2½ lbs. bone-in chicken thighs
- ½ tsp. pepper
- ½ tsp. salt
- 1 Tbsp. canola oil
- 1 large onion, chopped
- 1 garlic clove, minced
- 10 cups chicken broth
- 4 celery ribs, chopped
- 4 medium carrots, chopped
- 2 bay leaves
- 1 tsp. minced fresh thyme or ¼ tsp. dried thyme
- 3 cups uncooked kluski or other egg noodles (about 8 oz.)
- 1 Tbsp. chopped fresh parsley
- 1 Tbsp. lemon juice
  Optional: Additional salt and pepper

**1.** Pat the chicken dry with paper towels; sprinkle with pepper and salt. In a 6-qt. stockpot, heat oil over medium-high heat. Add chicken in batches, skin side down; cook until dark golden brown, 3-4 minutes. Remove chicken from pot; remove and discard skin. Discard drippings, reserving 2 Tbsp.
**2.** Add onion to the drippings; cook and stir over medium-high heat until tender, 4-5 minutes. Add garlic; cook 1 minute longer. Add broth, stirring to loosen any browned bits. Bring to a boil. Return chicken to the pot. Add celery, carrots, bay leaves and thyme. Reduce heat; simmer, covered, until chicken is tender, 25-30 minutes.
**3.** Transfer the chicken to a plate. Remove soup from heat. Add the noodles; let stand, covered, until noodles are tender, 20-22 minutes.
**4.** When chicken is cool enough to handle, remove meat from bones; discard bones. Shred meat into bite-sized pieces and return to pot. Stir in parsley and lemon juice. If desired, adjust seasoning with salt and pepper. Discard bay leaves.

**1⅓ cups:** 239 cal., 12g fat (3g sat. fat), 68mg chol., 1176mg sod., 14g carb. (3g sugars, 2g fiber), 18g pro.

## Hearty Sausage Minestrone

As a teacher, I appreciate quick and easy recipes. When there are more people at the table, every last spoonful of this soup is eaten!
—*Tami Stoudt, Evans, CO*

**Takes:** 30 min.
**Makes:** 8 servings

- 1 lb. bulk Italian sausage
- 1 medium onion, chopped
- 2 celery ribs, chopped
- 2 medium carrots, chopped
- 3 cans (14½ oz. each) diced tomatoes with basil, oregano and garlic, undrained
- 2 cans (16 oz. each) kidney beans, rinsed and drained
- 2 cans (14½ oz. each) chicken broth
- ¼ tsp. garlic powder
- ¼ tsp. pepper
- 1 cup ditalini or other small pasta

**1.** In a Dutch oven, cook sausage, onion, celery and carrots over medium heat for 8-10 minutes or until sausage is no longer pink and onion is tender, breaking the sausage into crumbles; drain.
**2.** Stir in tomatoes, beans, broth, garlic powder and pepper; bring to a boil. Add pasta; cook, covered, 6-8 minutes or until pasta is tender.
**Freeze option:** Freeze cooled minestrone in freezer containers. To use, partially thaw in refrigerator overnight. Heat through in a saucepan, stirring occasionally; add a little broth if necessary.
**1¾ cups:** 372 cal., 13g fat (4g sat. fat), 33mg chol., 1481mg sod., 44g carb. (9g sugars, 9g fiber), 18g pro.

## Quick Cream of Mushroom Soup

My daughter-in-law, a gourmet cook, served this soup as the first course for a holiday dinner. She had received the recipe from her mom and then graciously shared it with me. Now I'm happy to share it, too!
—*Anne Kulick, Phillipsburg, NJ*

**Takes:** 30 min. • **Makes:** 6 servings

- 2 Tbsp. butter
- ½ lb. sliced fresh mushrooms
- ¼ cup chopped onion
- 6 Tbsp. all-purpose flour
- ½ tsp. salt
- ⅛ tsp. pepper
- 2 cans (14½ oz. each) chicken broth
- 1 cup half-and-half cream

**1.** In a large saucepan, heat butter over medium-high heat; saute mushrooms and onion until tender.
**2.** Mix flour, salt, pepper and 1 can of broth until smooth; stir into the mushroom mixture. Stir in the remaining can of broth. Bring to a boil; cook and stir until thickened, about 2 minutes. Reduce heat; stir in cream. Simmer, uncovered, until flavors are blended, about 15 minutes, stirring occasionally.
**1 cup:** 136 cal., 8g fat (5g sat. fat), 33mg chol., 842mg sod., 10g carb. (3g sugars, 1g fiber), 4g pro.

QUICK CREAM OF MUSHROOM SOUP

IRISH BEEF STEW

1. In a stockpot, cook bacon over medium heat until crisp. Using a slotted spoon, remove to paper towels. In a large shallow dish, combine flour, salt and pepper. Add beef, a few pieces at a time, and turn to coat. Brown beef in the bacon drippings. Remove and set aside.

2. In the same pot, saute mushrooms, leeks, carrots and celery in oil until tender. Add garlic; cook 1 minute longer. Stir in tomato paste until blended. Add the broth, beer, bay leaves, thyme, parsley and rosemary. Return the beef and the bacon to pot. Bring to a boil. Reduce heat; cover and simmer for 2 hours or until beef is tender.

3. Add potatoes. Return to a boil. Reduce heat; cover and simmer 1 hour longer or until potatoes are tender. Combine cornstarch and water until smooth; stir into stew. Bring to a boil; cook and stir until thickened, 2 minutes. Add peas; heat through. Discard bay leaves.

**1 cup:** 301 cal., 13g fat (4g sat. fat), 66mg chol., 441mg sod., 21g carb. (3g sugars, 2g fiber), 23g pro.

Debate over what constitutes a "real" Irish stew rages—whether it should be broth-based or thickened, and what kind of meat should be used. Potatoes and onions are the only must-haves. Some cooks use starchy potatoes and forgo any thickener like flour or cornstarch. For those who prefer their Irish stew made with lamb, it's simple to just substitute cubed lamb stew meat for the beef in this recipe.

## Irish Beef Stew

Rich and hearty with beef that is incredibly tender, this stew is my husband's favorite. It is an ideal cool-weather meal and is perfect for any Irish holiday.
—*Carrie Karleen, St. Nicolas, QC*

**Prep:** 40 min. • **Cook:** 3¼ hours
**Makes:** 15 servings

- 8 bacon strips, diced
- ⅓ cup all-purpose flour
- 1 tsp. salt
- ½ tsp. pepper
- 3 lbs. beef stew meat, cut into 1-in. cubes
- 1 lb. whole fresh mushrooms, quartered
- 3 medium leeks (white portion only), chopped
- 2 medium carrots, chopped
- ¼ cup chopped celery
- 1 Tbsp. canola oil
- 4 garlic cloves, minced
- 1 Tbsp. tomato paste
- 4 cups reduced-sodium beef broth
- 1 cup dark stout beer or additional reduced-sodium beef broth
- 2 bay leaves
- 1 tsp. dried thyme
- 1 tsp. dried parsley flakes
- 1 tsp. dried rosemary, crushed
- 2 lbs. Yukon Gold potatoes, cut into 1-in. cubes
- 2 Tbsp. cornstarch
- 2 Tbsp. cold water
- 1 cup frozen peas

HEARTY MANHATTAN
CLAM CHOWDER

CHUNKY CREAMY
CHICKEN SOUP

## Hearty Manhattan Clam Chowder

This veggie-packed chowder is savory and satisfying. Butter some crusty bread for a complete meal.
—*Carol Bullick, Royersford, PA*

**Prep:** 20 min. • **Cook:** 7 hours
**Makes:** 6 servings

- 1½ lbs. potatoes (about 3 medium), peeled and cut into ¾-in. cubes
- 1 large onion, chopped
- 2 medium carrots, shredded (about ¾ cup)
- 3 celery ribs, sliced
- 4 cans (6½ oz. each) chopped clams, undrained
- 5 bacon strips, cooked and crumbled
- 1 Tbsp. dried parsley flakes
- 1 bay leaf
- 1½ tsp. dried thyme
- ¼ tsp. coarsely ground pepper
- 1 can (28 oz.) diced tomatoes, undrained

Place all ingredients in a 4- or 5-qt. slow cooker. Cook, covered, on low until the vegetables are tender, 7-9 hours. Remove the bay leaf before serving.

**1½ cups:** 203 cal., 4g fat (1g sat. fat), 50mg chol., 995mg sod., 29g carb. (8g sugars, 5g fiber), 15g pro.

# Chunky Creamy Chicken Soup

I am a stay-at-home mom who relies on my slow cooker for nutritious meals with minimal prep time and cleanup. I knew this recipe was a hit when there were no leftovers and my husband asked me to make it again!
—*Nancy Clow, Mallorytown, ON*

**Prep:** 15 min. • **Cook:** 4½ hours
**Makes:** 7 servings

1½  lbs. boneless skinless chicken breasts, cut into 2-in. strips
 2  tsp. canola oil
 ⅔  cup finely chopped onion
 2  medium carrots, chopped
 2  celery ribs, chopped
 1  cup frozen corn
 2  cans (10¾ oz. each) condensed cream of potato soup, undiluted
1½  cups chicken broth
 1  tsp. dill weed
 1  cup frozen peas
 ½  cup half-and-half cream

**1.** In a large skillet over medium-high heat, brown chicken in oil. Transfer to a 5-qt. slow cooker; add the onion, carrots, celery and corn.
**2.** In a large bowl, whisk the soup, broth and dill until blended; stir into slow cooker. Cover and cook on low until the chicken and vegetables are tender, about 4 hours .
**3.** Stir in peas and cream. Cover and cook until heated through, about 30 minutes longer.

**1 cup:** 229 cal., 7g fat (3g sat. fat), 66mg chol., 629mg sod., 17g carb. (5g sugars, 3g fiber), 24g pro.

CLASSIC FRENCH
ONION SOUP

## Stuffed Pepper Soup

At the restaurant where I work, some of my fellow cooks and I were talking about stuffed peppers. We decided to stir up similar ingredients for a soup. The response from our customers was overwhelming!
—*Krista Muddiman, Meadville, PA*

**Prep:** 15 min. • **Cook:** 45 min.
**Makes:** 8 servings

- 2  lbs. ground beef
- 6  cups water
- 1  can (28 oz.) tomato sauce
- 1  can (28 oz.) diced tomatoes, undrained
- 2  cups chopped green peppers
- ¼  cup packed brown sugar
- 2  tsp. salt
- 2  tsp. beef bouillon granules
- 1  tsp. pepper
- 2  cups cooked long grain rice
   Chopped fresh parsley, optional

**1.** In a Dutch oven over medium heat, cook and stir beef until no longer pink, breaking into crumbles; drain. Stir in next 8 ingredients; bring to a boil. Reduce heat; simmer, uncovered, until peppers are tender, about 30 minutes.
**2.** Add the cooked rice; simmer, uncovered, 10 minutes longer. If desired, sprinkle with chopped fresh parsley.
**1 cup:** 337 cal.,14g fat (5g sat. fat), 70mg chol., 1466mg sod., 30g carb. (13g sugars, 4g fiber), 24g pro.

## Classic French Onion Soup

Enjoy my signature soup the way my granddaughter Becky does. I serve it for her in a French onion soup bowl complete with garlic croutons and gobs of melted Swiss cheese on top.
—*Lou Sansevero, Ferron, UT*

**Prep:** 20 min. • **Cook:** 2 hours
**Makes:** 12 servings

- 5  Tbsp. olive oil, divided
- 1  Tbsp. butter
- 8  cups thinly sliced onions (about 3 lbs.)
- 3  garlic cloves, minced
- ½  cup port wine
- 2  cartons (32 oz. each) beef broth
- ½  tsp. pepper
- ¼  tsp. salt
- 24  slices French bread baguette (½ in. thick)
- 2  large garlic cloves, peeled and halved
- ¾  cup shredded Gruyere or Swiss cheese

**1.** In a Dutch oven, heat 2 Tbsp. oil and the butter over medium heat. Add the onions; cook and stir until softened, 10-13 minutes. Reduce heat to medium-low; cook, stirring occasionally, until deep golden brown, 30-40 minutes. Add minced garlic; cook 2 minutes longer.
**2.** Stir in wine. Bring to a boil; cook until liquid is reduced by half. Add broth, pepper and salt; return to a boil. Reduce heat. Simmer, covered, stirring occasionally, for 1 hour.
**3.** Place the baguette slices on a baking sheet; brush both sides with remaining oil. Bake at 400° until toasted, 3-5 minutes on each side. Rub toasts with halved garlic.
**4.** To serve, place twelve 8-oz. broiler-safe bowls or ramekins on baking sheets; place 2 toasts in each. Ladle with soup; top with cheese. Broil 4 in. from heat until cheese is melted.
**¾ cup soup with 1 slice bread and 1 Tbsp. cheese:** 172 cal., 9g fat (3g sat. fat), 10mg chol., 773mg sod., 16g carb. (3g sugars, 1g fiber), 6g pro.

STUFFED
PEPPER SOUP

## Crab Soup with Sherry

Everybody loves this rich, comforting soup that's a tradition in the South. It is brimming with crab and has a smooth texture.
—*Regina Huggins, Summerville, SC*

**Prep:** 15 min. • **Cook:** 30 min.
**Makes:** 6 servings

- 1 lb. fresh or frozen crabmeat, thawed
- 6 Tbsp. sherry or chicken broth
- 1 small onion, grated
- ¼ cup butter, cubed
- ¼ cup all-purpose flour
- ½ tsp. salt
- 2 cups 2% milk
- 2 chicken bouillon cubes
- 3 cups half-and-half cream
- 2 Tbsp. minced fresh parsley

**1.** In a small bowl, combine crabmeat and sherry; set aside.
**2.** In a large saucepan, saute onion in butter until tender. Stir in flour and salt until blended; gradually add milk and bouillon. Bring to a boil; cook and stir for 2 minutes or until thickened. Stir in cream and the crab mixture; heat through. Sprinkle servings with parsley.
**1 cup:** 382 cal., 23g fat (14g sat. fat), 162mg chol., 936mg sod., 14g carb. (9g sugars, 0 fiber), 23g pro.

 **TIP**
Fresh and frozen crabmeat are more flavorful than the more economical canned, so one of those is preferred for this recipe. But if you do opt for canned, make sure you buy jumbo or lump crabmeat. You can also boost the flavor by soaking the crabmeat in ice water for 10 minutes before patting it dry and adding it to your recipe.

SEAFOOD CIOPPINO

## Seafood Cioppino

If you're looking for a terrific seafood recipe for your slow cooker, this is just the ticket. It's brimming with clams, crab, fish and shrimp, and it is fancy enough to be an elegant meal.
—*Lisa Moriarty, Wilton, NH*

**Prep:** 20 min. • **Cook:** 4½ hours
**Makes:** 8 servings

- 1 can (28 oz.) diced tomatoes, undrained
- 2 medium onions, chopped
- 3 celery ribs, chopped
- 1 bottle (8 oz.) clam juice
- 1 can (6 oz.) tomato paste
- ½ cup white wine or ½ cup vegetable broth
- 5 garlic cloves, minced
- 1 Tbsp. red wine vinegar
- 1 Tbsp. olive oil
- 1 to 2 tsp. Italian seasoning
- 1 bay leaf
- ½ tsp. sugar
- 1 lb. haddock fillets, cut into 1-in. pieces
- 1 lb. uncooked shrimp (41-50 per lb.), peeled and deveined
- 1 can (6 oz.) chopped clams, undrained
- 1 can (6 oz.) lump crabmeat, drained
- 2 Tbsp. minced fresh parsley

**1.** In a 4- or 5-qt. slow cooker, combine the first 12 ingredients. Cook, covered, on low 4-5 hours.
**2.** Stir in seafood. Cook, covered, until fish just begins to flake easily with a fork and the shrimp turn pink, 20-30 minutes longer.
**3.** Remove bay leaf. Stir in parsley.
**1¼ cups:** 205 cal., 3g fat (1g sat. fat), 125mg chol., 483mg sod., 15g carb. (8g sugars, 3g fiber), 29g pro.
**Diabetic exchanges:** 3 lean meat, 2 vegetable.

# Chicken Matzo Ball Soup

The key to great chicken matzo ball soup is slow-cooking the soup and using boxed matzo ball mix. Some people swear by seltzer, but I find it's not necessary. The boxed mix makes perfect, fluffy matzo balls every time due to the baking powder in the mix. Add chicken fat (schmaltz) for extra-authentic flavor straight from Grandma's kitchen.

—Shannon Sarna, South Orange, NJ

**Prep:** 30 min. + chilling
**Cook:** 1½ hrs. + simmering
**Makes:** 26 servings

- 1 broiler/fryer chicken (3 to 4 lbs.)
- 1 lb. chicken wings
- 6 qt. water
- 3 large carrots, chopped
- 2 medium parsnips, peeled and chopped
- 1 medium turnip, peeled and chopped
- 1 large onion, chopped
- 1 bunch fresh dill sprigs
- 1 bunch fresh parsley sprigs
- 1½ tsp. whole peppercorns
- 3 tsp. salt

**MATZO BALLS**

- 1 pkg. (5 oz.) matzo ball mix
- 4 large eggs, room temperature
- ¼ cup safflower oil
- ¼ cup rendered chicken fat
- 2 Tbsp. snipped fresh dill
- 2 Tbsp. minced fresh parsley
- 10 cups water

**1.** Place chicken and wings in a stockpot; add water, vegetables, herbs and seasonings. Slowly bring to a boil. Reduce heat; simmer, covered, 1-2 hours.

**2.** Remove chicken and wings and let cool. Strain broth through a cheesecloth-lined colander; reserve vegetables. Skim fat. Remove meat from bones and cut into bite-sized pieces; discard bones. Return broth, vegetables and meat to pot. Skim fat. (Or cool broth, then refrigerate 8 hours or overnight; remove the fat from surface before using. Broth may be refrigerated up to 3 days or frozen 4-6 months.)

**3.** Meanwhile, in a large bowl, beat matzo ball mix, eggs, oil, chicken fat, dill and parsley until combined. Cover and refrigerate for at least 30 minutes.

**4.** In another stockpot, bring water to a boil. Drop rounded tablespoonfuls of matzo ball dough into boiling water. Reduce heat; cover and simmer until a toothpick inserted into a matzo ball comes out clean (do not lift cover while simmering), 20-25 minutes.

**5.** To serve, carefully remove matzo balls from water with a slotted spoon; place 1 matzo ball in each soup bowl. Add soup.

**1 cup:** 167 cal., 10g fat (2g sat. fat), 60mg chol., 523mg sod., 8g carb. (1g sugars, 1g fiber), 11g pro.

CHICKEN MATZO BALL SOUP

CHICKPEA TORTILLA
SOUP, P. 36

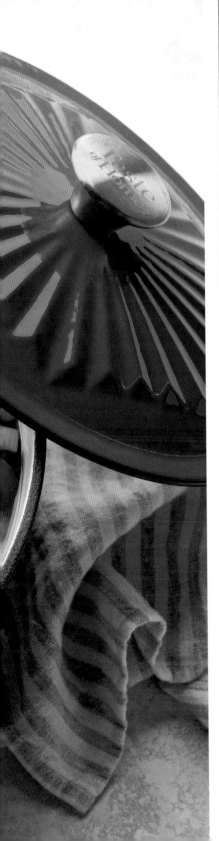

# Beans
# & Lentils

Ladle up your favorite legumes to
make every bowlful more filling,
nutritious and delicious.

ARBORIO RICE
& WHITE BEAN
SOUP, P. 42

QUICK
MEXICAN BEAN SOUP

## Quick Mexican Bean Soup

It never hurts to have a few meals that you can whip up in very little time, and this fabulous soup is one of my busy-day favorites. Green chiles and chili powder give it some oomph.
—*Colleen Delawder, Herndon, VA*

**Takes:** 20 min. • **Makes:** 4 servings

- 1 can (16 oz.) butter beans, rinsed and drained
- 1 can (15½ oz.) small white beans or navy beans, rinsed and drained
- 1 can (14½ oz.) no-salt-added diced tomatoes, undrained
- 1 can (4 oz.) chopped green chiles
- 1 Tbsp. minced fresh cilantro
- 1½ tsp. chili powder
- ½ tsp. onion powder
- 1½ cups vegetable stock
  Optional: Crumbled queso fresco and additional cilantro

In a large saucepan, combine the first 8 ingredients; bring to a boil. Reduce heat; simmer, covered, until flavors are blended, about 10 minutes. If desired, top with cheese and additional cilantro.

**1⅓ cups:** 214 cal., 1g fat (0 sat. fat), 0 chol., 893mg sod., 45g carb. (4g sugars, 12g fiber), 14g pro.

## Fiesta Chorizo-Chicken Soup

Place some crusty rolls on the table when you serve this soup and you'll have a hearty, comforting meal that will chase away winter's chill with just the right amount of heat.
—*Kathy Rodenbeck, Fort Wayne, IN*

**Prep:** 30 min. • **Cook:** 35 min.
**Makes:** 12 servings

FIESTA CHORIZO-CHICKEN SOUP

- 1 lb. uncooked chorizo, casings removed, or bulk spicy pork sausage
- 2 cups sliced fresh carrots
- 1 medium onion, chopped
- 4 garlic cloves, minced
- 1 lb. boneless skinless chicken breasts, cubed
- 1 tsp. salt
- ¼ tsp. pepper
- 2 Tbsp. olive oil
- 3 medium sweet potatoes, peeled and cubed
- 1 pkg. (10 oz.) frozen corn
- 1 medium sweet red pepper, chopped
- 1 carton (32 oz.) reduced-sodium chicken broth
- 1 can (16 oz.) butter beans, rinsed and drained
- 1 can (15 oz.) black beans, rinsed and drained
- 1 can (14½ oz.) fire-roasted diced tomatoes, undrained
- 1 can (5½ oz.) reduced-sodium V8 juice
- 1 tsp. hot pepper sauce
- 2 cups fresh spinach, chopped

**1.** Crumble the chorizo into a Dutch oven. Add the carrots, onion and garlic. Cook over medium heat until chorizo is fully cooked. Drain; remove and set aside.

**2.** In the same pot, saute the chicken, salt and pepper in oil until the meat is no longer pink, 5-10 minutes. Add the sweet potatoes, corn and red pepper; cook 5 minutes longer.

**3.** Stir in the chorizo mixture, broth, beans, tomatoes, V8 juice and pepper sauce. Bring to a boil. Reduce heat; simmer, uncovered, for 15 minutes or until vegetables are tender. Stir in spinach; cook until wilted.

**1½ cups:** 336 cal., 15g fat (5g sat. fat), 54mg chol., 1190mg sod., 29g carb. (8g sugars, 6g fiber), 22g pro.

## Lentil-Tomato Soup

Double the recipe and share this fabulous soup with friends and neighbors on cold nights. I serve it with cornbread for dunking.
—*Michelle Curtis, Baker City, OR*

**Prep:** 15 min. • **Cook:** 30 min.
**Makes:** 6 servings

- 4½ cups water
- 4 medium carrots, sliced
- 1 medium onion, chopped
- ⅔ cup dried brown lentils, rinsed
- 1 can (6 oz.) tomato paste
- 2 Tbsp. minced fresh parsley
- 1 Tbsp. brown sugar
- 1 Tbsp. white vinegar
- 1 tsp. garlic salt
- ½ tsp. dried thyme
- ¼ tsp. dill weed
- ¼ tsp. dried tarragon
- ¼ tsp. pepper

**1.** In a large saucepan, combine the water, carrots, onion and lentils; bring to a boil. Reduce heat; cover and simmer for 20-25 minutes or until the vegetables and lentils are tender.

**2.** Stir in remaining ingredients; return to a boil. Reduce heat; simmer, uncovered, for 5 minutes to allow flavors to blend.

**¾ cup:** 138 cal., 0 fat (0 sat. fat), 0 chol., 351mg sod., 27g carb. (9g sugars, 9g fiber), 8g pro. **Diabetic exchanges:** 1 starch, 1 lean meat, 1 vegetable.

**For sausage variation:** Stir in ½ pound chopped fully cooked turkey sausage; heat through.

**For kale variation:** Stir in 3 cups chopped fresh kale; cook, uncovered, until kale is tender.

**For spiced variation:** Add ¾ tsp. garam masala when adding other seasonings.

CHICKPEA TORTILLA SOUP

## Chickpea Tortilla Soup

This vegan tortilla soup recipe is healthy, filling and family-friendly! We love how flavorful it is. Each time it's served we play around with the different toppings we add.
—*Julie Peterson, Crofton, MD*

**Takes:** 30 min.
**Makes:** 8 servings

- 1 Tbsp. olive oil
- 1 medium red onion, chopped
- 4 garlic cloves, minced
- 1 to 2 jalapeno peppers, seeded and chopped, optional
- ¼ tsp. pepper
- 8 cups vegetable broth
- 1 cup red quinoa, rinsed
- 2 cans (15 oz. each) no-salt-added chickpeas or garbanzo beans, rinsed and drained
- 1 can (15 oz.) no-salt-added black beans, rinsed and drained
- 3 medium tomatoes, chopped
- 1 cup fresh or frozen corn
- ⅓ cup minced fresh cilantro
  Optional ingredients: Crushed tortilla chips, cubed avocado, lime wedges and additional chopped cilantro

Heat the oil in a Dutch oven over medium-high heat. Add the red onion, garlic, jalapeno if desired, and pepper; cook and stir until tender, 3-5 minutes. Add broth and quinoa. Bring to a boil; reduce heat. Simmer, uncovered, until quinoa is tender, about 10 minutes. Add the chickpeas, beans, tomatoes, corn and cilantro; heat through. If desired, serve with optional ingredients.

**1½ cups:** 289 cal., 5g fat (0 sat. fat), 0 chol., 702mg sod., 48g carb. (5g sugars, 9g fiber), 13g pro.

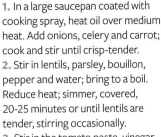

❄️
# Italian-Style Lentil Soup

I cook with lentils often because they're a nutritious, inexpensive source of protein. This low-fat soup is one of my favorite ways to use them. To make it even heartier, add ground beef, cooked sausage or leftover cubed chicken.

—*Rachel Keller, Roanoke, VA*

-----------------------------------------

**Prep:** 20 min. • **Cook:** 40 min.
**Makes:** 6 servings

- 2 tsp. olive oil
- 2 medium onions, chopped
- 2 celery ribs, thinly sliced
- 1 medium carrot, chopped
- 1 cup dried lentils, rinsed
- ¼ cup minced fresh parsley
- 1 Tbsp. reduced-sodium beef bouillon granules
- ½ tsp. pepper
- 5¼ cups water
- 1 can (6 oz.) tomato paste
- 2 Tbsp. white vinegar
- 2 tsp. brown sugar
- ½ tsp. salt
- 2 Tbsp. shredded Parmesan cheese

**1.** In a large saucepan coated with cooking spray, heat oil over medium heat. Add onions, celery and carrot; cook and stir until crisp-tender.

**2.** Stir in lentils, parsley, bouillon, pepper and water; bring to a boil. Reduce heat; simmer, covered, 20-25 minutes or until lentils are tender, stirring occasionally.

**3.** Stir in the tomato paste, vinegar, brown sugar and salt; heat through. Serve with cheese.

**Freeze option:** Freeze cooled soup in freezer containers. To use, partially thaw in a refrigerator overnight. Heat through in a saucepan, stirring occasionally; add water if necessary.

**1 cup:** 122 cal., 2g fat (1g sat. fat), 1mg chol., 420mg sod., 21g carb. (11g sugars, 6g fiber), 6g pro.
**Diabetic exchanges:** 2 vegetable, 1 starch.

 **TIP**

Unlike dried beans, lentils don't have to be soaked before using. They are a quick-cooking source of iron, vitamin B complex and fiber.

ITALIAN-STYLE LENTIL SOUP

## Pumpkin-Lentil Soup

I was really craving a hot delicious soup—something substantial and healthy. I looked around my kitchen for a few ingredients and then created this recipe. Pumpkin adds creamy richness and body.
—*Amy Blom, Marietta, GA*

- - - - - - - - - - - - - - - - - - - - - - - - - -

**Prep:** 15 min. • **Cook:** 45 min.
**Makes:** 6 servings

| | |
|---|---|
| 3 | **cups water** |
| 3 | **cups reduced-sodium chicken broth** |
| ⅔ | **cup dried lentils, rinsed** |
| 2 | **large garlic cloves, minced** |
| 1 | **Tbsp. ground cumin** |
| 2 | **tsp. dried oregano** |
| 1 | **can (15 oz.) pinto beans, rinsed and drained** |
| 1 | **can (15 oz.) black beans, rinsed and drained** |
| 1 | **can (15 oz.) pumpkin** |
| ½ | **cup mild salsa** |
| ½ | **tsp. salt** |
| 5 | **cups fresh spinach, lightly packed** |

**1.** In a 6-qt. stockpot, bring the first 6 ingredients to a boil. Cook, covered, over medium heat until the lentils are tender, 20-25 minutes.

**2.** Stir in beans, pumpkin, salsa and salt until blended; return to a boil. Reduce heat; simmer, uncovered, 20 minutes, stirring occasionally. Stir in spinach; cook until wilted, 3-5 minutes.

**1⅓ cups:** 244 cal., 1g fat (0 sat. fat), 0 chol., 857mg sod., 44g carb. (6g sugars, 11g fiber), 15g pro.

**PUMPKIN-LENTIL SOUP**

WHITE BEAN
FENNEL SOUP

## White Bean Fennel Soup

Friends often request this filling soup when I make dinner. A hint of fennel enhances the flavor, while spinach and tomatoes add color.
—*Donna Quinn,*
*Round Lake Beach, IL*

- - - - - - - - - - - - - - - - - - - - - - - - -

**Prep:** 10 min. • **Cook:** 45 min.
**Makes:** 5 servings

- 1 large onion, chopped
- 1 small fennel bulb, thinly sliced
- 1 Tbsp. olive oil
- 5 cups reduced-sodium chicken broth or vegetable broth
- 1 can (15 oz.) cannellini beans, rinsed and drained
- 1 can (14½ oz.) diced tomatoes, undrained
- 1 tsp. dried thyme
- ¼ tsp. pepper
- 1 bay leaf
- 3 cups shredded fresh spinach

**1.** In a large saucepan, saute onion and fennel in oil until tender. Add the broth, beans, tomatoes, thyme, pepper and bay leaf; bring to a boil. Reduce heat; cover and simmer for 30 minutes or until fennel is tender.
**2.** Discard bay leaf. Add spinach; cook 3-4 minutes longer or until the spinach is wilted.

**1½ cups:** 152 cal., 3g fat (0 sat. fat), 0 chol., 976mg sod., 23g carb. (0 sugars, 7g fiber), 8g pro.

FAST REFRIED BEAN SOUP

## Fast Refried Bean Soup

This recipe combines the heartiness of chili with the ease of convenient canned ingredients. It will fill you up on cold evenings or make a wonderful last-minute lunch. If you like it spicier, use medium or hot green chiles instead of mild.
—Darlene Brenden, Salem, OR

- - - - - - - - - - - - - - - - - - - - - - - - - - - -

**Takes:** 25 min.
**Makes:** 8 servings

- 1   can (16 oz.) spicy fat-free refried beans
- 1   can (15¼ oz.) whole kernel corn, drained
- 1   can (15 oz.) black beans, rinsed and drained
- 1   can (14½ oz.) chicken broth
- 1   can (14½ oz.) stewed tomatoes, cut up
- ½   cup water
- 1   can (4 oz.) chopped green chiles
- ¼   cup salsa
     Tortilla chips

In a large saucepan, combine the first 8 ingredients. Bring to a boil. Reduce heat; simmer, uncovered, until heated through, 8-10 minutes. Serve with tortilla chips.
**1 cup:** 117 cal., 1g fat (0 sat. fat), 1mg chol., 720mg sod., 21g carb. (6g sugars, 4g fiber), 5g pro.

## Easy Portuguese-Style Bean Soup

One day when looking at Portuguese recipes, I decided to put together a bean soup with the bright and spicy flavors of Portugal. It quickly became a classic in our household. The sausage, vegetables and herbs can all be prepped in minutes with a food processor.
—Steven Vance, Woodland, WA

- - - - - - - - - - - - - - - - - - - - - - - - - - - -

**Prep:** 30 min. • **Cook:** 7 hours
**Makes:** 17 servings

- 4   cans (15½ oz. each) navy beans, rinsed and drained
- 5   cups chicken stock
- 1   lb. linguica sausage or smoked sausage, thinly sliced
- 2   cans (14½ oz. each) petite diced tomatoes, undrained
- 1   large onion, halved and thinly sliced
- 1   large sweet red pepper, thinly sliced
- 2   celery ribs, thinly sliced
- 2   medium carrots, thinly sliced
- 1   cup dry white wine or additional chicken stock
- 4   garlic cloves, minced
- 2   bay leaves
- 1   orange zest strip (3 in.)
- 1   lemon zest strip (3 in.)
- 1   Tbsp. sweet paprika
- 1   Tbsp. hot pepper sauce
- 1   tsp. dried savory
- 1   tsp. dried thyme
- ½   tsp. ground cumin
- ½   tsp. salt
- ¼   tsp. pepper
- ½   cup chopped green onions
- ½   cup minced fresh cilantro
- ½   cup minced fresh parsley

**1.** Place the first 20 ingredients in a 7-qt. slow cooker. Cook, covered, on low until vegetables are tender, 7-9 hours. Remove bay leaves and orange and lemon zest strips.
**2.** Transfer 4 cups soup to a blender; cool slightly. Cover; process until smooth. Return to slow cooker; add green onions, cilantro and parsley. Heat through.
**Freeze option:** Freeze cooled soup in freezer containers. To use, partially thaw in a refrigerator overnight. Heat through in a saucepan, stirring occasionally; add broth if necessary.
**1 cup:** 235 cal., 8g fat (3g sat. fat), 18mg chol., 893mg sod., 28g carb. (4g sugars, 7g fiber), 14g pro.

EASY PORTUGUESE-STYLE
BEAN SOUP

## Zesty Garbanzo Sausage Soup

Even the busiest home cooks will have time to prepare this Cajun-inspired soup. If your family prefers spicier flavors, use medium salsa instead of mild.
—*Priscilla Doyle, Lutz, FL*

**Prep:** 20 min. • **Cook:** 6½ hours
**Makes:** 7 servings

- 2  cans (15 oz. each) garbanzo beans or chickpeas, rinsed and drained
- 3  cups water
- 1  jar (16 oz.) mild salsa
- 1  can (14½ oz.) diced tomatoes, undrained
- 2  celery ribs, chopped
- 1  cup sliced fresh or frozen okra
- 1  medium onion, chopped
- 2  tsp. Cajun seasoning
- 1  lb. smoked kielbasa or Polish sausage, cut into 1-in. pieces

In a 5-qt. slow cooker, combine the first 8 ingredients. Cover and cook on low until vegetables are tender, 6-8 hours. Stir in kielbasa. Cover and cook until heated through, about 30 minutes longer.
**1½ cups:** 370 cal., 20g fat (6g sat. fat), 43mg chol., 1514mg sod., 32g carb. (9g sugars, 6g fiber), 14g pro.

## Arborio Rice & White Bean Soup

Soup is the ultimate comfort food. This satisfying soup with arborio rice is low in fat and comes together in less than 30 minutes.
—*Deanna McDonald, Muskegon, MI*

**Takes:** 30 min. • **Makes:** 4 servings

- 1  Tbsp. olive oil
- 3  garlic cloves, minced
- ¾  cup uncooked arborio rice
- 1  carton (32 oz.) vegetable broth
- ¾  tsp. dried basil
- ½  tsp. dried thyme
- ¼  tsp. dried oregano
- 1  pkg. (16 oz.) frozen broccoli-cauliflower blend
- 1  can (15 oz.) cannellini beans, rinsed and drained
- 2  cups fresh baby spinach
    Lemon wedges, optional

**1.** In a large saucepan, heat oil over medium heat; saute garlic 1 minute. Add rice; cook and stir 2 minutes. Stir in the broth and herbs; bring to a boil. Reduce heat; simmer, covered, until rice is al dente, about 10 minutes.
**2.** Stir in the frozen vegetables and beans; cook, covered, over medium heat until heated through and the rice is tender, 8-10 minutes, stirring occasionally. Stir in the spinach until wilted. If desired, serve with lemon wedges.
**1¾ cups:** 303 cal., 4g fat (1g sat. fat), 0 chol., 861mg sod., 52g carb. (2g sugars, 6g fiber), 9g pro.

ARBORIO RICE & WHITE BEAN SOUP

SWISS CHARD
BEAN SOUP

## Swiss Chard Bean Soup

This robust soup combines nutritious Swiss chard with other terrific garden favorites. Its light broth is surprisingly rich in flavor and the grated Parmesan packs an additional punch.
—Taste of Home *Test Kitchen*

**Prep:** 25 min. • **Cook:** 30 min.
**Makes:** 10 servings

- 1 medium carrot, coarsely chopped
- 1 small zucchini, coarsely chopped
- 1 small yellow summer squash, coarsely chopped
- 1 small red onion, chopped
- 2 Tbsp. olive oil
- 2 garlic cloves, minced
- 3 cans (14½ oz. each) reduced-sodium chicken broth
- 4 cups chopped Swiss chard
- 1 can (15½ oz.) great northern beans, rinsed and drained
- 1 can (14½ oz.) diced tomatoes, undrained
- 1 tsp. dried thyme
- ½ tsp. salt
- ½ tsp. dried oregano
- ¼ tsp. pepper
- ¼ cup grated Parmesan cheese

In a Dutch oven, saute the carrot, zucchini, yellow squash and onion in oil until tender. Add garlic; saute 1 minute longer. Add the broth, Swiss chard, beans, tomatoes, thyme, salt, oregano and pepper. Bring to a boil. Reduce heat; simmer, uncovered, for 15 minutes or until the chard is tender. Just before serving, sprinkle with cheese.

**1 cup:** 94 cal., 4g fat (1g sat. fat), 2mg chol., 452mg sod., 12g carb. (3g sugars, 4g fiber), 5g pro.

## Southwest Barley & Lentil Soup

My family has been making lentil soup every new year since I was little. We have tweaked it over time, so now all our family and friends love it, too.
—*Kristen Heigl, Staten Island, NY*

**Prep:** 15 min. • **Cook:** 55 min.
**Makes:** 12 servings

- 1 Tbsp. olive oil
- 1 pkg. (14 oz.) smoked kielbasa or Polish sausage, halved lengthwise and sliced
- 4 medium carrots, chopped
- 1 medium onion, chopped
- 2 garlic cloves, minced
- ¾ tsp. ground cumin
- 1 can (28 oz.) crushed tomatoes
- 1 pkg. (16 oz.) dried brown lentils, rinsed
- 1 can (15 oz.) black beans, rinsed and drained
- ¾ cup medium pearl barley
- ½ cup frozen corn
- 10 cups reduced-sodium chicken broth

**1.** In a 6-qt. stockpot, heat oil over medium heat. Add the kielbasa; cook and stir 6-8 minutes or until browned. Remove from pot with a slotted spoon.
**2.** Add carrots and onion to same pot; cook and stir 6-8 minutes or until tender. Add garlic and cumin; cook 1 minute longer. Stir in kielbasa and remaining ingredients; bring to a boil. Reduce heat; simmer, covered, for 35-45 minutes or until lentils and barley are tender, stirring occasionally.
**1½ cups:** 366 cal., 11g fat (3g sat. fat), 22mg chol., 904mg sod., 48g carb. (7g sugars, 17g fiber), 21g pro.

SPICED SPLIT
PEA SOUP

WHITE BEAN & CHICKEN
ENCHILADA SOUP

## Spiced Split Pea Soup

A hint of curry adds the perfect amount of kick to this family-pleasing soup. Just assemble the ingredients in the slow cooker and go about your day while it cooks.
—*Sue Mohre, Mount Gilead, OH*

**Prep:** 25 min. • **Cook:** 8 hours
**Makes:** 10 servings

- 1 cup dried green split peas
- 2 medium potatoes, chopped
- 2 medium carrots, halved and thinly sliced
- 1 medium onion, chopped
- 1 celery rib, thinly sliced
- 3 garlic cloves, minced
- 3 bay leaves
- 4 tsp. curry powder
- 1 tsp. ground cumin
- ½ tsp. coarsely ground pepper
- ½ tsp. ground coriander
- 1 carton (32 oz.) reduced-sodium chicken broth
- 1 can (28 oz.) diced tomatoes, undrained

**1.** In a 4-qt. slow cooker, combine first 12 ingredients. Cook, covered, on low until the peas are tender, 8-10 hours.
**2.** Stir in the tomatoes; heat through. Discard bay leaves.
**1 cup:** 139 cal., 0 fat (0 sat. fat), 0 chol., 347mg sod., 27g carb. (7g sugars, 8g fiber), 8g pro.
**Diabetic exchanges:** 1 starch, 1 lean meat, 1 vegetable.

## White Bean & Chicken Enchilada Soup

I made this soup to satisfy my daughters' craving for creaminess, my husband's for spice and mine for white beans. Garnish with jalapenos, sour cream and green onions.
—*Darcy Gonzalez, Palmdale, CA*

- - - - - - - - - - - - - - - - - - - - - - - - - - - - -

**Prep:** 15 min. • **Cook:** 20 min.
**Makes:** 8 servings

- 4 cans (15½ oz. each) great northern beans, rinsed and drained
- 3 boneless skinless chicken breasts (6 oz. each), cubed
- ½ medium onion, chopped
- 1 garlic clove, minced
- 2 cups frozen corn, thawed
- 1 can (10¾ oz.) condensed cream of chicken soup, undiluted
- 1 carton (32 oz.) reduced-sodium chicken broth
- 1 Tbsp. ground cumin
- 2 seeded and chopped jalapeno peppers, divided
- 1 tsp. pepper
- 2 green onions, chopped
  Toppings: Sour cream, shredded cheddar cheese and tortilla chips
  Fresh cilantro leaves, optional

**1.** In a large stockpot, combine the first 8 ingredients. Add 1 chopped jalapeno and the ground pepper. Bring to a boil. Reduce heat; simmer, covered, until the chicken is no longer pink and the soup is heated through, 15-20 minutes.

**2.** Serve with the remaining chopped jalapeno and the green onions. Top with sour cream, cheese and tortilla chips. If desired, add cilantro leaves.

**1½ cups:** 301 cal., 5g fat (1g sat. fat), 41mg chol., 1121mg sod., 37g carb. (1g sugars, 12g fiber), 25g pro.

ITALIAN MEATBALL
& BEAN SOUP

## Italian Meatball & Bean Soup

I made meatball soup when I worked in an Italian restaurant years ago—and I've been playing with the recipe ever since! This is a taste sensation the whole family will love.
—*Amanda Bowyer, Caldwell, ID*

**Prep:** 30 min. • **Cook:** 5 hours
**Makes:** 6 servings

- 1 large egg
- 3 Tbsp. 2% milk
- ⅓ cup seasoned bread crumbs
- 1 lb. bulk Italian sausage
- ½ lb. ground turkey
- 2 cans (14½ oz. each) diced tomatoes
- 1 can (15 oz.) cannellini beans, rinsed and drained
- 1 can (15 oz.) black beans, rinsed and drained
- 1 can (8 oz.) tomato sauce
- 1 cup water
- 2 green onions, thinly sliced
- 1 tsp. Italian seasoning
- 1 tsp. dried minced garlic
- ½ tsp. crushed red pepper flakes
  Additional thinly sliced green onions, optional

1. In a large bowl, combine the egg, milk and bread crumbs. Crumble sausage and turkey over mixture and mix well. Shape into 1-in. balls. In a large skillet, brown meatballs in batches; drain.
2. Transfer the meatballs to a 3-qt. slow cooker. Stir in the remaining ingredients. Cover and cook on low until a thermometer inserted in a meatball reaches 160°, 5-6 hours. If desired, top with additional thinly sliced green onion.
**1½ cups:** 529 cal., 31g fat (11g sat. fat), 119mg chol., 1273mg sod., 35g carb. (6g sugars, 8g fiber), 27g pro.

BRATWURST SOUP

## Bratwurst Soup

I came up with this recipe one day to make use of some leftover bratwurst. It has been a favorite of my husband's ever since and is requested whenever the guys are hanging out.
—*Anna Miller, Churdan, IA*

**Prep:** 10 min. • **Cook:** 25 min.
**Makes:** 8 servings

- 1 lb. uncooked bratwurst links, casings removed
- ½ cup chopped onion
- 1 medium carrot, chopped
- 2 cans (15½ oz. each) navy beans, rinsed and drained
- ¼ cup pickled jalapeno slices, chopped
- ½ tsp. pepper
- 2 cups reduced-sodium chicken broth
- ¼ cup all-purpose flour
- 1½ cups 2% milk, divided
- 12 slices American cheese

1. In a Dutch oven, cook and crumble bratwurst with onion and carrot over medium heat until meat is no longer pink, 5-10 minutes; drain.
2. Stir in the beans, jalapeno, pepper and broth; bring to a boil. Whisk together flour and ½ cup milk until smooth; stir into soup. Bring to a boil, stirring constantly; cook and stir until thickened, about 5 minutes. Gradually stir in the remaining milk. Add cheese; cook and stir over low heat until melted.
**1 cup:** 468 cal., 25g fat (11g sat. fat), 53mg chol., 1322mg sod., 33g carb. (5g sugars, 6g fiber), 25g pro.

## Spicy Kielbasa Soup

Should you have any left over, this soup is fantastic reheated—the flavors will have had more time to blend. I like to serve steaming bowls with fresh rye bread.
—*Carol Custer, Clifton Park, NY*

**Prep:** 15 min. • **Cook:** 8 hours
**Makes:** 5 servings

- ½ lb. reduced-fat smoked turkey kielbasa, sliced
- 1 medium onion, chopped
- 1 medium green pepper, chopped
- 1 celery rib with leaves, thinly sliced
- 4 garlic cloves, minced
- 2 cans (14½ oz. each) reduced-sodium chicken broth
- 1 can (15½ oz.) great northern beans, rinsed and drained
- 1 can (14½ oz.) stewed tomatoes, cut up
- 1 small zucchini, sliced
- 1 medium carrot, shredded
- 1 Tbsp. dried parsley flakes
- ¼ tsp. crushed red pepper flakes
- ¼ tsp. pepper

**1.** In a nonstick skillet, cook the kielbasa over medium heat until lightly browned. Add onion, green pepper and celery; cook and stir for 3 minutes. Add the garlic; cook for 1 minute longer.
**2.** Transfer to a 5-qt. slow cooker. Stir in the remaining ingredients. Cover and cook on low for 8-9 hours or until the vegetables are tender.
**1½ cups:** 192 cal., 3g fat (1g sat. fat), 28mg chol., 1210mg sod., 27g carb. (8g sugars, 7g fiber), 16g pro.

FRENCH LENTIL & CARROT SOUP

## French Lentil & Carrot Soup

It's crazy how just a few ingredients can make such a difference. Using finely chopped rotisserie chicken in this recipe makes it perfect for a busy weeknight meal, but you can leave the chicken out altogether if you prefer.
—*Colleen Delawder, Herndon, VA*

**Prep:** 15 min. • **Cook:** 6¼ hours
**Makes:** 6 servings

- 5 large carrots, peeled and sliced
- 1½ cups dried green lentils, rinsed
- 1 shallot, finely chopped
- 2 tsp. herbes de Provence
- ½ tsp. pepper
- ¼ tsp. kosher salt
- 6 cups reduced-sodium chicken broth
- 2 cups cubed rotisserie chicken
- ¼ cup heavy whipping cream

**1.** Combine the first 7 ingredients in a 5- or 6-qt. slow cooker; cover. Cook on low until the lentils are tender, 6-8 hours.
**2.** Stir in chicken and cream. Cover and continue cooking until heated through, about 15 minutes.
**1½ cups:** 338 cal., 8g fat (3g sat. fat), 53mg chol., 738mg sod., 39g carb. (5g sugars, 7g fiber), 29g pro.
**Diabetic exchanges:** 3 lean meat, 2 starch, 1 vegetable.

## Hearty Black Bean Soup

Cumin and chili powder give spark to this thick soup. Make it vegetarian by using vegetable broth. Or if you are serving meat lovers, toss in some leftover smoked sausage, browned ground beef or roast for the last 30 minutes of cooking.
—*Amy Chop, Oak Grove, LA*

- - - - - - - - - - - - - - - - - - - - - - - - - - -

**Prep:** 10 min. • **Cook:** 9 hours
**Makes:** 8 servings

- 3 medium carrots, halved and thinly sliced
- 2 celery ribs, thinly sliced
- 1 medium onion, chopped
- 4 garlic cloves, minced
- 1 can (30 oz.) black beans, rinsed and drained
- 2 cans (14½ oz. each) reduced-sodium chicken broth or vegetable broth
- 1 can (15 oz.) crushed tomatoes
- 1½ tsp. dried basil
- ½ tsp. dried oregano
- ½ tsp. ground cumin
- ½ tsp. chili powder
- ½ tsp. hot pepper sauce
  Hot cooked rice

In a 3-qt. slow cooker, combine the first 12 ingredients. Cover and cook on low for 9-11 hours or until the vegetables are tender. Serve with rice.

**1 cup:** 129 cal., 0 fat (0 sat. fat), 0 chol., 627mg sod., 24g carb. (6g sugars, 6g fiber), 8g pro. **Diabetic exchanges:** 1½ starch, 1 lean meat.

## Tortilla Chicken Bean Soup

Tasty toppings jazz up this no-fuss soup that has Mexican flair. The recipe for this sure-to-please soup was given to me by a friend. I make it often for company, and everyone asks for the recipe. You can use pinto beans in red chili sauce instead of the regular pinto beans and cumin if you prefer.
—*Michelle Larson, Greentown, IN*

- - - - - - - - - - - - - - - - - - - - - - - - - - -

**Takes:** 10 min. • **Makes:** 5 servings

- 1 can (10½ oz.) condensed chicken with rice soup, undiluted
- 1⅓ cups water
- 1 cup salsa
- 1 cup canned pinto beans, rinsed and drained
- 1 cup canned black beans, rinsed and drained
- 1 cup frozen corn
- 1 cup frozen diced cooked chicken, thawed
- 1 tsp. ground cumin
  Toppings: Crushed tortilla chips, shredded cheddar cheese and sour cream

In a large saucepan, combine the first 8 ingredients. Cook over medium-high heat for 5-7 minutes or until heated through. Serve with tortilla chips, cheese and sour cream.

**1 cup:** 193 cal., 2g fat (1g sat. fat), 19mg chol., 869mg sod., 30g carb. (3g sugars, 5g fiber), 13g pro.

HEARTY BLACK BEAN SOUP

## Lima Bean Soup

A yearly Lima Bean Festival in West Cape May honors the growers there and showcases different recipes using their crops. This comforting chowder was a contest winner at the festival several years ago.
—*Kathleen Olsack,*
*North Cape May, NJ*

- - - - - - - - - - - - - - - - - - - - - - - - -

**Prep:** 10 min. • **Cook:** 30 min.
**Makes:** 12 servings

LIMA BEAN
SOUP

- 3 cans (14½ oz. each) chicken broth
- 2 cans (15¼ oz. each) lima beans, rinsed and drained
- 3 medium carrots, thinly sliced
- 2 medium potatoes, peeled and diced
- 2 small sweet red peppers, chopped
- 2 small onions, chopped
- 2 celery ribs, thinly sliced
- ¼ cup butter
- 1½ tsp. dried marjoram
- ½ tsp. salt
- ½ tsp. pepper
- ½ tsp. dried oregano
- 1 cup half-and-half cream
- 3 bacon strips, cooked and crumbled

**1.** In a Dutch oven or soup kettle, combine the first 12 ingredients; bring to a boil over medium heat. Reduce heat; cover and simmer for 25-35 minutes or until vegetables are tender.

**2.** Add cream; heat through but do not boil. Sprinkle with bacon just before serving.

**1 cup:** 110 cal., 7g fat (4g sat. fat), 22mg chol., 431mg sod., 9g carb. (3g sugars, 2g fiber), 3g pro.

PESTO BEAN
SOUP

## Pesto Bean Soup

This is one of my favorite vegetarian recipes, especially on those cold winter evenings. I make large batches and freeze it. Homemade pesto is tasty, but you can keep things really simple by using store-bought. This soup is delicious served with garlic toast and a green salad.
—*Liz Bellville, Tonasket, WA*

**Prep:** 10 min. • **Cook:** 4 hours
**Makes:** 8 servings

- 1 carton (32 oz.) reduced-sodium vegetable broth
- 1 large white onion, chopped
- 4 garlic cloves, minced
- 2½ cups sliced baby portobello mushrooms
- 3 cans (15 to 15½ oz. each) cannellini beans, rinsed and drained
- ¾ cup prepared pesto, divided
- ¼ cup grated Parmigiano Reggiano cheese
- Optional: Additional pesto and cheese

In a 4-qt. slow cooker, combine the first 5 ingredients. Stir in ½ cup pesto. Cook, covered, on low until vegetables are tender, 4-6 hours. Before serving, stir in remaining pesto and cheese. If desired, serve with additional pesto and cheese.
**1¼ cups:** 244 cal., 9g fat (2g sat. fat), 2mg chol., 586mg sod., 30g carb. (3g sugars, 8g fiber), 9g pro.
**Diabetic exchanges:** 2 starch, 1½ fat, 1 lean meat.

**GREENS & BEANS TURKEY SOUP**

3. Add the beans, spinach, chopped onion, bouillon, salt and pepper. Bring to a boil. Reduce heat; simmer, covered, 10 minutes.

**1 cup:** 105 cal., 2g fat (0 sat. fat), 22mg chol., 568mg sod., 10g carb. (1g sugars, 3g fiber), 10g pro. **Diabetic exchanges:** 1 lean meat, ½ starch.

## Country Sausage Soup

Savory pork sausage, two kinds of beans and diced tomatoes make this soup one I prepare time and again. It's a perfect solution when I don't know what to prepare for supper.
—*Grace Meyer, Galva, KS*

-----

**Takes:** 20 min.
**Makes:** 4 servings

- ¾ lb. bulk pork sausage
- 1 can (14½ oz.) diced tomatoes, undrained
- 1 can (14½ oz.) chicken broth
- 1 tsp. dried thyme
- ¾ to 1 tsp. dried rosemary, crushed
- ¼ tsp. pepper
- 1 can (15½ oz.) great northern beans, rinsed and drained
- 1 can (15 oz.) garbanzo beans or chickpeas, rinsed and drained

In a large saucepan, cook sausage over medium heat until no longer pink, 5-10 minutes, breaking into crumbles; drain. Stir in the tomatoes, broth, thyme, rosemary and pepper. Bring to a boil. Stir in the beans; heat through.

**1½ cups:** 387 cal., 18g fat (6g sat. fat), 31mg chol., 1279mg sod., 39g carb. (7g sugars, 11g fiber), 17g pro.

## Greens & Beans Turkey Soup

Whenever we serve turkey at a holiday meal, I use the leftover carcass to make a flavorful stock for this satisfying soup. We look forward to it almost as much as the turkey dinner!
—*Susan Albert, Jonesburg, MO*

-----

**Prep:** 15 min. • **Cook:** 2½ hours
**Makes:** 10 servings

- 1 leftover turkey carcass (from a 12-lb. turkey)
- 9 cups water
- 2 celery ribs, cut into ½-in. pieces
- 1 medium onion, cut into chunks
- 1 can (15½ oz.) great northern beans, rinsed and drained
- 1 pkg. (10 oz.) frozen chopped spinach, thawed and squeezed dry
- 3 Tbsp. chopped onion
- 2 tsp. chicken bouillon granules
- 1 tsp. salt
- ¼ tsp. pepper

1. Place turkey carcass in a stockpot; add water, celery and onion. Slowly bring to a boil. Reduce heat; simmer, covered, 2 hours.
2. Remove carcass and cool. Strain broth through a cheesecloth-lined colander; discard vegetables. Skim fat. Remove meat from bones and cut into bite-sized pieces; discard the bones. Return broth and meat to pot.

COUNTRY
SAUSAGE SOUP

## Lentil Pepperoni Stew

Turkey pepperoni nicely spices this thick lentil stew with its rich tomato broth. The recipe is a stick-to-our-ribs mainstay at our house.

—Diane Hixon, Niceville, FL

**Prep:** 5 min. • **Cook:** 1 hour 40 min.
**Makes:** 6 servings

HAM & LENTIL SOUP

- 6 cups water
- 1½ cups lentils, rinsed
- 1 medium onion, chopped
- ¼ lb. sliced turkey pepperoni, quartered
- 1 can (6 oz.) tomato paste
- ¾ tsp. salt
- ¼ tsp. dried oregano
- ¼ tsp. rubbed sage
- ⅛ tsp. cayenne pepper
- 2 medium tomatoes, chopped
- 1 celery rib with leaves, chopped
- 1 medium carrot, chopped

**1.** In a Dutch oven, combine the water, lentils, onion, pepperoni, tomato paste and seasonings; bring to a boil. Reduce heat; cover and simmer for 30 minutes.

**2.** Add tomatoes, celery and carrot; cover and simmer 35-45 minutes longer or until vegetables are tender.

**1½ cups:** 261 cal., 3g fat (1g sat. fat), 23mg chol., 681mg sod., 41g carb. (6g sugars, 7g fiber), 20g pro.
**Diabetic exchanges:** 2 starch, 2 vegetable, 1 lean meat.

## Ham & Lentil Soup

This is a combination of two soup recipes I came across and adapted. I often serve it for Sunday dinner, making enough to have leftovers. My husband is a bricklayer who regularly works outside during the winter—this soup in his lunch thermos keeps him warm!

—Andi Haug, Hendrum, MN

**Prep:** 5 min. • **Cook:** 2 hours 10 min.
**Makes:** 12 servings

- 1 meaty ham bone
- 6 cups water
- 1¼ cups dried lentils, rinsed
- 1 can (28 oz.) diced tomatoes, undrained
- 2 to 3 carrots, sliced
- 2 celery ribs, sliced
- ¼ cup chopped green onions
- ½ tsp. salt
- ½ tsp. garlic powder
- ½ tsp. dried oregano
- ⅛ tsp. pepper
- 12 oz. bulk pork sausage, cooked and drained
- 2 Tbsp. chopped fresh parsley

**1.** In a Dutch oven, bring ham bone and water to a boil. Reduce heat; cover and simmer for 1½ hours.

**2.** Remove ham bone. Add the lentils, tomatoes, carrots, celery, onions and seasonings; return to a boil. Reduce heat; cover and simmer until the lentils and vegetables are tender, 30-40 minutes.

**3.** Meanwhile, remove the meat from the ham bone; coarsely chop. Add ham, sausage and parsley to soup; heat through.

**1 cup:** 173 cal., 7g fat (3g sat. fat), 20mg chol., 355mg sod., 16g carb. (4g sugars, 7g fiber), 11g pro.

# Summer Squash & White Bean Soup

I love using summer squash in soups. This soup is hearty as is, but stir in chopped ham for an extra wallop of flavor. Serve this warm or chilled.
—*Sara Hornbeck, Knoxville, TN*

- - - - - - - - - - - - - - - - - - - - - - - - - -

**Takes:** 30 min.
**Makes:** 6 servings

2 Tbsp. butter
2 Tbsp. olive oil
2 large sweet onions, chopped (about 4 cups)
2 garlic cloves, minced
4 medium yellow summer squash, cubed (about 6 cups)
1 carton (32 oz.) chicken broth
2 cans (15 oz. each) cannellini beans, rinsed and drained, divided

¼ cup minced fresh parsley
1 to 2 Tbsp. minced fresh tarragon
¾ tsp. salt
¾ cup plain Greek yogurt

**1.** In a 6-qt. stockpot, heat butter and oil over medium heat. Add onions; cook and stir 6-8 minutes or until tender. Add garlic; cook 1 minute longer.
**2.** Add squash and broth; bring to a boil. Reduce heat; simmer, uncovered, 10-12 minutes or until the squash is tender. Stir in 1 can of beans, parsley, tarragon and salt.
**3.** Puree soup using an immersion blender. Or cool soup slightly and puree in batches in a blender, then return to pot. Stir in the remaining can of beans and heat through. Top each serving with yogurt.

**Freeze option:** Freeze cooled soup in freezer containers. To use, partially thaw in a refrigerator overnight. Heat through in a saucepan, stirring occasionally; add a little broth if necessary.

**1½ cups with 2 Tbsp. yogurt:** 290 cal., 12g fat (5g sat. fat), 21mg chol., 1187mg sod., 36g carb. (11g sugars, 8g fiber), 10g pro.

**TIP**

If you love pureed soups, an immersion blender is a wonderful tool to have. The hand-held power tool is lowered into the soup pot, eliminating the need for potentially messy transfers back and forth to the blender.

SUMMER SQUASH & WHITE BEAN SOUP

CREAM OF
CAULIFLOWER
SOUP, P. 69

# Cheesy & Creamy

*Mmm!* Indulge your craving for a bowl of rich, golden goodness with one of these irresistible recipes.

ONION CHEESE SOUP, P. 78

SPEEDY CREAM OF
WILD RICE SOUP

## Speedy Cream of Wild Rice Soup

Add homemade touches to a can of potato soup to get comfort food on the table quickly. The result is a thick and creamy treat textured with wild rice and flavored with smoky bacon.
—*Joanne Eickhoff, Pequot Lakes, MN*

**Takes:** 20 min. • **Makes:** 2 servings

- ½ cup water
- 4½ tsp. dried minced onion
- ⅔ cup condensed cream of potato soup, undiluted
- ½ cup shredded Swiss cheese
- ½ cup cooked wild rice
- ½ cup half-and-half cream
- 2 bacon strips, cooked and crumbled

In a small saucepan, bring water and onion to a boil. Reduce heat. Stir in the potato soup, cheese, rice and cream; heat through (do not boil). Garnish with bacon.
**1 cup:** 333 cal., 18g fat (11g sat. fat), 68mg chol., 835mg sod., 24g carb. (5g sugars, 2g fiber), 15g pro.

**TIP**

To cook wild rice on the stovetop, use 3 parts liquid (water or broth) to 1 part rice. Bring the liquid to a boil, add the rice and then simmer, covered, for 40-45 minutes. Fluff with a fork 5 minutes before it's finished cooking.

When finished cooking, the kernels will have burst to show the cream-colored center. The rice may not absorb all the cooking liquid; be sure to drain before using.

CREAMY HERBED TOMATO SOUP

## Creamy Herbed Tomato Soup

No one will ever guess a soup this smooth and creamy could be low in fat! The savory herb flavors blend so well, making this soup a keeper.
—*Taste of Home Test Kitchen*

**Takes:** 30 min. • **Makes:** 4 servings

- 1 can (14½ oz.) diced tomatoes, undrained
- 2 Tbsp. minced fresh parsley
- 1 Tbsp. finely chopped onion
- ¾ tsp. dried basil
- ½ tsp. salt
- ⅛ tsp. pepper
- ¼ cup tomato paste
- ¾ cup nonfat dry milk powder
- 3 Tbsp. all-purpose flour
- 2 cups 2% milk

**1.** In a large saucepan, combine the first 6 ingredients; bring to a boil. Reduce heat; simmer, uncovered, for 10 minutes.
**2.** Stir in tomato paste until blended. In a small bowl, combine milk powder and flour; stir in milk until smooth. Gradually stir into soup. Cook and stir until thickened and heated through.
**1 cup:** 201 cal., 3g fat (2g sat. fat), 14mg chol., 621mg sod., 31g carb. (24g sugars, 3g fiber), 14g pro.
**Diabetic exchanges:** 2 vegetable, 1 starch, 1 fat-free milk.

## Asparagus Leek Chowder

To us, asparagus is the taste of spring, so we enjoy it in as many meals as we can during the season. When this thick and creamy chowder is on the table, we know spring has arrived.
—*Elisabeth Harders, West Allis, WI*

------------------------------------------

**Takes:** 20 min. • **Makes:** 7 servings

- 1 lb. fresh asparagus, trimmed and cut into 1-in. pieces
- 3 cups sliced fresh mushrooms
- 3 large leeks (white portion only), sliced
- 6 Tbsp. butter
- ¼ cup all-purpose flour
- ½ tsp. salt
  Dash pepper
- 2 cups chicken broth
- 2 cups half-and-half cream
- 1 can (11 oz.) whole kernel corn, drained
- 1 Tbsp. chopped pimientos

**1.** In a large saucepan, saute the asparagus, mushrooms and leeks in butter for 10 minutes or until tender. Stir in the flour, salt and pepper until blended.

**2.** Gradually stir in chicken broth and cream. Bring to a boil. Reduce heat; cook and stir for 2 minutes or until thickened. Stir in corn and pimientos; heat through.

**1 cup:** 269 cal., 17g fat (11g sat. fat), 62mg chol., 686mg sod., 19g carb. (7g sugars, 2g fiber), 6g pro.

## Zippy Chicken & Corn Chowder

Gently spiced corn chowder is always a good option for kids, but adults can rev up their servings with hot pepper sauce. It's my go-to on busy nights.
—*Andrea Early, Harrisonburg, VA*

------------------------------------------

**Prep:** 15 min. • **Cook:** 25 min.
**Makes:** 8 servings

- ¼ cup butter
- 1 large onion, chopped
- 1 medium green pepper, chopped
- ¼ cup all-purpose flour
- 1 Tbsp. paprika
- 2 medium potatoes, peeled and chopped
- 1 carton (32 oz.) chicken broth
- 1 skinned rotisserie chicken, shredded
- 6 cups fresh or frozen corn
- 1 Tbsp. Worcestershire sauce
- ½ to 1 tsp. hot pepper sauce
- 1 tsp. salt
- 1 cup 2% milk

**1.** In a stockpot, heat butter over medium-high heat. Add the chopped onion and pepper; cook, stirring, until the vegetables are crisp-tender, 3-4 minutes. Stir in flour and paprika until blended.

**2.** Add potatoes; stir in broth. Bring to a boil; reduce heat and simmer, covered, until tender, 12-15 minutes.

**3.** Stir in chicken, corn, sauces and salt; bring to a boil. Reduce heat and cook, uncovered, until corn is tender, 4-6 minutes. Add milk; heat through (do not boil).

**1½ cups:** 351 cal., 12g fat (5g sat. fat), 75mg chol., 920mg sod., 39g carb. (7g sugars, 4g fiber), 25g pro.

ZIPPY CHICKEN & CORN CHOWDER

AUNT NANCY'S
CREAM OF CRAB SOUP

## Aunt Nancy's Cream of Crab Soup

My sister, Nancy, is one of the best cooks I know. When my daughter was getting married, I put together a cookbook of her favorite family recipes—and Nancy's soup was a definite must-have! Our family often had this with a salad before Christmas Eve services.
—*Lynne German, Buford, GA*

**Prep:** 10 min. • **Cook:** 25 min.
**Makes:** 6 servings

- ¼ cup butter, cubed
- 1 tsp. chicken bouillon granules
- 2 Tbsp. finely grated onion
- ¼ cup cornstarch
- 4 cups half-and-half cream
- 1 lb. jumbo lump crabmeat, drained
- 1 Tbsp. grated Parmesan cheese
- 2 tsp. seafood seasoning
- ¼ tsp. salt
- ¼ tsp. ground nutmeg
- ⅛ tsp. pepper
- 3 Tbsp. sherry
  Additional nutmeg

**1.** In a large saucepan, heat butter and bouillon over medium heat. Add onion; cook and stir until tender, 1-2 minutes. Stir in cornstarch until blended; gradually whisk in cream. Bring just to a boil, stirring constantly. Stir in crab, cheese and seasonings. Reduce heat; simmer, uncovered, to allow flavors to blend, about 20 minutes, stirring occasionally.
**2.** Stir in sherry; heat 1-2 minutes longer. Sprinkle individual servings with additional nutmeg.
**¾ cup:** 383 cal., 25g fat (16g sat. fat), 175mg chol., 1089mg sod., 12g carb. (6g sugars, 0 fiber), 19g pro.

## Cheddar Cheese & Beer Soup

The subtle taste of the beer is just enough to complement the cheese in this rich soup. If you want a slightly sweeter version, use apple juice instead of beer.
—*Holly Lewis, Swink, CO*

**Prep:** 15 min. • **Cook:** 25 min.
**Makes:** 6 servings

- ¼ cup butter, cubed
- ¾ lb. potatoes, peeled and chopped (about 2 cups)
- 4 celery ribs, chopped (about 2 cups)
- 2 medium onions, chopped (about 1½ cups)
- 2 medium carrots, sliced (about 1 cup)
- ½ cup all-purpose flour
- 1½ tsp. salt
- 1 tsp. ground mustard
- ⅛ tsp. cayenne pepper
- 3 cups chicken stock
- 3 cups shredded sharp cheddar cheese
- 2 cups 2% milk
- ½ cup beer or apple juice

**1.** In a 6-qt. stockpot, heat butter over medium-high heat. Add the potatoes, celery, onions and carrots; cook and stir for 5-7 minutes or until onions are tender.
**2.** Stir in flour, salt, mustard and cayenne until blended; gradually stir in stock. Bring to a boil, stirring occasionally. Reduce heat; simmer, uncovered, 10-12 minutes or until potatoes are tender. Add remaining ingredients; cook and stir until cheese is melted.
**1½ cups:** 452 cal., 29g fat (17g sat. fat), 84mg chol., 1346mg sod., 28g carb. (9g sugars, 3g fiber), 21g pro.

## Bacon Cheeseburger Soup

This creamy recipe brings two of my absolute favorite foods together in one! The tomato, fresh lettuce and crisp bacon toppers make this soup taste just like burger time.
—*Geoff Bales, Hemet, CA*

-------------------------------------

**Prep:** 20 min. • **Cook:** 4 hours
**Makes:** 6 servings

- 1½ lbs. lean ground beef (90% lean)
- 1 large onion, chopped
- ⅓ cup all-purpose flour
- ½ tsp. pepper
- 2½ cups chicken broth
- 1 can (12 oz.) evaporated milk
- 1½ cups shredded cheddar cheese
- 8 slices process American cheese, chopped
- 1½ cups shredded lettuce
- 2 medium tomatoes, chopped
- 6 bacon strips, cooked and crumbled

**1.** In a large skillet, cook and crumble the ground beef with chopped onion over medium-high heat until meat is no longer pink, 6-8 minutes; drain. Stir in flour and pepper; transfer to a 5-qt. slow cooker.

**2.** Stir in the chicken broth and milk. Cook, covered, on low 4-5 hours or until flavors are blended. Stir in the cheeses until melted. Top servings with remaining ingredients.

**1 cup:** 557 cal., 32g fat (17g sat. fat), 135mg chol., 1160mg sod., 18g carb. (10g sugars, 1g fiber), 42g pro.

BACON
CHEESEBURGER
SOUP

CHEDDAR
PEAR SOUP

## Cheddar Pear Soup

Fresh pears and sharp cheddar have always been one of my favorite flavor combos. This recipe brings the two together in a creamy, delicious soup. I like to serve it with a warm baguette and some fresh fruit for lunch or a light supper.
—*Trisha Kruse, Eagle, ID*

**Prep:** 15 min. • **Cook:** 35 min.
**Makes:** 8 servings

- ¼ cup butter, cubed
- 1 large onion, chopped
- 2 garlic cloves, minced
- ⅓ cup all-purpose flour
- 2 tsp. smoked paprika
- 5 cups chicken broth
- 3 medium ripe pears, peeled and chopped
- 3 cups sharp cheddar cheese, shredded
- ¼ tsp. freshly ground pepper
  Fresh pear slices, optional

**1.** In a Dutch oven, heat butter over medium-high heat; saute onion and garlic until tender, 7-9 minutes. Stir in flour and paprika until blended; cook and stir 2 minutes. Gradually stir in broth. Add chopped pears; bring to a boil. Reduce heat; simmer, covered, until pears are tender, about 15 minutes, stirring occasionally.
**2.** Puree soup using an immersion blender, or cool slightly and puree soup in batches in a blender; return to pot. Add cheese and pepper; cook and stir over low heat until cheese is melted, 3-5 minutes. If desired, top with pear slices.

**1 cup:** 299 cal., 20g fat (12g sat. fat), 60mg chol., 938mg sod., 18g carb. (8g sugars, 3g fiber), 12g pro.

**3.** Process the soup in batches in a blender until smooth. Return all to pan. Stir in dill; heat through. If desired, top with chives, lemon peel, dill and croutons.

**1¼ cups:** 183 cal., 11g fat (6g sat. fat), 45mg chol., 729mg sod., 13g carb. (6g sugars, 2g fiber), 6g pro.

# Chicken Gnocchi Pesto Soup

After tasting a similar soup at a restaurant, I created my own quick and tasty version.
—Deanna Smith, Des Moines, IA

- - - - - - - - - - - - - - - - - - - - - - - - -

**Takes:** 25 min.
**Makes:** 4 servings

- 1  jar (15 oz.) roasted garlic Alfredo sauce
- 2  cups water
- 2  cups rotisserie chicken, roughly chopped
- 1  tsp. Italian seasoning
- ¼  tsp. salt
- ¼  tsp. pepper
- 1  pkg. (16 oz.) potato gnocchi
- 3  cups coarsely chopped fresh spinach
- 4  tsp. prepared pesto

In a large saucepan, combine the first 6 ingredients; bring to a gentle boil, stirring occasionally. Stir in gnocchi and spinach; cook until the gnocchi float, 3-8 minutes. Top individual servings with pesto.

**1½ cups:** 586 cal., 26g fat (11g sat. fat), 158mg chol., 1650mg sod., 56g carb. (3g sugars, 4g fiber), 31g pro.

CREAMY CAULIFLOWER & GOAT CHEESE SOUP

# Creamy Cauliflower & Goat Cheese Soup

Here's an elegant choice to serve for a first course or even a light meatless dinner. The goat cheese adds an extra-special touch.
—Roxanne Chan, Albany, CA

- - - - - - - - - - - - - - - - - - - - - - - - -

**Prep:** 20 min. • **Cook:** 30 min.
**Makes:** 6 servings

- 1  Tbsp. olive oil
- 1  small onion, chopped
- 1  medium head cauliflower, broken into florets
- 1  small potato, peeled and cubed
- 2  cans (14½ oz. each) vegetable broth
- 1  Tbsp. Dijon mustard
- ½  tsp. white pepper
- 2  cups half-and-half cream
- 1  log (4 oz.) fresh goat cheese, crumbled
- 2  Tbsp. snipped fresh dill
   Optional: Minced chives, lemon peel strips, snipped fresh dill and croutons

**1.** In a large saucepan, heat oil over medium-high heat. Add the chopped onion; cook and stir until tender. Stir in the cauliflower and potato; cook and stir 4-5 minutes.
**2.** Stir in broth, mustard and white pepper. Bring to a boil. Reduce heat; simmer, covered, 15-20 minutes or until vegetables are tender. Remove from heat; stir in cream and cheese. Cool slightly.

CHICKEN GNOCCHI
PESTO SOUP

## Slow-Cooker Cordon Bleu Soup

I've taken this soup to potlucks and teacher luncheons, and I bring home an empty crock every time. When my son's school recently created a cookbook, this was the first recipe he asked me to submit for it, and his teachers were glad he did!
—*Erica Winkel, Ada, MI*

**Prep:** 40 min. + cooling
**Cook:** 3 hours
**Makes:** 8 servings

SLOW-COOKER CORDON BLEU SOUP

| 3 | Tbsp. butter, melted |
| ¼ | tsp. garlic powder |
| ¼ | tsp. pepper |
| 4 | cups cubed French bread |

**SOUP**

| 1 | small onion, diced |
| 1 | celery rib, diced |
| 1 | garlic clove, minced |
| ¼ | tsp. salt |
| ¼ | tsp. pepper |
| 3 | cans (14½ oz. each) reduced-sodium chicken broth |
| ⅓ | cup all-purpose flour |
| ⅓ | cup water |
| ¼ | cup white wine or additional reduced-sodium chicken broth |
| 8 | oz. reduced-fat cream cheese, cubed |
| 1½ | cups Swiss cheese, shredded |
| ½ | cup shredded cheddar cheese |
| ½ | lb. diced rotisserie chicken |
| ½ | lb. diced deli ham |

**1.** For croutons, preheat oven to 375°. In a large bowl, mix butter, garlic powder and pepper. Add the bread cubes; toss to coat. Transfer to a 15x10x1-in. baking pan; bake, stirring every 5 minutes, until golden brown, 15-20 minutes. Remove from pan to wire racks to cool completely.

**2.** Meanwhile, in a 4- or 5-qt. slow cooker, combine the next 5 ingredients; pour in broth. Cook, covered, on low for about 2 hours, until the vegetables are tender.
**3.** Increase heat setting to high. Mix flour and water until smooth; whisk flour mixture into broth. Cook until thickened, 30-40 minutes. Stir in the wine. Whisk in cheeses until melted. Add chicken and ham; heat through. Serve with croutons.
**Freeze option:** Before adding the croutons, freeze cooled soup in freezer containers. Freeze croutons separately. To use, partially thaw soup in refrigerator overnight. When thawed, soup may start to separate, but a good stir will smooth it out.

Heat through in a saucepan, stirring occasionally; add broth or water if necessary. While the soup is heating, thaw croutons at room temperature; sprinkle over soup.
**1¼ cups plus ½ cup croutons:** 384 cal., 23g fat (13g sat. fat), 100mg chol., 1112mg sod., 15g carb. (3g sugars, 1g fiber), 29g pro.

 **TIP**

Add some shredded carrots for a little pop of color and a boost of Vitamin A!

# Broccoli Beer Cheese Soup

Whether you include the beer or not, this soup tastes wonderful. I always make extra and pop some individual servings into the freezer.
—*Lori Lee, Brooksville, FL*

**Prep:** 20 min. • **Cook:** 30 min.
**Makes:** 10 servings

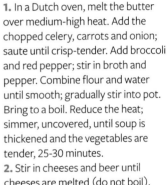

- 3 Tbsp. butter
- 5 celery ribs, finely chopped
- 3 medium carrots, finely chopped
- 1 small onion, finely chopped
- 4 cups fresh broccoli florets, chopped
- ¼ cup chopped sweet red pepper
- 4 cans (14½ oz. each) chicken broth
- ½ tsp. pepper
- ½ cup all-purpose flour
- ½ cup water
- 3 cups shredded cheddar cheese
- 1 pkg. (8 oz.) cream cheese, cubed
- 1 bottle (12 oz.) beer or nonalcoholic beer
- Optional: Additional shredded cheddar cheese, cooked and crumbled bacon strips, chopped green onions, sour cream and salad croutons

**1.** In a Dutch oven, melt the butter over medium-high heat. Add the chopped celery, carrots and onion; saute until crisp-tender. Add broccoli and red pepper; stir in broth and pepper. Combine flour and water until smooth; gradually stir into pot. Bring to a boil. Reduce the heat; simmer, uncovered, until soup is thickened and the vegetables are tender, 25-30 minutes.

**2.** Stir in cheeses and beer until cheeses are melted (do not boil). Top with additional shredded cheese, bacon, green onions, sour cream and croutons as desired.

**Freeze option:** Before adding the toppings, cool the soup; transfer to freezer containers. Freeze for up to 3 months. To use, partially thaw in refrigerator overnight; heat through in a large saucepan over medium-low heat, stirring occasionally (do not boil). Add toppings as desired.

**1 cup:** 316 cal., 23g fat (13g sat. fat), 69mg chol., 1068mg sod., 13g carb. (5g sugars, 2g fiber), 12g pro.

BROCCOLI BEER CHEESE SOUP

CHEESY CREAM OF
ASPARAGUS SOUP

CREAM OF
CAULIFLOWER SOUP

## Cheesy Cream of Asparagus Soup

Kids may not want to try a vegetable soup, but once they spoon up a mouthful of this cheesy variety, the flavor will keep them coming back for more.

—*Muriel Lerdal, Humboldt, IA*

**Takes:** 25 min. • **Makes:** 6 servings

- 2 pkg. (12 oz. each) frozen cut asparagus
- ¼ cup butter
- 2 Tbsp. all-purpose flour
- 4 cups whole milk
- 1 cup shredded Monterey Jack cheese
- 4 to 5 drops hot pepper sauce
- 1½ tsp. salt
- ¾ to 1 tsp. pepper
  Roasted asparagus tips, optional

**1.** Prepare asparagus according to package directions; drain and set aside. In a large saucepan, melt butter. Stir in flour until smooth; gradually add milk. Bring to a boil; cook and stir until thickened, about 2 minutes. Cool slightly.

**2.** Pour half of the milk mixture into a blender; add half of the asparagus. Cover and process until very smooth; return soup to the saucepan. Repeat with the remaining milk mixture and asparagus. Stir in the cheese, hot pepper sauce, salt and pepper; heat through (do not boil). If desired, top with roasted asparagus tips.

**¾ cup:** 261 cal., 19g fat (12g sat. fat), 59mg chol., 852mg sod., 12g carb. (9g sugars, 1g fiber), 12g pro.

## Cream of Cauliflower Soup

This mildly cheesy cauliflower soup is a favorite of mine. I make it often in summer, although it's good anytime.
—*Karen Brown, West Lafayette, OH*

**Takes:** 20 min. • **Makes:** 6 servings

- ⅓ cup thinly sliced green onions (tops only)
- 2 Tbsp. butter
- 2 Tbsp. all-purpose flour
- ½ tsp. salt
- 2 cups chicken broth
- 2¼ cups frozen cauliflower, thawed and chopped
- 2 cups 1% milk
- 1½ cups shredded reduced-fat cheddar cheese
- 2 Tbsp. dry sherry, optional
- 1 Tbsp. minced chives

**1.** In a saucepan, saute onions in butter until tender. Stir in flour and salt until blended. Gradually add broth. Bring to a boil; cook and stir for 2 minutes or until thickened. Reduce heat.

**2.** Add the cauliflower; simmer for 2 minutes. Add the milk and cheese; cook and stir until cheese is melted. Stir in sherry if desired. Garnish with chives.

**1 cup:** 186 cal., 11g fat (6g sat. fat), 36mg chol., 792mg sod., 10g carb. (6g sugars, 1g fiber), 13g pro.

CREAMY
RED PEPPER
SOUP

## Creamy Red Pepper Soup

Everyone loves this soup's taste, but no one guesses that the secret ingredient is pears!
—*Connie Summers, Augusta, MI*

**Prep:** 15 min.
**Cook:** 30 min. + cooling
**Makes:** 12 servings

- 2 large onions, chopped
- ¼ cup butter, cubed
- 4 garlic cloves, minced
- 2 large potatoes, peeled and diced
- 2 jars (7 oz. each) roasted red peppers, drained, patted dry and chopped
- 5 cups chicken broth
- 2 cans (15 oz. each) pears in juice
- ⅛ tsp. cayenne pepper
- ⅛ tsp. black pepper
  Optional: Chopped chives, heavy cream and croutons

**1.** In a Dutch oven, saute onions in butter until tender. Add garlic; cook 1 minute longer. Add the potatoes, red peppers and broth. Bring to a boil. Reduce heat; cover and simmer for 15-20 minutes or until vegetables are tender. Remove from the heat. Add pears; let cool.

**2.** Using a blender, puree the soup in batches. Return to the pan. Stir in the cayenne and black pepper. Cook until the soup is heated through. If desired, serve with chopped chives, heavy cream and croutons.

**1 cup:** 127 cal., 4g fat (2g sat. fat), 10mg chol., 494mg sod., 20g carb. (9g sugars, 2g fiber), 3g pro.

MEXICAN LEEK SOUP

## Mexican Leek Soup

This soup is so satisfying! You can use other beans, swap kale for the spinach, or add corn. For brunch, I put a fried egg on top.
—*Donna Ahnert, Scotia, NY*

**Takes:** 20 min. • **Makes:** 2 servings

- 1 can (15 oz.) pinto beans, rinsed and drained
- 2 medium leeks (white portion only), chopped
- ½ cup water
- ¾ cup coarsely chopped fresh spinach
- 1 cup shredded cheddar cheese
- 2 Tbsp. grated Parmesan cheese
- 2 Tbsp. grated Romano cheese
- ½ tsp. ground cumin
- ½ tsp. coarsely ground pepper
- ¼ tsp. cayenne pepper
- ⅛ tsp. salt
- ¼ cup heavy whipping cream
- ¼ cup french-fried onions
- 2 bacon strips, cooked and crumbled
  Chopped fresh cilantro, optional

**1.** Place the beans, leeks and water in a 1-qt. microwave-safe bowl. Cover and microwave on high until tender, 4-5 minutes.

**2.** In a blender, process the bean mixture and spinach until smooth. Return to the bowl; add cheeses and seasonings. Whisk in cream. Cover and microwave on high until heated through, 2-3 minutes, stirring once. Sprinkle with onions and bacon and, if desired, chopped cilantro.

**1½ cups:** 641 cal., 34g fat (19g sat. fat), 100mg chol., 1240mg sod., 54g carb. (9g sugars, 11g fiber), 34g pro.

## Onion Soup with Sausage

With a slice of mozzarella cheese bread on top, this hearty soup makes such an impressive luncheon or light supper. It looks great, and it tastes wonderful, too.
—*Sundra Hauck, Bogalusa, LA*

----------------------------------------

**Takes:** 20 min. • **Makes:** 4 servings

- ½  lb. pork sausage links, cut into ½-in. pieces
- 1  lb. sliced fresh mushrooms
- 1  cup sliced onion
- 2  cans (14½ oz. each) beef broth
- 4  slices Italian bread
- ½  cup shredded part-skim mozzarella cheese

**1.** In a large saucepan, cook sausage over medium heat until no longer pink; drain. Add sliced mushrooms and onion; cook for 4-6 minutes or until tender. Stir in the broth. Bring to a boil. Reduce the heat; simmer, uncovered, for 4-6 minutes or until heated through.

**2.** Ladle into four 2-cup ovenproof bowls. Top each with a slice of bread; sprinkle with cheese. Broil until the cheese is melted.

**1½ cups:** 378 cal., 23g fat (9g sat. fat), 58mg chol., 1325mg sod., 23g carb. (5g sugars, 3g fiber), 21g pro.

## Cheesy Chicken Chowder

I like to serve this chowder with some garlic bread and a salad. The rich, mild flavor and the tender vegetables and chicken appeal even to children and picky eaters.
—*Hazel Fritchie, Palestine, IL*

----------------------------------------

**Prep:** 10 min. • **Cook:** 25 min.
**Makes:** 8 servings

- 3  cups chicken broth
- 2  cups diced peeled potatoes
- 1  cup diced carrots
- 1  cup diced celery
- ½  cup diced onion
- 1½ tsp. salt
- ¼  tsp. pepper
- ¼  cup butter, cubed
- ⅓  cup all-purpose flour
- 2  cups whole milk
- 2  cups shredded cheddar cheese
- 2  cups diced cooked chicken

**1.** In a 4-qt. saucepan, bring chicken broth to a boil. Reduce heat; add the potatoes, carrots, celery, onion, salt and pepper. Cover and simmer for 12-15 minutes or until vegetables are tender.

**2.** Meanwhile, melt the butter in a medium saucepan; stir in the flour until smooth. Gradually stir in milk. Bring to a boil over medium heat; cook and stir for 2 minutes or until thickened. Reduce heat; add cheese, stirring until melted; add to the broth along with chicken. Cook and stir until heated through.

**1 cup:** 322 cal., 19g fat (12g sat. fat), 85mg chol., 1100mg sod., 18g carb. (6g sugars, 2g fiber), 21g pro.

CHEESY CHICKEN CHOWDER

CREAMY CREMINI-
SPINACH SOUP

## Mac & Cheese Soup

I came across this recipe a few years ago and made some changes to suit our tastes. Because it starts with packaged macaroni and cheese, it's ready in a jiffy.
—*Nancy Daugherty, Cortland, OH*

**Takes:** 30 min.
**Makes:** 8 servings

- 1 pkg. (14 oz.) deluxe macaroni and cheese dinner mix
- 9 cups water, divided
- 1 cup fresh broccoli florets
- 2 Tbsp. finely chopped onion
- 1 can (10¾ oz.) condensed cheddar cheese soup, undiluted
- 2½ cups 2% milk
- 1 cup chopped fully cooked ham

**1.** Set aside cheese sauce packet from macaroni and cheese mix. In a large saucepan, bring 8 cups water to a boil. Add macaroni; cook for 8-10 minutes or until tender.
**2.** Meanwhile, in another large saucepan, bring remaining water to a boil. Add broccoli and onion; cook, uncovered, for 3 minutes. Stir in the soup, milk, chopped ham and contents of cheese sauce packet; heat through. Drain macaroni; stir into soup.

**1 cup:** 263 cal., 9g fat (4g sat. fat), 28mg chol., 976mg sod., 32g carb. (6g sugars, 2g fiber), 13g pro.

## Creamy Cremini-Spinach Soup

This elegant twist on mushroom soup is a great option for parties, especially if you're putting on a buffet. You can make it ahead, then warm and finish it on the day of the party.
—*Susan Jordan, Denver, CO*

**Prep:** 15 min. • **Cook:** 30 min.
**Makes:** 6 servings

- ¼ cup butter, cubed
- ½ lb. sliced baby portobello mushrooms
- 2 Tbsp. finely chopped celery
- 2 Tbsp. finely chopped onion
- 2 Tbsp. all-purpose flour
- 2½ cups vegetable stock
- 1 pkg. (6 oz.) fresh baby spinach, chopped
- 1½ cups half-and-half cream
- ½ cup sour cream
- 1½ tsp. salt
- ¼ tsp. pepper
- 1 Tbsp. minced fresh parsley

**1.** In a large saucepan, heat butter over medium-high heat. Add the mushrooms, celery and onion; cook and stir until tender, 4-6 minutes. Stir in flour until blended; cook and stir until lightly browned, 2-3 minutes. Gradually whisk in stock. Bring to a boil. Reduce heat; simmer, covered, 10 minutes.
**2.** Add spinach; cook and stir until wilted, 2-4 minutes. Gradually stir in cream, sour cream, salt and pepper; heat through (do not allow to boil). Sprinkle with parsley.

**¾ cup:** 219 cal., 18g fat (11g sat. fat), 55mg chol., 952mg sod., 8g carb. (4g sugars, 1g fiber), 5g pro.

CHEESY
MEATBALL
SOUP

### Cheesy Meatball Soup

With meat, potatoes and other vegetables, this rich-tasting soup is really a meal in one. The cheese dip makes it taste like a cheeseburger! I serve this soup with a nice crusty loaf of French bread.

—*Ione Sander, Carlton, MN*

- - - - - - - - - - - - - - - - - - - - - - - - - - - - - -

**Prep:** 15 min. • **Cook:** 45 min.
**Makes:** 6 servings

- 1 large egg
- ¼ cup dry bread crumbs
- ½ tsp. salt
- 1 lb. ground beef
- 2 cups water
- 1 cup diced celery
- 1 cup whole kernel corn, drained
- 1 cup cubed peeled potatoes
- ½ cup sliced carrot
- ½ cup chopped onion
- 2 beef bouillon cubes
- ½ tsp. hot pepper sauce
- 1 jar (16 oz.) cheese dip

**1.** In a large bowl, combine the egg, bread crumbs and salt. Crumble beef over egg mixture and mix well. Shape into 1-in. balls.

**2.** In a large saucepan, brown the meatballs; drain. Add the water, celery, corn, potatoes, carrot, onion, bouillon and hot pepper sauce; bring to a boil. Reduce the heat; cover and simmer until meat is no longer pink and the potatoes are tender, about 25 minutes. Stir in the cheese dip; heat through.

**1⅓ cups:** 421 cal., 24g fat (15g sat. fat), 118mg chol., 1959mg sod., 23g carb. (6g sugars, 2g fiber), 26g pro.

**SQUASH
HOMINY SOUP**

## Squash Hominy Soup

Using frozen cooked winter squash speeds up the preparation time in this delicious soup.

—Taste of Home *Test Kitchen*

- - - - - - - - - - - - - - - - - - - - - - - - - -

**Takes:** 20 min. • **Makes:** 4 servings

⅔  cup chopped onion
1  tsp. minced garlic
1  Tbsp. butter
2  pkg. (10 oz. each) frozen cooked winter squash, thawed
2  cups chicken broth
1  can (15½ oz.) hominy, rinsed and drained
1  tsp. salt
¼  tsp. pepper
¼  tsp. each ground ginger, cinnamon and nutmeg
¼  cup heavy whipping cream

In a large saucepan, saute the onion and garlic in butter until tender. Stir in the squash, broth, hominy and seasonings. Bring to a boil. Reduce heat; cover and simmer 15 minutes. Remove from the heat; stir in cream.

**1¼ cups:** 203 cal., 9g fat (5g sat. fat), 28mg chol., 1558mg sod., 29g carb. (8g sugars, 7g fiber), 4g pro.

**TIP**

There are many varieties of winter squash, with thick, hard skins and soft yellow to orange flesh. Acorn and butternut squash would both work equally well for this recipe, but feel free to experiment with a less common variety, such as Hubbard or kabocha.

SWISS
POTATO
SOUP

## Buffalo Chicken Wing Soup

We love Buffalo chicken wings, so we created a soup that has the same zippy flavor. Start with a small amount of hot sauce—you can always add more to suit your family's tastes.
—*Pat Farmer, Falconer, NY*

**Prep:** 5 min. • **Cook:** 4 hours
**Makes:** 8 servings

- 5 cups 2% milk
- 3 cans (10¾ oz. each) condensed cream of chicken soup, undiluted
- 3 cups shredded cooked chicken (about 1 lb.)
- 1 cup sour cream
- ¼ to ½ cup Louisiana-style hot sauce
  Sliced celery, optional

In a 5-qt. slow cooker, mix all of the ingredients. Cook, covered, on low for 4-5 hours or until heated through and flavors are blended. If desired, top servings with additional hot sauce and celery.

**1 serving:** 572 cal., 29g fat (11g sat. fat), 180mg chol., 1308mg sod., 18g carb. (9g sugars, 2g fiber), 57g pro.

## Swiss Potato Soup

You have a few options when it comes to whipping up this soup—it can also be made in the microwave or started in a slow cooker in the morning.
—*Krista Musser, Orrville, OH*

**Takes:** 30 min. • **Makes:** 4 servings

- 5 bacon strips, diced
- 1 medium onion, chopped
- 2 cups water
- 4 medium potatoes, peeled and cubed
- 1½ tsp. salt
- ⅛ tsp. pepper
- ⅓ cup all-purpose flour
- 2 cups 2% milk
- 1 cup shredded Swiss cheese

**1.** In a large saucepan, cook bacon until crisp; remove to paper towels with a slotted spoon. Drain, reserving 1 Tbsp. drippings.
**2.** Saute the onion in drippings until tender. Add water, potatoes, salt and pepper. Bring to a boil. Reduce heat; simmer, uncovered, for 12 minutes or until potatoes are tender.
**3.** Combine the flour and milk until smooth; gradually stir in the potato mixture. Bring to a boil; cook and stir for 2 minutes or until thickened and bubbly. Remove from the heat; stir in cheese until melted. Sprinkle with bacon.

**1 cup:** 455 cal., 17g fat (9g sat. fat), 46mg chol., 1218mg sod., 57g carb. (12g sugars, 4g fiber), 21g pro.

BUFFALO CHICKEN
WING SOUP

## Brie Mushroom Soup

Simmer up the earthy flavor of fresh mushrooms and the richness of Brie cheese in one delicious, creamy soup. I serve big bowlfuls to warm everyone up on chilly days.
—*Maria Emmerich, River Falls, WI*

- - - - - - - - - - - - - - - - - - - - - - - -

**Prep:** 15 min. • **Cook:** 20 min.
**Makes:** 4 servings

¼ cup butter, cubed
1 lb. sliced fresh mushrooms
2 large onions, chopped
1 can (14½ oz.) chicken broth
1 Tbsp. paprika
1 Tbsp. reduced-sodium soy sauce
2 tsp. dill weed
3 Tbsp. all-purpose flour
1 cup milk
4 oz. Brie cheese, rind removed, cubed
¼ cup minced fresh parsley
2 tsp. lemon juice
½ tsp. salt
¼ tsp. pepper

**1.** In a Dutch oven, heat butter over medium-high heat. Add mushrooms and onions; cook and stir until tender. Stir in broth, paprika, soy sauce and dill weed. Bring to a boil. Reduce heat; simmer, covered, 5 minutes.
**2.** In a small bowl, whisk flour and milk until smooth. Stir into the mushroom mixture. Bring to a boil; cook and stir until thickened, 1-2 minutes. Reduce heat; add the remaining ingredients. Cook and stir until cheese is melted (do not boil).
**1¼ cups:** 328 cal., 22g fat (14g sat. fat), 67mg chol., 1192mg sod., 21g carb. (9g sugars, 3g fiber), 14g pro.

## Onion Cheese Soup

I came across an onion soup recipe in a local cookbook and made a few tweaks. It's rich, buttery and cheesy.
—*Janice Pogozelski, Cleveland, OH*

- - - - - - - - - - - - - - - - - - - - - - - -

**Takes:** 25 min. • **Makes:** 6 servings

1 large onion, chopped
3 Tbsp. butter
3 Tbsp. all-purpose flour
½ tsp. salt
Pepper to taste
4 cups whole milk
2 cups shredded Colby-Monterey Jack cheese

Seasoned salad croutons
Optional: Grated Parmesan cheese and minced chives

**1.** In a large saucepan, saute the onion in butter. Stir in the flour, salt and pepper until blended. Gradually add milk. Bring to a boil; cook and stir for 2 minutes or until thickened.
**2.** Stir in cheese until melted. Serve with croutons. If desired, top with Parmesan cheese and minced chives.
**1 cup:** 308 cal., 22g fat (15g sat. fat), 65mg chol., 540mg sod., 14g carb. (9g sugars, 1g fiber), 14g pro.

ONION CHEESE SOUP

CREAMY CHICKEN
& BROCCOLI STEW

1. Place chicken in a 4-qt. slow cooker. Combine the salad dressing, wine, 4 Tbsp. butter, onion, garlic powder, Italian seasoning, ½ tsp. salt and ½ tsp. pepper in a small bowl; pour over chicken.

2. Cover and cook on low for 5 hours. Skim fat. Remove chicken from slow cooker with slotted spoon; shred chicken with 2 forks and return to slow cooker. Combine the soup, cream cheese and 2 cups of liquid from the slow cooker in a small bowl until blended; add to the slow cooker. Cover and cook 45 minutes longer or until chicken is tender, adding the broccoli during the last 30 minutes of cooking.

3. Meanwhile, place the potatoes in a large saucepan and cover with water. Bring to a boil. Reduce heat; cover and simmer until tender, 15-20 minutes. Drain and return to pan. Mash potatoes with the remaining butter, salt and pepper.

4. Serve the chicken and broccoli mixture over mashed potatoes.

**1 serving:** 572 cal., 36g fat (14g sat. fat), 142mg chol., 1126mg sod., 28g carb. (5g sugars, 3g fiber), 29g pro.

 **TIP**

One of the big concerns in making a meal in a slow cooker is not introducing too much liquid. With the lid in place, moisture released from the food as it cooks will not evaporate. Using a condensed soup is a great way to create a flavorful sauce in the slow cooker. Just don't mix it with water or milk first!

## Creamy Chicken & Broccoli Stew

No one ever guesses how easy this homey, comforting stew is to make. My husband, who doesn't like many chicken dishes, requests it regularly.
—*Mary Watkins, Little Elm, TX*

**Prep:** 15 min. • **Cook:** 6 hours
**Makes:** 8 servings

- 8 bone-in chicken thighs, skin removed (about 3 lbs.)
- 1 cup Italian salad dressing
- ½ cup white wine or chicken broth
- 6 Tbsp. butter, melted, divided
- 1 Tbsp. dried minced onion
- 1 Tbsp. garlic powder
- 1 Tbsp. Italian seasoning
- ¾ tsp. salt, divided
- ¾ tsp. pepper, divided
- 1 can (10¾ oz.) condensed cream of mushroom soup, undiluted
- 1 pkg. (8 oz.) cream cheese, softened
- 2 cups frozen broccoli florets, thawed
- 2 lbs. red potatoes, quartered

SLOW-COOKER
QUINOA CHILI, P. 97

# Chilis

Get your chili on! Beefy, cheesy, spicy and vegetarian—they're all here for you to dig in to and enjoy.

THAI-STYLE
CHICKEN
CHILI, P. 102

MEATY
MUSHROOM
CHILI

## Meaty Mushroom Chili

Since our two daughters did not like beans in their chili, I adapted a recipe to suit our whole family's tastes. We all agree that mushrooms are an appealing alternative.
—*Marjol Burr, Catawba, OH*

**Prep:** 5 min. • **Cook:** 70 min.
**Makes:** 8 servings

- 1 lb. bulk Italian sausage
- 1 lb. ground beef
- 1 cup chopped onion
- 1 lb. fresh mushrooms, sliced
- 1 can (46 oz.) V8 juice
- 1 can (6 oz.) tomato paste
- 1 tsp. sugar
- 1 tsp. Worcestershire sauce
- 1 tsp. salt
- 1 tsp. garlic powder
- 1 tsp. dried oregano
- ½ tsp. dried basil
- ½ tsp. pepper
  Optional: Sour cream and thinly sliced green onions

In a Dutch oven, cook the sausage, beef and onion over medium heat until meat is no longer pink; drain. Stir in the mushrooms, V8 juice, tomato paste, sugar, Worcestershire sauce and seasonings. Bring to a boil. Reduce heat; cover and simmer for 1 hour. If desired, top with the sour cream and green onions.

**1 cup:** 364 cal., 23g fat (9g sat. fat), 71mg chol., 1189mg sod., 17g carb. (11g sugars, 3g fiber), 21g pro.

 **TIP**

The V8 vegetable juice adds a boost of flavor to this hearty chili, but feel free to replace it with tomato juice if you'd like.

GAME-STOPPER CHILI

## Game-Stopper Chili

A hearty chili with sausage, beef, beans and barley is perfect for the halftime food rush. People actually cheer when they see me coming with my slow cooker!
—*Barbara Lento, Houston, PA*

**Prep:** 25 min. • **Cook:** 6 hours
**Makes:** 12 servings

- 1 can (28 oz.) diced tomatoes, undrained
- 1 can (15 oz.) black beans, rinsed and drained
- 1 can (15 oz.) kidney beans, rinsed and drained
- 1 lb. boneless beef chuck steak, cut into 1-in. cubes
- 1 lb. bulk spicy pork sausage, cooked and drained
- 2 medium onions, chopped
- 1 medium sweet red pepper, chopped
- 1 medium green pepper, chopped
- 1 cup hot chunky salsa
- ⅓ cup medium pearl barley
- 2 Tbsp. chili powder
- 2 tsp. jarred roasted minced garlic
- 1 tsp. salt
- 1 tsp. ground cumin
- 4 cups beef stock
- 2 cups shredded Mexican cheese blend
  Corn chips

**1.** Place all ingredients except the cheese and chips in a 6-qt. slow cooker. Cook, covered, on low for 6-8 hours or until the beef is tender.
**2.** Stir in cheese until melted. Serve with chips.

**Freeze option:** Freeze cooled chili in freezer containers. To use, partially thaw in refrigerator overnight. Heat chili through in a saucepan, stirring occasionally.

**1⅓ cups:** 359 cal., 18g fat (7g sat. fat), 62mg chol., 1062mg sod., 26g carb. (6g sugars, 6g fiber), 23g pro.

## Kielbasa Chili

This easy creation combines the flavors of chili dogs in a bowl! I make it when I need a hot, hearty meal in a hurry. It's also great when you're watching a football game.
—Audra Duvall, Las Vegas, NV

**Takes:** 20 min. • **Makes:** 7 servings

- 1 lb. smoked kielbasa or Polish sausage, halved and sliced
- 2 cans (14½ oz. each) diced tomatoes, undrained
- 1 can (15 oz.) chili with beans
- 1 can (8¾ oz.) whole kernel corn, drained
- 1 can (2¼ oz.) sliced ripe olives, drained

In a Dutch oven coated with cooking spray, saute kielbasa until browned. Stir in the remaining ingredients. Bring to a boil. Reduce heat; simmer, uncovered, for 4-5 minutes or until heated through.

**Freeze option:** Cool chili and transfer to freezer containers. Freeze for up to 3 months. To use, thaw chili in the refrigerator. Place in a saucepan and heat through.

**1 cup:** 319 cal., 20g fat (7g sat. fat), 49mg chol., 1308mg sod., 20g carb. (6g sugars, 5g fiber), 14g pro.

## Lamb & White Bean Chili

I created a fresh take on chili using lamb and Moroccan seasoning with a feta and almond garnish. My family found it so delicious, I made a second batch almost right away. If you like a spicier chili, add harissa paste or use medium salsa instead of mild.
—Arlene Erlbach, Morton Grove, IL

**Prep:** 25 min. • **Cook:** 6¼ hours
**Makes:** 4 servings

- 1 lb. ground lamb
- 1 cup coarsely chopped red onion
- 1 can (15 oz.) cannellini beans, undrained
- 1 jar (16 oz.) mild chunky salsa
- 3 Tbsp. Moroccan seasoning (ras el hanout), divided
- 4½ tsp. finely chopped lemon zest, divided
- 3 Tbsp. orange marmalade
- ¼ cup minced fresh parsley
- ¼ cup crumbled goat cheese
- 2 Tbsp. sliced almonds
  Optional: Additional chopped red onion and toasted naan flatbread or pita bread

**1.** In a large nonstick skillet, cook lamb and onion over medium-high heat 6-8 minutes or until meat is no longer pink, breaking into crumbles; drain. Transfer lamb mixture to a 3- or 4-qt. slow cooker. Add beans.

**2.** In a small bowl, combine salsa, 1½ Tbsp. Moroccan seasoning and 3 tsp. lemon zest. Pour over beans and lamb; stir until well combined. Cook, covered, on low about 6 hours or until onions are tender.

**3.** In a small bowl, combine the orange marmalade with remaining Moroccan seasoning and lemon zest; stir into slow cooker. Cook, covered, 15 minutes longer. Sprinkle each serving with parsley, cheese and almonds. If desired, serve with the additional red onion and naan or pita bread.

**1 cup:** 438 cal., 18g fat (8g sat. fat), 84mg chol., 840mg sod., 39g carb. (16g sugars, 7g fiber), 28g pro.

LAMB & WHITE BEAN CHILI

TEX-MEX CHILI

1. In a large skillet, brown beef in oil in batches. Add garlic; cook 1 minute longer. Transfer to a 6-qt. slow cooker.

2. Stir in the beans, tomato sauce, tomatoes, water, tomato paste, salsa verde and seasonings. Cover and cook on low for 6-8 hours or until meat is tender. Garnish each serving with cheese, cilantro, sour cream, peppers and additional salsa verde if desired.

**Freeze option** Before adding toppings, cool chili. Freeze chili in freezer containers. To use, partially thaw in refrigerator overnight. Heat through in a saucepan, stirring occasionally and adding a little broth or water if necessary. Sprinkle each serving with cheese, cilantro and other toppings as desired.

**1⅓ cups:** 334 cal., 9g fat (3g sat. fat), 70mg chol., 1030mg sod., 31g carb. (7g sugars, 8g fiber), 32g pro. **Diabetic exchanges:** 3 lean meat, 1 starch, 1 vegetable.

## Tex-Mex Chili

Hearty and spicy, this is a man's chili for sure. You can also simmer it up on the stovetop—the longer you cook it, the better it tastes!
—*Eric Hayes, Antioch, CA*

- - - - - - - - - - - - - - - - - - - - - - - - - - - - - -

**Prep:** 20 min. • **Cook:** 6 hours
**Makes:** 12 servings

- 3 lbs. beef stew meat
- 1 Tbsp. canola oil
- 3 garlic cloves, minced
- 3 cans (16 oz. each) kidney beans, rinsed and drained
- 3 cans (15 oz. each) tomato sauce
- 1 can (14½ oz.) diced tomatoes, undrained
- 1 cup water
- 1 can (6 oz.) tomato paste
- ¾ cup salsa verde
- 1 envelope chili seasoning
- 2 tsp. dried minced onion
- 1 tsp. chili powder
- ½ tsp. crushed red pepper flakes
- ½ tsp. ground cumin
- ½ tsp. cayenne pepper
- Optional: Shredded cheddar cheese, minced fresh cilantro, sour cream, sliced jalapeno or fresno peppers and additional salsa verde

BEEF &
LENTIL CHILI

## Beef & Lentil Chili

Lentils were one of the crops on my dad's farm when we were growing up, and they're the best-kept secret in this delicious chili recipe. This quick, easy dish is great for a large family meal but any leftovers freeze well.
—*Cindy Agee, Lewiston, ID*

- - - - - - - - - - - - - - - - - - - - - - - - - - - -

**Prep:** 10 min. • **Cook:** 1 hour
**Makes:** 8 servings

- 2   lbs. ground beef
- 1   medium onion, chopped
- 1   garlic clove, minced
- 2   cans (14½ oz. each) stewed tomatoes, chopped
- 1   can (15 oz.) tomato sauce
- 3   Tbsp. chili powder
- 1   oz. semisweet chocolate
- ¼   tsp. salt
- 1   cup dried lentils, rinsed
- 2   cups water

In a Dutch oven, cook ground beef and onion, crumbling meat, over medium-high heat until beef is no longer pink, 6-8 minutes. Add garlic; cook 1 minute longer. Drain. Add next 5 ingredients; bring to a boil. Add lentils and water. Reduce heat; simmer, covered, until lentils are soft, about 1 hour, stirring often. Add water if mixture seems too dry.

**1¼ cups:** 367 cal., 16g fat (6g sat. fat), 70mg chol., 655mg sod., 29g carb. (8g sugars, 6g fiber), 29g pro.

 **TIP**

For a fast appetizer, reheat leftover chili in the microwave with a bit of salsa and lots of shredded cheese. Once the cheese is melted, you'll have a great dip for tortilla chips.

SPICY PEANUT
CHICKEN CHILI

## Spicy Peanut Chicken Chili

After spending time in the Southwest, I discovered Mexican peanut chicken and thought it would be fun to make it into a chili. Chipotle peppers give it a nice spice that's extra warming on a cold winter day.

—*Crystal Schlueter, Northglenn, CO*

- - - - - - - - - - - - - - - - - - - - - - - - - - - -

**Takes:** 30 min.
**Makes:** 6 servings

1 can (15 oz.) pinto beans, rinsed and drained
1 can (14½ oz.) Mexican diced tomatoes, undrained
1 can (14½ oz.) no-salt-added diced tomatoes, undrained
1 can (14½ oz.) reduced-sodium chicken broth
1 pkg. (12 oz.) frozen Southwestern corn
3 Tbsp. creamy peanut butter
1 to 2 Tbsp. minced chipotle peppers in adobo sauce
2 tsp. chili powder
½ tsp. ground cinnamon
3 cups coarsely shredded rotisserie chicken
6 Tbsp. reduced-fat sour cream
Minced fresh cilantro, optional

Place first 9 ingredients in a 6-qt. stockpot; bring to a boil. Reduce heat; simmer, covered, until flavors are blended, about 15 minutes. Stir in chicken; heat through. Serve with the sour cream and, if desired, fresh cilantro.

**1⅓ cups chili with 1 Tbsp. sour cream:** 368 cal., 13g fat (3g sat. fat), 67mg chol., 797mg sod., 33g carb. (11g sugars, 6g fiber), 30g pro.

CHUNKY CHIPOTLE
PORK CHILI

## White Chili with a Kick

Store-bought rotisserie chicken
makes this spicy chili easy, but you
could also cook your own if you prefer.
We like to top our bowls with sour
cream, green onions, cheese or salsa.
—*Emmajean Anderson,
Mendota Heights, MN*

**Prep:** 20 min. • **Cook:** 15 min.
**Makes:** 9 servings

- 1 large onion, chopped
- 6 Tbsp. butter, cubed
- 2 Tbsp. all-purpose flour
- 2 cups chicken broth
- ¾ cup half-and-half cream
- 1 rotisserie chicken, cut up
- 2 cans (15 oz. each) cannellini
  beans, rinsed and drained
- 1 can (11 oz.) white corn,
  drained
- 2 cans (4 oz. each) chopped
  green chiles
- 2 tsp. ground cumin
- 1 tsp. chili powder
- ½ tsp. salt
- ½ tsp. white pepper
- ½ tsp. hot pepper sauce
- 1½ cups shredded pepper jack
  cheese
  **Optional: Salsa and chopped
  green onions**

**1.** In a Dutch oven, saute onion in
butter. Stir in flour until blended;
cook and stir until golden brown,
about 3 minutes. Gradually add broth
and cream. Bring to a boil; cook and
stir until thickened, about 2 minutes.
**2.** Add the chicken, beans, corn,
chiles, cumin, chili powder, salt,
pepper and pepper sauce; heat
through. Stir in cheese until melted.
**3.** If desired, garnish each serving
with salsa and green onions.
**1 cup:** 424 cal., 21g fat (11g sat. fat),
113mg chol., 896mg sod., 26g carb.
(3g sugars, 5g fiber), 31g pro.

❄

## Chunky Chipotle
## Pork Chili

Perfect for using leftover pork roast,
this tasty, easy recipe can be made
ahead and reheated. It's even better
the second day.
—*Peter Halferty, Corpus Christi, TX*

**Prep:** 15 min. • **Cook:** 20 min.
**Makes:** 4 servings

- 1 medium green pepper,
  chopped
- 1 small onion, chopped
- 1 chipotle pepper in adobo
  sauce, finely chopped
- 1 Tbsp. canola oil
- 3 garlic cloves, minced
- 1 can (16 oz.) red beans,
  rinsed and drained
- 1 cup beef broth
- ½ cup salsa
- 2 tsp. ground cumin
- 2 tsp. chili powder
- 2 cups shredded cooked pork
- ¼ cup sour cream
  Sliced jalapeno pepper,
  optional

**1.** In a large saucepan, saute the
green pepper, onion and chipotle
pepper in oil until tender. Add the
garlic; cook 1 minute longer.
**2.** Add the red beans, beef broth,
salsa, ground cumin and chili powder.
Bring to a boil. Reduce heat; simmer,
uncovered, for 10 minutes or until
thickened. Add pork; heat through.
Serve with sour cream.
**Freeze option:** Cool the chili and
transfer to freezer containers. Freeze
for up to 3 months. To use, thaw chili
in the refrigerator. Transfer to a large
saucepan; heat through. Add water to
thin if desired. Serve with sour cream
and, if desired, jalapeno slices.
**1 cup:** 340 cal., 14g fat (4g sat. fat),
73mg chol., 834mg sod., 24g carb.
(3g sugars, 7g fiber), 27g pro.

WHITE CHILI
WITH A KICK

## Southwest Chili con Carne

This thick, meaty chili recipe makes two generous bowls. Because it takes only 20 minutes to prepare, it's handy for whipping up a hot lunch.
—*Marline Emmal, Vancouver, BC*

**Takes:** 20 min. • **Makes:** 2 servings

½ lb. lean ground beef (90% lean)
1½ cups reduced-sodium tomato juice
¾ cup kidney beans, rinsed and drained
2 Tbsp. chopped onion
1 tsp. chili powder
¼ tsp. ground cumin
¼ tsp. minced garlic
2 to 3 drops hot pepper sauce
Thinly sliced green onion, optional

In a large saucepan, cook beef over medium heat until no longer pink; drain. Stir in remaining ingredients. Bring to a boil. Reduce heat; simmer, uncovered, for 10 minutes or until mixture is slightly thickened, stirring occasionally. Garnish with green onion if desired.

**1 cup:** 299 cal., 8g fat (3g sat. fat), 56mg chol., 346mg sod., 24g carb. (8g sugars, 6g fiber), 30g pro. **Diabetic exchanges:** 3 lean meat, 2 vegetable, 1 starch.

TURKEY WHITE CHILI

## Turkey White Chili

Growing up in a Pennsylvania Dutch area, I was surrounded by excellent cooks and wonderful foods. I enjoy experimenting with new recipes, like this change-of-pace chili.
—*Kaye Whiteman, Charleston, WV*

**Prep:** 15 min. • **Cook:** 70 min.
**Makes:** 6 servings (1 ½ qt. )

2 Tbsp. canola oil
½ cup chopped onion
3 garlic cloves, minced
2½ tsp. ground cumin
1 lb. boneless skinless turkey breast, cut into 1-in. cubes
½ lb. ground turkey
3 cups chicken broth
1 can (15 oz.) garbanzo beans or chickpeas, rinsed and drained
1 Tbsp. minced jalapeno pepper
½ tsp. dried marjoram
¼ tsp. dried savory
2 tsp. cornstarch
1 Tbsp. water
Optional: Shredded Monterey Jack cheese and sliced red onion

**1.** In a large saucepan or Dutch oven, heat canola oil over medium heat. Add onion; saute until tender, about 5 minutes. Add garlic; cook 1 minute more. Stir in cumin; cook 5 minutes. Add turkey; cook until no longer pink. Add chicken broth, beans, jalapeno, marjoram and savory. Bring to a boil. Reduce heat; simmer, covered, for 45 minutes, stirring occasionally. **2.** Uncover; cook 15 minutes more. Dissolve cornstarch in water; stir into chili. Bring to a boil. Cook and stir for 2 minutes. If desired, serve chili with cheese and sliced red onion.

**1 cup:** 288 cal., 12g fat (2g sat. fat), 73mg chol., 635mg sod., 15g carb. (3g sugars, 3g fiber), 29g pro. **Diabetic exchanges:** 3 lean meat, 1 starch, 1 fat.

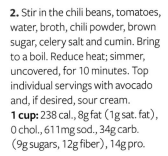

# Hearty Vegetarian Chili

Rich and flavorful, this hearty chili is absolutely packed with veggies such as mushrooms, beans and sun-dried tomatoes. It's so filling, you'll win over any meat lover.
—*Pam Ivbuls, Elkhorn, NE*

- - - - - - - - - - - - - - - - - - - - - - - - -

**Takes:** 30 min.
**Makes:** 9 servings

1¾ cups chopped baby portobello mushrooms
1   medium onion, finely chopped
½   cup chopped sun-dried tomatoes (not packed in oil)
2   Tbsp. olive oil
2   garlic cloves, minced
1   pkg. (12 oz.) frozen vegetarian meat crumbles
2   cans (16 oz. each) chili beans, undrained
2   cans (14½ oz. each) no-salt-added diced tomatoes
½   cup water
½   cup vegetable broth
4½ tsp. chili powder
2   tsp. brown sugar
½   tsp. celery salt
½   tsp. ground cumin
1   medium ripe avocado, peeled and finely chopped
    Reduced-fat sour cream, optional

**1.** In a Dutch oven, saute the baby portobello mushrooms, chopped onion and sun-dried tomatoes in oil until tender. Add minced garlic; cook 1 minute longer. Add meat crumbles; heat through.

**2.** Stir in the chili beans, tomatoes, water, broth, chili powder, brown sugar, celery salt and cumin. Bring to a boil. Reduce heat; simmer, uncovered, for 10 minutes. Top individual servings with avocado and, if desired, sour cream.

**1 cup:** 238 cal., 8g fat (1g sat. fat), 0 chol., 611mg sod., 34g carb. (9g sugars, 12g fiber), 14g pro.

# Chili with Cornbread Topping

Cornbread and chili just belong together—and this recipe proves it! You can have this on the table in less than 40 minutes.
—Taste of Home *Test Kitchen*

- - - - - - - - - - - - - - - - - - - - - - - - -

**Prep:** 20 min. • **Bake:** 15 min.
**Makes:** 2 servings

⅓   lb. lean ground beef (90% lean)
¼   cup chopped onion
1   can (15 oz.) chili with beans
½   cup water
¾   cup cornbread/muffin mix
3   Tbsp. 2% milk
2   Tbsp. beaten egg
⅓   cup shredded cheddar cheese
¼   cup frozen corn, thawed

**1.** In a large skillet, cook beef and onion over medium heat until meat is no longer pink; drain. Stir in chili and water. Bring to a boil. Reduce heat; cover and simmer for 10 minutes. Pour into two 2-cup baking dishes.
**2.** In a small bowl, combine the cornbread mix, milk and egg. Stir in cheese and corn just until combined. Spread batter evenly over chili.
**3.** Bake at 400° for 15-18 minutes or until topping is golden brown.

**1 serving:** 657 cal., 19g fat (8g sat. fat), 85mg chol., 1714mg sod., 80g carb. (21g sugars, 9g fiber), 41g pro.

HEARTY VEGETARIAN CHILI

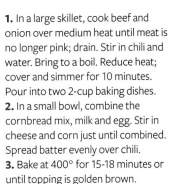

## Beer Brat Chili

My husband and I love this chili because it smells so good as it simmers in the slow cooker all day. I can't think of a better way to use up leftover brats. He can't think of a better way to eat them!
—*Katrina Krumm, Apple Valley, MN*

**Prep:** 10 min. • **Cook:** 5 hours
**Makes:** 8 servings

- 1 can (15 oz.) cannellini beans, rinsed and drained
- 1 can (15 oz.) pinto beans, rinsed and drained
- 1 can (15 oz.) Southwestern black beans, undrained
- 1 can (14½ oz.) Italian diced tomatoes, undrained
- 1 can (10 oz.) diced tomatoes and green chiles, undrained
- 1 pkg. (14 oz.) fully cooked beer bratwurst links, sliced
- 1½ cups frozen corn
- 1 medium sweet red pepper, chopped
- 1 medium onion, finely chopped
- ¼ cup chili seasoning mix
- 1 garlic clove, minced

In a 5-qt. slow cooker, combine all ingredients. Cook, covered, on low 5-6 hours.

**1¼ cups:** 383 cal., 16g fat (5g sat. fat), 34mg chol., 1256mg sod., 42g carb. (7g sugars, 10g fiber), 17g pro.

BEER BRAT CHILI

BLACK BEAN, CHORIZO & SWEET POTATO CHILI

### Black Bean, Chorizo & Sweet Potato Chili

Chili is one of my favorite dishes. This recipe takes chili to the next level by changing up the flavors and adding a surprise—sweet potatoes!
—*Julie Merriman, Seattle, WA*

- - - - - - - - - - - - - - - - - - - - - - - - - - - - -

**Prep:** 20 min. • **Cook:** 6 hours
**Makes:** 16 servings

- 1 lb. uncooked chorizo, casings removed, or spicy bulk pork sausage
- 1 large onion, chopped
- 2 poblano peppers, finely chopped
- 2 jalapeno peppers, seeded and finely chopped
- 3 Tbsp. tomato paste
- 3 large sweet potatoes, peeled and cut into ½-in. cubes
- 4 cans (14½ oz. each) fire-roasted diced tomatoes, undrained
- 2 cans (15 oz. each) black beans, rinsed and drained
- 2 cups beef stock
- 2 Tbsp. chili powder
- 1 Tbsp. dried oregano
- 1 Tbsp. ground coriander
- 1 Tbsp. ground cumin
- 1 Tbsp. smoked paprika
- ¼ cup lime juice
  Optional: Chopped jalapenos, chopped red onion and crumbled queso fresco

**1.** In a large skillet, cook and stir the chorizo, onion, poblanos and jalapenos over medium heat for 8-10 minutes or until chorizo is cooked. Using a slotted spoon, transfer to a 6-qt. slow cooker.
**2.** Stir in tomato paste. Add sweet potatoes, tomatoes, beans, stock and spices; stir to combine. Cover and cook on low for 6-7 hours or until potatoes are tender. Stir in lime juice. If desired, top servings with chopped jalapenos, chopped red onion and crumbled queso fresco.
**1 cup:** 263 cal., 9g fat (3g sat. fat), 25mg chol., 823mg sod., 33g carb. (11g sugars, 6g fiber), 12g pro.

CHEESY CHILI

## Cheesy Chili

My six grandchildren enjoy feasting on big bowls of this zesty chili. It's so creamy and comforting you can even serve it as a dip at parties.
—*Codie Ray, Tallulah, LA*

**Takes:** 25 min.
**Makes:** 12 servings

- 2 lbs. ground beef
- 2 medium onions, chopped
- 2 garlic cloves, minced
- 3 cans (10 oz. each) diced tomatoes and green chiles, undrained
- 1 can (28 oz.) diced tomatoes, undrained
- 2 cans (4 oz. each) chopped green chiles
- ½ tsp. pepper
- 2 lbs. Velveeta, cubed
  Optional: Sour cream, sliced jalapeno pepper, chopped tomato and minced fresh cilantro

**1.** In a large saucepan, cook the beef, onions and garlic until the meat is no longer pink; drain. Stir in tomatoes, chiles and pepper; bring to a boil.
**2.** Reduce heat; simmer, uncovered, for 10-15 minutes. Stir in cheese until melted. Serve immediately. If desired, top chili with sour cream, jalapenos, tomatoes and cilantro.
**Freeze option:** Freeze the cooled chili in freezer containers for up to 3 months. To use, partially thaw in refrigerator overnight. Heat through in a saucepan, stirring occasionally; add a little broth or water if necessary.
**1 cup:** 396 cal., 25g fat (15g sat. fat), 85mg chol., 1166mg sod., 13g carb. (9g sugars, 2g fiber), 29g pro.

STEAK & BEER CHILI

## Steak & Beer Chili

A cup of chili is always a pleasant way to warm up on a cold day. This one has a combination of budget-friendly chuck steak and brats in a spicy broth. If you ask me, this is guy food at its very best.
—*Elizabeth King, Duluth, MN*

**Prep:** 20 min. • **Cook:** 40 min.
**Makes:** 10 servings

- 1 boneless beef chuck steak (1 lb.), cubed
- 2 Tbsp. canola oil, divided
- 1 lb. uncooked bratwurst links, sliced
- 1 medium onion, chopped
- 4 garlic cloves, minced
- 3 cans (14½ oz. each) diced tomatoes with mild green chiles, undrained
- 2 cans (16 oz. each) hot chili beans, undrained
- 1 bottle (12 oz.) beer or 1½ cups beef broth
- 1 can (14¾ oz.) cream-style corn
- 1 can (8 oz.) pizza sauce
- ½ tsp. chili powder
- ½ tsp. ground cumin
- ¼ tsp. crushed red pepper flakes
  Sour cream, optional

**1.** In a Dutch oven, brown steak in 1 Tbsp. oil. Remove and keep warm.
**2.** Add the bratwurst, onion and remaining oil to the pan; cook and stir over medium heat until sausage is no longer pink. Add the garlic; cook 1 minute longer.
**3.** Return steak to the pan. Stir in the tomatoes, beans, beer, corn, pizza sauce, chili powder, cumin and pepper flakes.
**4.** Bring to a boil. Reduce heat; simmer, uncovered, until heated through, 25-30 minutes. Serve with sour cream if desired.
**1⅓ cups:** 431 cal., 21g fat (7g sat. fat), 63mg chol., 1317mg sod., 39g carb. (12g sugars, 8g fiber), 23g pro.

## White Bean & Chicken Chili

I adapted three different recipes to create this popular dish. It's mild, so everyone can enjoy it. In fact, it's actually won a few ribbons at chili cook-off competitions.
—*Julie White, Yacolt, WA*

- - - - - - - - - - - - - - - - - - - - - - - - - - - -

**Takes:** 20 min. • **Makes:** 6 servings

3 **cans (15 oz. each) cannellini beans, undrained**
1 **can (4 oz.) chopped green chiles**
3 **tsp. chicken bouillon granules**
3 **tsp. ground cumin**
2 **cups water**
3 **cups cubed cooked chicken or turkey**
   **Minced fresh cilantro, optional**

**1.** In a large saucepan, combine the first 5 ingredients; bring to a boil. Reduce heat; simmer, uncovered, 2-3 minutes to allow flavors to blend, stirring occasionally.
**2.** Stir in chicken; heat through. If desired, sprinkle with cilantro.
**Freeze option:** Freeze cooled chili in freezer containers. To use, partially thaw in refrigerator overnight. Heat through in a saucepan, stirring occasionally and adding a little water if necessary.
**1 cup:** 323 cal., 6g fat (1g sat. fat), 63mg chol., 1113mg sod., 34g carb. (3g sugars, 10g fiber), 34g pro.

## Chorizo Chili

I modified a bean soup recipe and came up with this wonderful chili. I make it mild, as that's how my family likes it, then I just add Tabasco sauce to spice up my bowl.
—*Jenne Delkus, Des Peres, MO*

- - - - - - - - - - - - - - - - - - - - - - - - - - - -

**Prep:** 20 min. • **Cook:** 5 hours
**Makes:** 8 servings

2 **cans (15 oz. each) black beans, rinsed and drained**
1 **can (16 oz.) kidney beans, rinsed and drained**
1 **jar (16 oz.) chunky salsa**
1 **can (15 oz.) whole kernel corn, drained**
1 **pkg. (12 oz.) fully cooked Spanish chorizo links, chopped**
1 **can (10 oz.) diced tomatoes and green chiles, undrained**
1 **cup reduced-sodium chicken broth**
2 **Tbsp. ground cumin**
1 **to 2 tsp. hot pepper sauce**
1 **medium ripe avocado, peeled and cubed**
6 **Tbsp. sour cream**
¼ **cup fresh cilantro leaves**

Combine first 9 ingredients in a 4- or 5-qt. slow cooker. Cook, covered, on low 5-6 hours or until flavors are blended. Serve with avocado, sour cream and cilantro.
**1 cup:** 366 cal., 17g fat (6g sat. fat), 30mg chol., 1262mg sod., 37g carb. (8g sugars, 10g fiber), 18g pro.

CHORIZO CHILI

SLOW-COOKER
QUINOA CHILI

**3.** Serve with the optional toppings as desired.

**1½ cups:** 318 cal., 7g fat (2g sat. fat), 37mg chol., 805mg sod., 41g carb. (7g sugars, 8g fiber), 21g pro. **Diabetic exchanges:** 2½ starch, 2 lean meat.

## Baked Bean Chili

Who says a good chili has to simmer all day? This zippy chili—with a mild hint of sweetness from the baked beans—can be made on the spur of the moment. It's an excellent standby when unexpected guests drop in. Served with bread and a salad, it's a hearty dinner everyone raves about.
—*Nancy Wall, Bakersfield, CA*

- - - - - - - - - - - - - - - - - - - - - - - - - - -

**Takes:** 30 min. • **Makes:** 24 servings

- 2 **lbs. ground beef**
- 3 **cans (28 oz. each) baked beans**
- 1 **can (46 oz.) tomato juice**
- 1 **can (11½ oz.) V8 juice**
- 1 **envelope chili seasoning**
  **Optional: Sour cream, shredded cheddar cheese and sliced jalapenos**

In a Dutch oven, cook beef over medium heat until no longer pink; drain. Stir in remaining ingredients. Bring to a boil. Reduce heat; simmer, uncovered, 10 minutes. If desired, serve with sour cream, cheddar cheese and jalapenos.

**1 cup:** 189 cal., 6g fat (2g sat. fat), 30mg chol., 721mg sod., 23g carb. (2g sugars, 6g fiber), 13g pro.

## Slow-Cooker Quinoa Chili

This is the recipe that turned my husband into a quinoa lover. I made it the day he received good news on a new job, and we'll always remember how excited we were as we enjoyed this beautiful meal.
—*Claire Gallam, Alexandria, VA*

- - - - - - - - - - - - - - - - - - - - - - - - - - -

**Prep:** 25 min. • **Cook:** 4 hours
**Makes:** 10 servings (about 3¾ qt.)

- 1 **lb. lean ground beef (90% lean)**
- 1 **medium onion, chopped**
- 2 **garlic cloves, minced**
- 1 **can (28 oz.) diced tomatoes with mild green chiles, undrained**
- 1 **can (14 oz.) fire-roasted diced tomatoes, undrained**
- 1 **can (15 oz.) garbanzo beans or chickpeas, rinsed and drained**
- 1 **can (15 oz.) black beans, rinsed and drained**
- 2 **cups reduced-sodium beef broth**
- 1 **cup quinoa, rinsed**
- 2 **tsp. onion soup mix**
- 1 **to 2 tsp. crushed red pepper flakes**
- 1 **tsp. garlic powder**
- ¼ **to ½ tsp. cayenne pepper**
- ¼ **tsp. salt**
  **Optional: Shredded cheddar cheese, chopped avocado, chopped red onion, sliced jalapeno, sour cream and cilantro**

**1.** In a large skillet, cook beef, onion and garlic over medium-high heat 6-8 minutes or until no longer pink, breaking into crumbles; drain.
**2.** Transfer the mixture to a 5- or 6-qt. slow cooker. Add the next 11 ingredients; stir to combine. Cook, covered, on low 4-5 hours or until quinoa is tender.

## Autumn Pumpkin Chili

We have this chili often as everyone loves it, even my picky little grandkids. It's a definite keeper in my book.
—*Kimberly Nagy, Port Hadlock, WA*

----------------------------------------

**Prep:** 20 min. • **Cook:** 7 hours
**Makes:** 4 servings

- 1 medium onion, chopped
- 1 small green pepper, chopped
- 1 small sweet yellow pepper, chopped
- 1 Tbsp. canola oil
- 1 garlic clove, minced
- 1 lb. ground turkey
- 1 can (15 oz.) solid-pack pumpkin
- 1 can (14½ oz.) diced tomatoes, undrained
- 4½ tsp. chili powder
- ¼ tsp. salt
- ¼ tsp. pepper

Optional: Shredded cheddar cheese, sour cream, corn chips and sliced green onions

**1.** Saute the onion and green and yellow peppers in oil in a large skillet until tender. Add minced garlic; cook 1 minute longer. Crumble turkey into skillet. Cook over medium heat until meat is no longer pink.

**2.** Transfer to a 3-qt. slow cooker. Stir in the pumpkin, diced tomatoes, chili powder, salt and pepper. Cover and cook on low for 7-9 hours. If desired, serve with toppings.

**1¼ cups:** 281 cal., 13g fat (3g sat. fat), 75mg chol., 468mg sod., 20g carb. (9g sugars, 7g fiber), 25g pro. **Diabetic exchanges:** 3 lean meat, 1 starch, 1 vegetable, 1 fat.

AUTUMN PUMPKIN CHILI

CINCINNATI CHILI

## Cincinnati Chili

Cinnamon and cocoa give deep, rich brown color to this hearty Cincinnati chili. This dish will warm you up on a cold day.
—*Edith Joyce, Parkman, OH*

**Prep:** 20 min. • **Cook:** 1¾ hours
**Makes:** 8 servings

- 1 lb. ground beef
- 1 lb. ground pork
- 4 medium onions, chopped
- 6 garlic cloves, minced
- 2 cans (16 oz. each) kidney beans, rinsed and drained
- 1 can (28 oz.) crushed tomatoes
- ¼ cup white vinegar
- ¼ cup baking cocoa
- 2 Tbsp. chili powder
- 2 Tbsp. Worcestershire sauce
- 4 tsp. ground cinnamon
- 3 tsp. dried oregano
- 2 tsp. ground cumin
- 2 tsp. ground allspice
- 2 tsp. hot pepper sauce
- 3 bay leaves
- 1 tsp. sugar
  Salt and pepper to taste
  Hot cooked spaghetti
  Optional: Shredded cheddar cheese, sour cream, chopped tomatoes and green onions

**1.** In a Dutch oven, cook the beef, pork and onions over medium heat until meat is no longer pink. Add garlic; cook 1 minute longer. Drain. Add the beans, tomatoes, vinegar, cocoa and seasonings; bring to a boil. Reduce heat; cover and simmer for 1½ hours or until heated through.
**2.** Discard bay leaves. Serve with spaghetti. If desired garnish with cheese, sour cream, tomatoes and onions.
**1 cup:** 421 cal., 16g fat (6g sat. fat), 75mg chol., 443mg sod., 38g carb. (7g sugars, 11g fiber), 32g pro.

LIME NAVY BEAN CHILI

**1 cup:** 250 cal., 2g fat (1g sat. fat), 30mg chol., 532mg sod., 37g carb. (5g sugars, 12g fiber), 22g pro. **Diabetic exchanges:** 3 lean meat, 2 starch, 1 vegetable.

## Spicy Fajita Chili

You'll want to serve this with rolls or cornbread to soak up every delicious drop. Like more heat? Just use spicier versions of V8 juice and chili beans.
—*Cathy Bell, Joplin, MO*

- - - - - - - - - - - - - - - - - - - - - - - - - - -

**Prep:** 15 min. • **Cook:** 30 min.
**Makes:** 8 servings

- 1½ lbs. ground pork
- 1 medium onion, chopped
- 1 medium green pepper, chopped
- 1 medium sweet red pepper, chopped
- 1 garlic clove, minced
- 2 cans (11½ oz. each) V8 juice
- 1 can (16 oz.) chili beans, undrained
- 1 can (10 oz.) diced tomatoes and green chiles
- 2 Tbsp. chili powder
- 1 tsp. seasoned salt
- ½ tsp. seasoned pepper
  Shredded cheddar cheese

**1.** In a Dutch oven, cook pork, onion and peppers over medium heat until meat is no longer pink. Add garlic; cook 1 minute longer. Drain.
**2.** Stir in V8 juice, beans, tomatoes, chili powder, seasoned salt and seasoned pepper. Bring to a boil. Reduce heat; simmer, uncovered, for 20 minutes or until slightly thickened. Serve with cheese.
**1 cup:** 273 cal., 13g fat (5g sat. fat), 57mg chol., 782mg sod., 20g carb. (6g sugars, 6g fiber), 20g pro.

## Lime Navy Bean Chili

I love using my slow cooker for tasty soups like this one. Just fill it in the morning and come home later to a wonderful, warm meal—no matter how busy the day!
—*Connie Thomas, Jensen, UT*

- - - - - - - - - - - - - - - - - - - - - - - - - - -

**Prep:** 15 min. + soaking
**Cook:** 5 hours • **Makes:** 6 servings

- 1¼ cups dried navy beans
- 3 cups water
- 2 bone-in chicken breast halves (7 oz. each), skin removed
- 1 cup frozen corn
- 1 medium onion, chopped
- 1 can (4 oz.) chopped green chiles
- 4 garlic cloves, minced
- 1 Tbsp. chicken bouillon granules
- 1 tsp. ground cumin
- ½ tsp. chili powder
- 2 Tbsp. lime juice
  Minced fresh cilantro, optional

**1.** Sort the navy beans and rinse with cold water. Place the beans in a large saucepan; add water to cover by 2 in. Bring to a boil; boil for 2 minutes. Remove from the heat; cover and let beans soak until beans are softened, 1-4 hours. Drain and rinse the beans, discarding liquid.
**2.** In a 3-qt. slow cooker, combine the beans, water, chicken, corn, onion, chiles, garlic, bouillon, cumin and chili powder. Cover and cook on low for 5-6 hours, until a thermometer reads 170° and beans are tender.
**3.** Remove chicken breasts; set aside until cool enough to handle. Remove meat from bones; discard bones. Cut chicken into bite-sized pieces; return to slow cooker. Stir in lime juice just before serving. If desired, serve with fresh cilantro.

SPICY FAJITA CHILI

## Hominy Beef Chili

Warm up during the cold of winter with my hearty chili. Featuring beef, hominy and corn, it's a complete meal in a bowl.
—*Steve Westphal, Wind Lake, WI*

**Prep:** 25 min. • **Cook:** 6 hours
**Makes:** 8 servings

- 2 Tbsp. canola oil
- 1 boneless beef chuck roast (3-4 lbs.), cut into 1-in. pieces
- 1 can (15½ oz.) hominy, rinsed and drained
- 1 can (14½ oz.) reduced-sodium beef broth
- 1 can (14½ oz.) diced tomatoes, undrained
- 1 large sweet red pepper, finely chopped
- ½ cup chopped onion
- 1 can (4 oz.) chopped green chiles
- 2 garlic cloves, minced
- 1 Tbsp. paprika
- 1 Tbsp. chili powder
- 2 tsp. ground cumin
- ½ tsp. salt
- ½ tsp. pepper
- 1½ cups frozen corn
  Optional: Shredded cheddar cheese and sour cream

**1.** In a large skillet, heat oil over medium heat. Brown beef in batches. Remove with a slotted spoon to a 5-qt. slow cooker; discard drippings.
**2.** Stir in hominy, broth, tomatoes, red pepper, onion, chiles, garlic and seasonings. Cook, covered on low 6-7 hours or until meat is tender. Stir in corn; heat through. If desired, serve with cheese and sour cream.
**1½ cups:** 401 cal., 20g fat (7g sat. fat), 112mg chol., 714mg sod., 18g carb. (4g sugars, 4g fiber), 36g pro.

THAI-STYLE CHICKEN CHILI

## Thai-Style Chicken Chili

I love this Asian take on a classic one-pot meal. It's quick, easy and so delicious.
—*Roxanne Chan, Albany, CA*

**Takes:** 30 min. • **Makes:** 6 servings

- 2 Tbsp. sesame oil
- 1 lb. boneless skinless chicken thighs, cut into 1-in. pieces
- 1 medium carrot, diced
- 1 celery rib, chopped
- 1 tsp. minced fresh gingerroot
- 1 large garlic clove, minced
- 1 can (28 oz.) diced tomatoes
- 1 can (13.66 oz.) light coconut milk
- 1 Tbsp. red curry paste
- ¾ tsp. salt
- ¼ tsp. pepper
- 1 cup frozen shelled edamame, thawed
- 2 cups fresh baby spinach
- 1 green onion, minced
- ½ tsp. grated lemon zest
  Fresh cilantro leaves
  Dry roasted peanuts

**1.** In a large saucepan, heat sesame oil over medium heat. Add chicken, carrot and celery; cook and stir until vegetables are slightly softened, 3-4 minutes. Add ginger and garlic; cook 1 minute more.
**2.** Stir in tomatoes, coconut milk, curry paste, salt and pepper. Bring to a boil. Reduce the heat; simmer, covered, 10 minutes. Add edamame; cook 5 minutes more. Stir in spinach, green onion and lemon zest until spinach wilts. Remove from heat; top with cilantro and peanuts.
**1⅓ cups:** 270 cal., 16g fat (6g sat. fat), 50mg chol., 635mg sod., 12g carb. (7g sugars, 4g fiber), 18g pro.

## Peanut Butter Chili

Want to mix things up? I eliminated beans from my standard chili recipe and added peanut butter and peanuts just for fun. Wow! It was amazing! I served it to my family and they all loved it.

—Nancy Heishman, Las Vegas, NV

- - - - - - - - - - - - - - - - - - - - - - - - - - -

**Prep:** 25 min. • **Cook:** 4 hours
**Makes:** 12 servings

PEANUT BUTTER
CHILI

1 Tbsp. peanut oil or canola oil
2½ lbs. lean ground beef (90% lean)
1 large green pepper, chopped
1 large red onion, chopped
1 large carrot, peeled and chopped
2 garlic cloves, minced
2 cans (15 oz. each) tomato sauce
2 cans (14½ oz. each) diced tomatoes with basil, oregano and garlic, undrained
2 cans (4 oz. each) chopped green chiles
½ cup creamy peanut butter
1 to 2 Tbsp. ground ancho chili pepper
1 tsp. kosher salt
1 tsp. smoked paprika
Optional: Shredded smoked cheddar cheese and chopped peanuts

**1.** In a large skillet, heat the oil over medium-high heat; add beef and cook in batches until no longer pink, 7-10 minutes, breaking beef into crumbles. Remove with a slotted spoon; drain. Add green pepper, onion and carrot; cook and stir until slightly browned, about 2 minutes. Add garlic; cook 1 minute longer. Transfer meat, vegetables and drippings to a 5- or 6-qt. slow cooker.
**2.** Stir in the next 7 ingredients until combined. Cook, covered, on low about 4 hours, until vegetables are tender. If desired, sprinkle servings with shredded cheese and peanuts.
**1 cup:** 279 cal., 15g fat (4g sat. fat), 59mg chol., 878mg sod., 13g carb. (6g sugars, 4g fiber), 23g pro.

 **TIP**
You can store peanut oil in the freezer to extend its shelf life.

CHICKEN ENCHILADA
SOUP, P. 125

# Cook It
# Fast or Slow

Use either a pressure cooker or a slow cooker for these versatile recipes. The choice is yours!

ENGLISH PUB
SPLIT PEA.
SOUP, P. 117

BEEFY CABBAGE
BEAN STEW

## Beefy Cabbage Bean Stew

While we were on a small group quilting retreat, a friend prepared this heartwarming stew one night for dinner. I've been passing around the recipe for others to enjoy ever since!

—Melissa Glancy, La Grange, KY

½ lb. lean ground beef (90% lean)
3 cups shredded cabbage or angel hair coleslaw mix
1 can (16 oz.) red beans, rinsed and drained
1 can (14½ oz.) diced tomatoes, undrained
1 can (8 oz.) tomato sauce
¾ cup salsa or picante sauce
1 medium green pepper, chopped
1 small onion, chopped
3 garlic cloves, minced
1 tsp. ground cumin
½ tsp. pepper
Optional: Shredded cheddar cheese and sliced jalapeno peppers

### Fast

**Prep:** 20 min. • **Cook:** 5 min. • **Makes:** 6 servings

**1.** Select saute or browning setting on a 6-qt. electric pressure cooker; adjust for medium heat. Cook the beef until no longer pink, 5-10 minutes, breaking into crumbles; drain. Press cancel. Return beef to pressure cooker. Stir in the next 10 ingredients.
**2.** Lock the lid; close pressure-release valve. Adjust to pressure-cook on high for 3 minutes. Quick-release pressure. If desired, top with shredded cheddar cheese and sliced jalapeno peppers.

### Slow

**Prep:** 20 min. • **Cook:** 6 hours • **Makes:** 6 servings

**1.** In a large skillet, cook beef over medium heat until no longer pink, 5-10 minutes, breaking into crumbles; drain.
**2.** Transfer meat to a 4-qt. slow cooker. Stir in the next 10 ingredients. Cook, covered, on low 6-8 hours or until cabbage is tender. If desired, top with shredded cheddar cheese and sliced jalapeno peppers.

**Freeze option:** Freeze cooled stew in freezer containers. To use, partially thaw in refrigerator overnight. Heat through in a saucepan, stirring occasionally; add a little water if necessary.
**1 cup:** 177 cal., 4g fat (1g sat. fat), 24mg chol., 591mg sod., 23g carb. (5g sugars, 7g fiber), 13g pro.
**Diabetic exchanges:** 2 lean meat, 1 starch, 1 vegetable.

## Potato Soup

I jazzed up a basic potato chowder by adding chopped roasted red peppers. The extra flavor gives a deliciously distinctive twist to an otherwise ordinary soup.
—*Mary Shivers, Ada, OK*

- 3  lbs. potatoes, peeled and cut into ½-in. cubes (about 8 cups)
- 1  large onion, chopped
- 1  jar (7 oz.) roasted sweet red peppers, drained and chopped
- 1  small celery rib, chopped
- 6  cups chicken broth
- ½  tsp. garlic powder
- ½  tsp. seasoned salt
- ½  tsp. pepper
- ⅛  tsp. rubbed sage
- ⅓  cup all-purpose flour
- 2  cups heavy whipping cream, divided
- 1  cup grated Parmesan cheese, divided
- 8  bacon strips, cooked and crumbled
- 2  Tbsp. minced fresh cilantro

POTATO SOUP

---

### Fast
**Prep:** 20 min. • **Cook:** 25 min. • **Makes:** 12 servings

**1.** Place first 9 ingredients in a 6-qt. electric pressure cooker. Lock lid; close pressure-release valve. Adjust pressure to pressure-cook on high for 15 minutes. Quick-release pressure.
**2.** Select saute setting and adjust for low heat. Mix flour and ½ cup cream until smooth; stir into soup. Stir in ¾ cup Parmesan cheese and the bacon, cilantro and remaining cream. Cook and stir until slightly thickened, 6-8 minutes. Serve with the remaining cheese.

### Slow
**Prep:** 20 min. • **Cook:** 5½ hours • **Makes:** 12 servings

**1.** Place first 9 ingredients in a 5- or 6-qt. slow cooker. Cook, covered, on low 5-6 hours or until the potatoes are tender.
**2.** Mix flour and ½ cup cream until smooth; stir into the soup. Stir in ¾ cup Parmesan cheese and the bacon, cilantro and remaining cream. Cook, covered, on low for about 30 minutes or until slightly thickened. Serve with the remaining cheese.

**1 cup:** 289 cal., 19g fat (11g sat. fat), 59mg chol., 848mg sod., 23g carb. (4g sugars, 1g fiber), 7g pro.

**TIP**
Any combination of potatoes will work in this recipe, but russet potatoes hold up best to the heat.

INDIAN-STYLE
CHICKEN & VEGETABLES

# Indian-Style Chicken & Vegetables

This easy Indian-influenced dish is one just about everybody will love.
Feel free to add more or less tikka masala sauce according to your taste.
—*Erica Polly, Sun Prairie, WI*

2 medium sweet potatoes, peeled and cut into 1½-in. pieces
½ cup water
2 medium sweet red peppers, cut into 1-in. pieces
3 cups fresh cauliflowerets

2 lbs. boneless skinless chicken thighs, cubed
2 jars (15 oz. each) tikka masala curry sauce
¾ tsp. salt
Optional: Minced fresh cilantro and naan flatbreads, warmed

---

## Fast
**Prep:** 15 min. • **Cook:** 5 min. • **Makes:** 8 servings

In a 6-qt. electric pressure cooker, combine the first 5 ingredients; add sauce and salt. Lock lid; close the pressure-release valve. Adjust to pressure-cook on high for 3 minutes. Quick-release pressure. A thermometer inserted in chicken should read at least 170°. If desired, top with cilantro and serve with warmed naan.

## Slow
**Prep:** 15 min. • **Cook:** 4 hours • **Makes:** 8 servings

**1.** Microwave sweet potatoes and water, covered, on high just until potatoes begin to soften, 3-4 minutes.
**2.** In a 5- or 6-qt. slow cooker, combine vegetables and chicken; add sauce and salt. Cook, covered, on low until the meat is tender, 4-5 hours. If desired, top with cilantro and serve with warmed naan.

**Freeze option:** Omitting cilantro and naan, freeze cooled vegetable and chicken mixture in freezer containers. To use, partially thaw in refrigerator overnight. Microwave, covered, on high in a microwave-safe dish until heated through, stirring gently; add a little water if necessary. If desired, sprinkle with cilantro and serve with warmed naan.
**1¼ cups:** 334 cal., 15g fat (4g sat. fat), 80mg chol., 686mg sod., 25g carb. (12g sugars, 5g fiber), 25g pro.
**Diabetic exchanges:** 3 lean meat, 2 fat, 1½ starch.

ITALIAN SAUSAGE & KALE SOUP

## Italian Sausage & Kale Soup

When I first made this colorful soup, our home smelled wonderful—and our meal tasted just as good! We immediately knew the recipe was a keeper to help us through cold winter days.
—Sarah Stombaugh, Chicago, IL

1   lb. bulk hot Italian sausage
6   cups chopped fresh kale
2   cans (15½ oz. each) great northern beans, rinsed and drained
1   can (28 oz.) crushed tomatoes
4   large carrots, finely chopped (about 3 cups)
1   medium onion, chopped
3   garlic cloves, minced
1   tsp. dried oregano
¼   tsp. salt
⅛   tsp. pepper
5   cups chicken stock
     Grated Parmesan cheese

---

### Fast
**Prep:** 20 min. • **Cook:** 15 min. + releasing
**Makes:** 8 servings

**1.** Select saute setting on a 6-qt. electric pressure cooker and adjust for medium heat. Add sausage. Cook and stir, crumbling meat until no longer pink, 5-10 minutes. Press cancel. Remove sausage; drain, then return sausage to the pressure cooker. Add the next 10 ingredients.
**2.** Lock lid; close the pressure-release valve. Adjust to pressure-cook on high for 10 minutes. Allow pressure to naturally release for 5 minutes, then quick-release any remaining pressure. Top each serving with cheese.

### Slow
**Prep:** 20 min. • **Cook:** 8 hours
**Makes:** 8 servings

**1.** In a large skillet, cook sausage over medium heat until no longer pink, 5-10 minutes, breaking into crumbles; drain. Transfer to a 5-qt. slow cooker.
**2.** Add kale, beans, tomatoes, carrots, onion, garlic, seasonings and stock to slow cooker. Cook, covered, on low for 8-10 hours or until vegetables are tender. Top each serving with cheese.

**1¾ cups:** 297 cal., 13g fat (4g sat. fat), 31mg chol., 1105mg sod., 31g carb. (7g sugars, 9g fiber), 16g pro.

## Manchester Stew

While in college, I studied abroad. I was a vegetarian at the time and pleasantly surprised by how delicious and diverse vegetarian food in Britain could be. After returning to the States, I re-created my favorite restaurant dish and named it after the University of Manchester. When the enticing aroma fills my kitchen, I feel as if I'm back in England!
—*Kimberly Hammond, Kingwood, TX*

MANCHESTER
STEW

- 2   Tbsp. olive oil
- 2   medium onions, chopped
- 2   garlic cloves, minced
- 1   tsp. dried oregano
- 1   cup dry red wine
- 1   lb. small red potatoes, quartered
- 1   can (16 oz.) kidney beans, rinsed and drained
- ½   lb. sliced fresh mushrooms
- 2   medium leeks (white portions only), sliced
- 1   cup fresh baby carrots
- 2½ cups water
- 1   can (14½ oz.) no-salt-added diced tomatoes
- 1   tsp. dried thyme
- ½   tsp. salt
- ¼   tsp. pepper
  Fresh basil leaves

---

### Fast
**Prep:** 25 min. • **Cook:** 5 min. + releasing • **Makes:** 6 servings

**1.** Select saute setting on a 6-qt. electric pressure cooker. Adjust for medium heat; add the oil. When oil is hot, cook and stir the onions until crisp-tender, 2-3 minutes. Add the garlic and oregano; cook and stir 1 minute longer. Stir in the wine. Bring to a boil; cook until liquid is reduced by half, 3-4 minutes. Press cancel.
**2.** Add potatoes, beans, mushrooms, leeks and carrots. Stir in water, tomatoes, thyme, salt and pepper. Lock lid; close pressure-release valve. Adjust to pressure-cook on high for 3 minutes. Allow pressure to release naturally for 10 minutes, then quick-release any remaining pressure. Top with basil.

### Slow
**Prep:** 25 min. • **Cook:** 8 hours • **Makes:** 6 servings

**1.** In a large skillet, heat the oil over medium-high heat. Add onions; cook and stir until crisp-tender, 2-3 minutes. Add garlic and oregano; cook and stir 1 minute longer. Stir in wine. Bring to a boil; cook until liquid is reduced by half, 3-4 minutes.
**2.** Transfer to a 5- or 6-qt. slow cooker. Add the potatoes, beans, mushrooms, leeks and carrots. Stir in the water, tomatoes, thyme, salt and pepper. Cook, covered, on low 8-10 hours or until the potatoes are tender. Top with basil.

---

**1⅔ cups:** 221 cal., 5g fat (1g sat. fat), 0 chol., 354mg sod., 38g carb. (8g sugars, 8g fiber), 8g pro.
**Diabetic exchanges:** 2 starch, 1 vegetable, 1 fat.

# Turkey Chili

I've taken my mother's milder recipe for chili and made it thicker and more robust. It's a favorite, especially in fall and winter.
—*Celesta Zanger, Bloomfield Hills, MI*

| | |
|---|---|
| 1 lb. lean ground turkey | 2 Tbsp. chili powder |
| ¾ cup chopped celery | 1 tsp. ground cumin |
| ¾ cup chopped onion | ¼ tsp. pepper |
| ¾ cup chopped green pepper | ⅛ to ¼ tsp. cayenne pepper |
| 1½ cups water | 1 can (16 oz.) hot chili beans, undrained |
| 2 cans (14½ oz. each) no-salt-added diced tomatoes, undrained | 1 can (16 oz.) kidney beans, rinsed and drained |
| 1 jar (24 oz.) meatless pasta sauce | 1 can (15 oz.) pinto beans, rinsed and drained |
| ½ cup frozen corn | Optional: Sour cream, cubed avocado, diced jalapeno peppers |

---

## Fast

**Prep:** 20 min. • **Cook:** 5 min. + releasing
**Makes:** 12 servings

**1.** Select saute or browning setting on a 6-qt. electric pressure cooker; adjust for medium heat. Cook turkey with celery, onion and pepper until meat is no longer pink, 5-10 minutes, breaking it into crumbles; drain. Add water to pressure cooker. Cook 1 minute; stir to loosen browned bits from pan. Return turkey mixture to pressure cooker. Stir in tomatoes, pasta sauce, corn, seasonings and beans.
**2.** Lock lid; close the pressure-release valve. Adjust to pressure-cook on high for 5 minutes. Allow pressure to release naturally for 10 minutes, then quick-release any remaining pressure. If desired, serve with sour cream, avocado and jalapeno.

## Slow

**Prep:** 20 min. • **Cook:** 6½ hours
**Makes:** 12 servings

**1.** In a large skillet, cook turkey with celery, onion and pepper over medium-high heat until turkey is no longer pink, 5-10 minutes, breaking meat into crumbles. Transfer to a 5-qt. slow cooker. Stir in water, tomatoes, pasta sauce, corn, seasonings and chili beans.
**2.** Cook, covered, on high 1 hour. Reduce setting to low; cook, covered, until the flavors are blended, 5-6 hours.
**3.** Stir in kidney and pinto beans; cook, covered, on low for 30 minutes longer. If desired, serve with sour cream, avocado and jalapeno.

**Freeze option:** Freeze cooled chili in freezer containers. To use, partially thaw in refrigerator overnight. Heat through in a saucepan, stirring occasionally; add a little water if necessary.
**1 cup:** 200 cal., 4g fat (1g sat. fat), 26mg chol., 535mg sod., 29g carb. (8g sugars, 8g fiber), 15g pro.

 **TIP**

It's important to rinse and drain canned beans because the thick, cloudy liquid inside often contains excess sodium and starch. Doing this can improve the taste, texture and nutritional content of a dish.

TURKEY CHILI

TURKEY SAUSAGE SOUP
WITH FRESH VEGETABLES

## Turkey Sausage Soup with Fresh Vegetables

Our family is big on soup. This favorite is very tasty and quick to make, giving me plenty of time to have fun with my kids and grandkids.
—*Nancy Heishman, Las Vegas, NV*

1 pkg. (19½ oz.) Italian turkey sausage links, casings removed
3 large tomatoes, chopped
1 can (15 oz.) garbanzo beans or chickpeas, rinsed and drained
3 medium carrots, thinly sliced
1½ cups cut fresh green beans (1-in. pieces)
1 medium zucchini, quartered lengthwise and sliced
1 large sweet red or green pepper, chopped
8 green onions, chopped
4 cups chicken stock
1 can (12 oz.) tomato paste
½ tsp. seasoned salt
⅓ cup minced fresh basil

### Fast

**Prep:** 30 min. • **Cook:** 5 min. + releasing
**Makes:** 10 servings

**1.** Select saute or browning setting on a 6-qt. electric pressure cooker; adjust for medium heat. Cook sausage until no longer pink, 5-10 minutes, breaking into crumbles; drain. Return to pressure cooker. Press cancel.
**2.** Add tomatoes, beans, carrots, green beans, zucchini, pepper and green onions. In a large bowl, whisk stock, tomato paste and seasoned salt; pour over vegetables.
**3.** Lock lid; close the pressure-release valve. Adjust to pressure-cook on high for 5 minutes. Allow pressure to release naturally for 10 minutes, then quick-release any remaining pressure. Just before serving, stir in basil.

### Slow

**Prep:** 30 min. • **Cook:** 6 hours
**Makes:** 10 servings

**1.** In a large skillet, cook the sausage over medium heat until no longer pink, 5-10 minutes, breaking into crumbles; drain and transfer to a 6-qt. slow cooker.
**2.** Add tomatoes, beans, carrots, green beans, zucchini, pepper and green onions. In a large bowl, whisk stock, tomato paste and seasoned salt; pour over vegetables. Cook, covered, on low 6-8 hours or until vegetables are tender. Just before serving, stir in basil.

**Freeze option:** Freeze cooled soup in freezer containers. To use, partially thaw in refrigerator overnight. Heat through in a saucepan, stirring occasionally; add a little stock if necessary.
**1⅓ cups:** 167 cal., 5g fat (1g sat. fat), 20mg chol., 604mg sod., 21g carb. (9g sugars, 5g fiber), 13g pro.
**Diabetic exchanges:** 2 lean meat, 2 vegetable, ½ starch.

## Provencal Ham & Bean Soup

There is nothing quite like the pleasant aroma of this delicious, rustic soup. And it's so easy to make!
—*Lyndsay Wells, Ladysmith, BC*

PROVENCAL HAM
& BEAN SOUP

2 cups assorted dried beans for soup
1 can (28 oz.) whole plum tomatoes, undrained
2 cups cubed fully cooked ham
1 large Yukon Gold potato, peeled and chopped
1 medium onion, chopped
1 cup chopped carrot
1 celery rib, chopped
2 garlic cloves, minced
2 tsp. herbes de Provence
1½ tsp. salt
1 tsp. pepper
1 carton (32 oz.) unsalted chicken stock
French bread

---

### Fast

**Prep:** 15 min. + soaking • **Cook:** 10 min. + releasing
**Makes:** 10 servings

**1.** Rinse and sort the beans; soak according to package directions. Drain and rinse the beans, discarding liquid.
**2.** Transfer beans to a 6-qt. electric pressure cooker. Add tomatoes; crush with a wooden spoon until chunky. Stir in ham, vegetables, garlic, seasonings and stock.
**3.** Lock lid; close the pressure-release valve. Adjust to pressure-cook on high for 10 minutes. Allow pressure to naturally release for 10 minutes, then quick-release any remaining pressure. Serve with bread.

### Slow

**Prep:** 15 min. + soaking • **Cook:** 7 hours
**Makes:** 10 servings

**1.** Rinse and sort beans; soak according to package directions. Drain and rinse beans, discarding liquid.
**2.** Transfer beans to a 6-qt. slow cooker. Add tomatoes; crush with a wooden spoon until chunky. Stir in ham, vegetables, garlic, seasonings and stock. Cook, covered, on low for 7-9 hours or until the beans are tender. Serve with bread.

**1⅓ cups:** 212 cal., 2g fat (0 sat. fat), 17mg chol., 887mg sod., 33g carb. (5g sugars, 9g fiber), 17g pro.

ENGLISH PUB
SPLIT PEA SOUP

# English Pub Split Pea Soup

This family favorite is the same basic recipe my grandmother used years ago, but I have adapted it for today's convenient appliances. Now I can spend just 15 minutes doing the prep, walk away for a bit and then the soup's on! Finish it with more milk if you like your soup a bit thinner.
—*Judy Batson, Tampa, FL*

- 1 meaty ham bone
- 1⅓ cups dried green split peas, rinsed
- 2 celery ribs, chopped
- 1 large carrot, chopped
- 1 sweet onion, chopped
- 4 cups water
- 1 bottle (12 oz.) light beer

- 1 Tbsp. prepared English mustard
- ½ cup 2% milk
- ¼ cup minced fresh parsley
- ½ tsp. salt
- ¼ tsp. pepper
- ¼ tsp. ground nutmeg
  Additional minced fresh parsley, optional

---

## Fast

**Prep:** 15 min. • **Cook:** 15 min. + releasing
**Makes:** 8 servings

**1.** Place ham bone in a 6-qt. electric pressure cooker. Add peas, celery, carrot, onion, water, beer and mustard. Lock lid; close pressure-release valve. Adjust to pressure-cook on high for 15 minutes. Allow pressure to release naturally, then quick-release any remaining pressure.
**2.** Remove the ham bone from the soup. Cool slightly, trim away fat and remove meat from bone; discard fat and bone. Cut meat into bite-sized pieces; return to pressure cooker. Stir in the remaining ingredients. If desired, top with additional minced parsley.

## Slow

**Prep:** 15 min. • **Cook:** 5 hours
**Makes:** 8 servings

**1.** Place the ham bone in a 4-qt. slow cooker. Add peas, celery, carrot and sweet onion. Combine water, beer and mustard; pour over the vegetables. Cook, covered, on high 5-6 hours or until peas are tender.
**2.** Remove the ham bone from the soup. Cool slightly, trim away fat and remove meat from bone; discard fat and bone. Cut meat into bite-sized pieces; return to slow cooker. Stir in remaining ingredients. If desired, top with additional minced parsley.

**1 cup:** 141 cal., 1g fat (0 sat. fat), 1mg chol., 193mg sod., 25g carb. (6g sugars, 9g fiber), 9g pro.
**Diabetic exchanges:** 1½ starch, 1 lean meat.

We used Colman's prepared mustard when testing this recipe. If you can't find English mustard, horseradish mustard is always a good substitute.

SPICY BEEF
VEGETABLE STEW

## Spicy Beef Vegetable Stew

This zesty ground beef and vegetable soup is flavorful and comes together so quickly. It makes a complete meal when served with warm cornbread, sourdough or French bread—if you can squeak in a few more calories!
—*Lynnette Davis, Tullahoma, TN*

- 1 lb. lean ground beef (90% lean)
- 1 cup chopped onion
- 3½ cups water
- 1 jar (24 oz.) meatless pasta sauce
- 1 pkg. (16 oz.) frozen mixed vegetables
- 1 can (10 oz.) diced tomatoes and green chiles, undrained
- 1 cup sliced celery
- 1 tsp. beef bouillon granules
- 1 tsp. pepper

### Fast

**Prep:** 10 min. • **Cook:** 5 min. + releasing
**Makes:** 8 servings

1. Select saute or browning setting on a 6-qt. electric pressure cooker; adjust for medium heat. Cook beef until no longer pink, 5-10 minutes, breaking it into crumbles; drain. Press cancel. Stir in remaining ingredients.
2. Lock lid; close the pressure-release valve. Adjust to pressure-cook on high for 5 minutes. Allow pressure to release naturally.

### Slow

**Prep:** 10 min. • **Cook:** 8 hours
**Makes:** 8 servings

1. In a large skillet, cook beef and onion over medium heat until meat is no longer pink, 5-10 minutes, breaking it into crumbles; drain.
2. Transfer to a 5-qt. slow cooker. Stir in the remaining ingredients. Cover and cook on low for 8 hours or until the vegetables are tender.

**Freeze option:** Freeze cooled stew in freezer containers. To use, partially thaw in refrigerator overnight. Heat through in a saucepan, stirring occasionally; add a little water if necessary.
**1½ cups:** 177 cal., 5g fat (2g sat. fat), 35mg chol., 675mg sod., 19g carb. (8g sugars, 5g fiber), 15g pro.
**Diabetic exchanges:** 2 lean meat, 1 starch.

## Burgundy Beef

When my adult children are coming over for dinner, this is their most-requested dish. All three of them, and their significant others, love this recipe.
—*Urilla Cheverie, Andover, MA*

- 4 lbs. beef top sirloin steak, cut into 1-in. cubes
- 3 large onions, sliced
- 1 cup water
- 1 cup burgundy wine or beef broth
- 1 cup ketchup
- ¼ cup quick-cooking tapioca
- ¼ cup packed brown sugar
- ¼ cup Worcestershire sauce
- 4 tsp. paprika
- 1½ tsp. salt
- 1 tsp. minced garlic
- 1 tsp. ground mustard
- 2 Tbsp. cornstarch
- 3 Tbsp. cold water
  Hot cooked noodles

BURGUNDY BEEF

---

### Fast

**Prep:** 10 min. • **Cook:** 25 min. + releasing
**Makes:** 10 servings

**1.** Combine the first 12 ingredients in a 6-qt. electric pressure cooker. Lock lid; close the pressure-release valve. Adjust to pressure-cook on high for 20 minutes. Allow pressure to release naturally for 10 minutes, then quick-release any remaining pressure. Press cancel.
**2.** Combine the cornstarch and water until smooth; stir into pressure cooker. Select saute setting and adjust for low heat. Simmer, stirring constantly, until thickened, 1-2 minutes. Serve with noodles.

### Slow

**Prep:** 10 min. • **Cook:** 8¼ hours
**Makes:** 10 servings

**1.** In a 5-qt. slow cooker, combine the first 12 ingredients. Cook, covered, on low until meat is tender, 8-9 hours.
**2.** Combine cornstarch and water until smooth; stir into pan juices. Cook, covered, on high until gravy is thickened, about 15 minutes. Serve with noodles.

**Freeze option:** Place beef in freezer containers; top with sauce. Cool and freeze. To use, partially thaw in refrigerator overnight. Heat through in a covered saucepan, stirring gently; add a little water if necessary.
**1 cup:** 347 cal., 8g fat (3g sat. fat), 74mg chol., 811mg sod., 24g carb. (15g sugars, 1g fiber), 40g pro.

# Pork Chile Verde

Pork stews with jalapenos, onion, green enchilada sauce and spices in this flavor-packed Mexican dish. It is fantastic on its own or stuffed into a warm tortilla with sour cream, grated cheese or olives on the side.
—*Kimberly Burke, Chico, CA*

3 Tbsp. canola oil
1 boneless pork sirloin roast (3 lbs.), cut into 1-in. cubes
4 medium carrot, sliced
1 medium onion, thinly sliced
4 garlic cloves, minced

1 can (28 oz.) green enchilada sauce
¼ cup cold water
2 jalapeno peppers, seeded and chopped
1 cup minced fresh cilantro
Hot cooked rice
Flour tortillas (8 in.)

---

## Fast

**Prep:** 25 min. • **Cook:** 30 min+ releasing • **Makes:** 8 servings

**1.** Select saute setting on a 6-qt. electric pressure cooker and adjust for high heat; add the oil. In batches, saute the pork, carrots, onion and garlic until meat is no longer pink, 5-10 minutes. Return all items to the pressure cooker. Add the enchilada sauce, water, jalapenos and cilantro.
**2.** Lock the lid; close the pressure-release valve. Adjust to pressure-cook on high for 30 minutes. Allow pressure to naturally release for 10 minutes, then quick-release any remaining pressure. Serve with rice and tortillas.

## Slow

**Prep:** 15 min. • **Cook:** 5 hours • **Makes:** 8 servings

**1.** In a large skillet, in oil saute the pork, carrots, onion and garlic in batches until meat is no longer pink, 5-10 minutes. Transfer to a 5-qt. slow cooker.
**2.** Add the enchilada sauce, water, jalapenos and cilantro. Cover and cook on low for 6 hours or until the meat is tender. Serve with rice and tortillas.

**1 cup:** 345 cal., 18g fat (4g sat. fat), 102mg chol., 545mg sod., 12g carb. (4g sugars, 1g fiber), 35g pro.

PORK CHILE VERDE

GENERAL
TSO'S STEW

## General Tso's Stew

I love Asian food and wanted a chili-style soup with the flavors of General Tso. You can use any meat you like—I use leftover pork but it's tasty with turkey, chicken or ground meats.

—Lori McLain, Denton, TX

- 1 cup tomato juice
- ½ cup water
- ½ cup pickled cherry peppers, chopped
- 2 Tbsp. soy sauce
- 2 Tbsp. hoisin sauce
- 1 Tbsp. peanut oil
- 1 to 2 tsp. crushed red pepper flakes
- 1 lb. boneless skinless chicken breast halves
- 1½ cups chopped onion
- 1 cup chopped fresh broccoli
- ¼ cup chopped green onions
- 1 tsp. sesame seeds, toasted

### Fast

**Prep:** 10 min. • **Cook:** 10 min. • **Makes:** 6 servings

**1.** In a 6-qt. electric pressure cooker, combine the first 7 ingredients. Top with the chicken, onion and broccoli. Lock the lid; close the pressure-release valve. Adjust to pressure-cook on high for 6 minutes. Quick-release pressure. A thermometer inserted in chicken should read at least 165°.
**2.** Remove chicken; shred with 2 forks. Return to pressure cooker; heat through. Top with green onions and sesame seeds to serve.

### Slow

**Prep:** 10 min. • **Cook:** 2 hours • **Makes:** 6 servings

In a 4- or 5-qt. slow cooker, combine the first 7 ingredients. Stir in chicken, onion and broccoli. Cook, covered, on low until the vegetables are tender, about 2 hours. Top with green onions and sesame seeds to serve.

**Freeze option:** Freeze cooled stew in freezer containers. To use, partially thaw in refrigerator overnight. Heat through in a saucepan, stirring occasionally; add a little water if necessary.
**1 cup:** 159 cal., 5g fat (1g sat. fat), 42mg chol., 762mg sod., 10g carb. (5g sugars, 2g fiber), 18g pro.
**Diabetic exchanges:** 2 lean meat, 2 vegetable, ½ fat.

# Lentil Pumpkin Soup

Plenty of herbs and spices brighten up my hearty pumpkin soup. It's just the thing we need on nippy days and nights.
—*Laura Magee, Houlton, WI*

LENTIL PUMPKIN
SOUP

1 lb. red potatoes (about 4 medium), cut into 1-in. pieces
1 can (15 oz.) pumpkin
1 cup dried lentils, rinsed
1 medium onion, chopped
3 garlic cloves, minced
½ tsp. ground ginger
½ tsp. pepper
⅛ tsp. salt
2 cans (14½ oz. each) vegetable broth
1½ cups water

---

## Fast
**Prep:** 10 min. • **Cook:** 15 min. + releasing
**Makes:** 6 servings

In a 6-qt. electric pressure cooker, combine all the ingredients. Lock the lid; close pressure-release valve. Adjust to pressure-cook on high for 12 minutes. Allow pressure to release naturally for 10 minutes, then quick-release any remaining pressure.

## Slow
**Prep:** 10 min. • **Cook:** 7 hours
**Makes:** 6 servings

In a 3- or 4-qt. slow cooker, combine all ingredients. Cook, covered, on low for 7-9 hours or until the potatoes and lentils are tender.

**1½ cups:** 210 cal., 1g fat (0 sat. fat), 0 chol., 463mg sod., 42g carb. (5g sugars, 7g fiber), 11g pro.
**Diabetic exchanges:** 3 starch, 1 lean meat.

 **TIP**
Serve with cornbread or a French baguette.

CHICKEN
ENCHILADA SOUP

# Chicken Enchilada Soup

This soup delivers a big bowl of fresh comfort. For my husband and me, tasty toppings like avocado, sour cream and tortilla strips are a must.
—*Heather Sewell, Harrisonville, MO*

| | |
|---|---|
| 1 Tbsp. canola oil | 2 Tbsp. tomato paste |
| 2 Anaheim or poblano peppers, finely chopped | 1 Tbsp. chili powder |
| 1 medium onion, chopped | 2 tsp. ground cumin |
| 3 garlic cloves, minced | ½ tsp. pepper |
| 1 lb. boneless skinless chicken breasts | ½ to 1 tsp. chipotle hot pepper sauce, optional |
| 1 carton (48 oz.) chicken broth | ⅓ cup minced fresh cilantro |
| 1 can (14½ oz.) Mexican diced tomatoes, undrained | Optional: Shredded cheddar cheese, cubed avocado, sour cream and tortilla strips |
| 1 can (10 oz.) enchilada sauce | |

---

## Fast

**Prep:** 25 min. • **Cook:** 20 min. + releasing
**Makes:** 8 servings

**1.** Select saute setting on a 6-qt. electric pressure cooker and adjust for high heat; add the oil. Add the peppers and onion; cook and stir 6-8 minutes or until tender. Add garlic; cook 1 minute longer. Add chicken, broth, tomatoes, enchilada sauce, tomato paste, seasonings and, if desired, pepper sauce. Stir.
**2.** Lock lid; close the pressure-release valve. Adjust to pressure-cook on high for 8 minutes. Allow pressure to naturally release for 7 minutes, then quick-release any remaining pressure.
**3.** Remove chicken from the pressure cooker. Shred with 2 forks; return to pressure cooker. Stir in the cilantro. Serve with toppings as desired.

## Slow

**Prep:** 25 min. • **Cook:** 6 hours
**Makes:** 8 servings

**1.** In a large skillet, heat the oil over medium heat. Add the peppers and onion; cook and stir until tender, 6-8 minutes. Add the garlic; cook 1 minute longer. Transfer the pepper mixture and chicken to a 5- or 6-qt. slow cooker. Stir in the broth, tomatoes, enchilada sauce, tomato paste, seasonings and, if desired, pepper sauce. Cook, covered, on low for 6-8 hours or until the chicken is tender (a thermometer should read at least 165°).
**2.** Remove chicken from slow cooker. Shred with 2 forks; return to slow cooker. Stir in cilantro. Serve with toppings as desired.

**Freeze option:** Freeze cooled soup in freezer containers. To use, partially thaw in refrigerator overnight. Heat through in a saucepan, stirring occasionally; add a little water if necessary.
**1½ cups:** 125 cal., 4g fat (1g sat. fat), 35mg chol., 1102mg sod., 9g carb. (4g sugars, 3g fiber), 14g pro.

To make a fresh garlic clove easy to peel, gently crush it with the flat side of a large knife blade to loosen the peel. If you don't have a large knife handy, crush the garlic with a small can. The peel will come right off!

LENTIL STEW

## Lentil Stew

This stew is perfect when you want a meatless meal. Adding the cream at the end results in a smoother texture.
—*Michelle Collins, Suffolk, VA*

2 Tbsp. canola oil
2 large onions, thinly sliced, divided
2 Tbsp. minced fresh gingerroot
3 garlic cloves, minced
8 plum tomatoes, chopped
2 tsp. ground coriander
1½ tsp. ground cumin
¼ tsp. cayenne pepper
3 cups vegetable broth
2 cups dried lentils, rinsed
2 cups water
1 can (4 oz.) chopped green chiles
¾ cup heavy whipping cream
2 Tbsp. butter
1 tsp. cumin seeds
6 cups hot cooked basmati or jasmine rice
   Optional: Sliced green onions or minced fresh cilantro

### Fast

**Prep:** 45 min. • **Cook:** 15 min. + releasing
**Makes:** 8 servings

**1.** Select saute setting on a 6-qt. electric pressure cooker. Adjust for medium heat; add oil. When oil is hot, cook and stir half the onions until crisp-tender, 2-3 minutes. Add ginger, garlic, plum tomatoes, coriander, cumin and cayenne; cook and stir 1 minute longer. Press cancel. Stir in broth, lentils, water, green chiles and remaining onion.
**2.** Lock the lid; close the pressure-release valve. Adjust to pressure-cook on high for 15 minutes. Allow pressure to release naturally.
**3.** In a small skillet, heat butter over medium heat. Add cumin seeds; cook and stir 1-2 minutes or until golden brown. Add to mixture. Just before serving, stir in cream.
**4.** To serve, spoon over rice. If desired, sprinkle with sliced green onions or minced cilantro.

### Slow

**Prep:** 45 min. • **Cook:** 6 hours
**Makes:** 8 servings

**1.** In a large skillet, in oil saute half the onions until tender. Add ginger and garlic; saute for 1 minute. Add the tomatoes, coriander, cumin and cayenne; cook and stir 5 minutes longer.
**2.** In a 4- or 5-qt. slow cooker, combine the vegetable broth, lentils, water, green chiles, tomato mixture and remaining onion. Cover and cook on low 6-8 hours or until the lentils are tender.
**3.** In a small skillet, heat the butter over medium heat. Add the cumin seeds; cook and stir until golden brown, 1-2 minutes. Add to lentil mixture. Just before serving, stir cream into slow cooker.
**4.** To serve, spoon over rice. If desired, sprinkle with sliced green onions or minced cilantro.

**1⅓ cups stew with ¾ cup rice:** 499 cal., 16g fat (7g sat. fat), 38mg chol., 448mg sod., 72g carb. (5g sugars, 17g fiber), 17g pro.

# Easy Pork Posole

Looking for a complete dinner in a bowl? Sit down and dig into a rich, hearty Mexican classic brimming with cubed pork, sliced sausage, hominy and more.
—*Greg Fontenot, The Woodlands, TX*

- 1 Tbsp. canola oil
- ½ lb. boneless pork shoulder butt roast, cubed
- ½ lb. fully cooked andouille sausage links, sliced
- 6 cups reduced-sodium chicken broth
- 2 medium tomatoes, seeded and chopped
- 1 can (15 oz.) hominy, rinsed and drained
- 1 cup minced fresh cilantro
- 1 medium onion, chopped
- 4 green onions, chopped
- 1 jalapeno pepper, seeded and chopped
- 2 garlic cloves, minced
- 1 Tbsp. chili powder
- 1 tsp. ground cumin
- ½ tsp. cayenne pepper
- ½ tsp. coarsely ground pepper
  Optional: Corn tortillas, chopped onion, minced fresh cilantro and lime wedges

EASY PORK POSOLE

---

## Fast

**Prep:** 30 min. • **Cook:** 10 min. + releasing
**Makes:** 8 servings

**1.** Select saute setting on a 6-qt. electric pressure cooker and adjust for medium heat. Add oil. When oil is hot, cook and stir pork cubes and sausage links until browned; drain. Return meats to the pressure cooker. Press cancel. Add the next 12 ingredients.
**2.** Lock lid; close the pressure-release valve. Adjust to pressure-cook on high for 10 minutes. Allow pressure to naturally release for 5 minutes, then quick-release any remaining pressure. If desired, serve with corn tortillas, chopped onion, minced cilantro and lime wedges.

## Slow

**Prep:** 30 min. • **Cook:** 6 hours
**Makes:** 8 servings

**1.** In a large skillet, heat oil over medium-high heat. Brown pork cubes and sausage links; drain. Transfer to a 4-qt. slow cooker.
**2.** Stir in the chicken broth, tomatoes, hominy, cilantro, onion, green onions, jalapeno, garlic, chili powder, cumin, cayenne and pepper. Cook, covered, on low 6-8 hours or until meat is tender. If desired, serve with corn tortillas, chopped onion, minced cilantro and lime wedges.

---

**Note:** Wear disposable gloves when cutting hot peppers; the oils can burn skin. Avoid touching your face.
**1 cup:** 190 cal., 11g fat (3g sat. fat), 54mg chol., 957mg sod., 12g carb. (2g sugars, 3g fiber), 14g pro.

## Chickpea & Potato Curry

I make chana masala, the classic Indian dish, in my slow cooker—and the recipe adapts nicely to a pressure-cooker as well. Browning the onion, ginger and garlic first really makes the sauce amazing.
—*Anjana Devasahayam, San Antonio, TX*

| | |
|---|---|
| 1 Tbsp. canola oil | 2½ cups vegetable stock |
| 1 medium onion, chopped | 2 cans (15 oz. each) chickpeas or |
| 2 garlic cloves, minced | garbanzo beans, rinsed and drained |
| 2 tsp. minced fresh gingerroot | 1 can (15 oz.) crushed tomatoes |
| 2 tsp. ground coriander | 1 large baking potato, peeled and |
| 1 tsp. garam masala | cut into ¾-in. cubes |
| 1 tsp. chili powder | 1 Tbsp. lime juice |
| ½ tsp. salt | Chopped fresh cilantro |
| ½ tsp. ground cumin | Hot cooked rice |
| ¼ tsp. ground turmeric | Optional: Sliced red onion and lime wedges |

--------------------------------------------------------

### Fast
**Prep:** 25 min. • **Cook:** 5 min. + releasing • **Makes:** 6 servings

**1.** Select saute setting on a 6-qt. electric pressure cooker. Adjust for medium heat; add oil. When oil is hot, cook and stir onion until crisp-tender, 2-4 minutes. Add garlic, ginger and dry seasonings; cook and stir 1 minute. Add stock to pressure cooker. Cook 30 seconds, stirring to loosen browned bits from pan. Press cancel. Stir in the chickpeas, tomatoes and potato.
**2.** Lock lid; close the pressure-release valve. Adjust to pressure-cook on high for 3 minutes. Let pressure release naturally for 10 minutes; quick-release any remaining pressure.
**3.** Stir in lime juice; sprinkle with cilantro. Serve with rice and, if desired, red onion and lime wedges.

### Slow
**Prep:** 25 min. • **Cook:** 6 hours • **Makes:** 6 servings

**1.** In a large skillet, heat oil over medium-high heat; saute onion until tender, 2-4 minutes. Add the garlic, ginger and dry seasonings; cook and stir 1 minute. Stir in stock; cook 30 seconds, stirring to loosen browned bits from pan. Transfer to a 3- or 4-qt. slow cooker.
**2.** Stir in chickpeas, tomatoes and potato. Cook, covered, on low until the potato is tender and flavors are blended, 6-8 hours.
**3.** Stir in lime juice; sprinkle with cilantro. Serve with rice and, if desired, red onion and lime wedges.

**1¼ cups chickpea mixture:** 240 cal., 6g fat (0 sat. fat), 0 chol., 767mg sod., 42g carb. (8g sugars, 9g fiber), 8g pro.

CHICKPEA &
POTATO CURRY

FROGMORE
STEW, P. 152

# Fish & Seafood

What's the catch of the day? Soups and stews brimming with fresh and flavorful ingredients, of course!

MARYLAND-STYLE
CRAB SOUP, P. 145

SWEET POTATO
& CRAB SOUP

## Orzo Shrimp Stew

My husband and I love seafood, so
I don't skimp on the shrimp in this
mildly seasoned stew. Broccoli,
tomatoes and pasta make this
a balanced meal in one bowl.
—*Lisa Stinger, Hamilton, NJ*

**Takes:** 20 min. • **Makes:** 4 servings

- 2½ cups reduced-sodium
  chicken broth
- 5 cups fresh broccoli florets
- 1 can (14½ oz.) diced tomatoes,
  undrained
- 1 cup uncooked orzo
- 1 lb. uncooked medium shrimp,
  peeled and deveined
- ¼ tsp. salt
- ¼ tsp. pepper
- 2 tsp. dried basil
- 2 Tbsp. butter

**1.** Bring broth to a boil in a Dutch
oven. Add the broccoli, tomatoes
and orzo. Reduce heat; simmer,
uncovered, for 5 minutes, stirring
occasionally.
**2.** Add the shrimp, salt and pepper.
Cover and cook for 4-5 minutes or
until shrimp turn pink and orzo is
tender. Stir in basil and butter.
**1¾ cups:** 387 cal., 8g fat (4g sat. fat),
153mg chol., 875mg sod., 48g carb.
(7g sugars, 5g fiber), 30g pro.

### TIP

Recipes for seafood-based soups
often call for chicken stock or
broth—you can use a seafood stock
instead or a combination of seafood
and chicken. Chicken broth is easier
to find and makes a terrific neutral
base; seafood broth has a more
delicate flavor and will bring out
the taste of the shrimp or fish.

## Sweet Potato & Crab Soup

This sweet and savory soup is easy
to prepare. You can use butternut
squash or pumpkin instead of the
sweet potatoes, depending on what
you have on hand.
—*Judy Armstrong, Prairieville, LA*

**Prep:** 15 min. • **Cook:** 35 min.
**Makes:** 8 servings

- 4 Tbsp. butter, divided
- 2 medium leeks (white portion
  only), finely chopped
- 3 garlic cloves, minced
- 4 cups cubed peeled sweet
  potatoes (about 1½ lbs.)
- 1 tsp. salt, divided
- ½ tsp. ground cinnamon
- ½ tsp. cayenne pepper
- 5 cups vegetable stock
- 2 cups heavy whipping cream
- 4 tsp. fresh thyme leaves,
  divided
- 12 oz. lump crabmeat, drained
  Croutons, optional

**1.** In a Dutch oven, heat 2 Tbsp.
butter over medium heat; saute
leeks and garlic until the leeks are
tender, 4-6 minutes.
**2.** Stir in sweet potatoes, ¾ tsp. salt,
the cinnamon, cayenne and stock;
bring to a boil. Reduce heat; simmer,
covered, until potatoes are tender,
15-20 minutes.
**3.** Puree soup using an immersion
blender or cool slightly and puree
soup in batches in a blender; return
to pan. Stir in cream and 2 tsp. thyme;
bring to a boil. Reduce heat; simmer,
uncovered, 5 minutes.
**4.** Meanwhile, in a large skillet, melt
the remaining butter over medium
heat. Add crab and the remaining salt
and thyme; cook 5 minutes, stirring
gently to combine. Top individual
servings of soup with crab mixture
and, if desired, croutons.
**1 cup:** 370 cal., 28g fat (18g sat. fat),
124mg chol., 994mg sod., 20g carb.
(5g sugars, 3g fiber), 11g pro.

ORZO SHRIMP
STEW

## Shrimp Egg Drop Soup

Who knew that egg drop soup could be so easy? Only three simple steps will give you this better-than-restaurant-quality soup with just the right blend of veggies and shrimp.
—Taste of Home *Test Kitchen*

**Takes:** 30 min.
**Makes:** 4 servings

    4   tsp. cornstarch
    ½   tsp. soy sauce
    ⅛   tsp. ground ginger
    1½  cups cold water, divided
    2   cans (14½ oz. each)
        chicken broth
    1½  cups frozen home-style
        egg noodles
    1   cup frozen broccoli florets,
        thawed and coarsely chopped
    ½   cup julienned carrot
    1   large egg, lightly beaten
    ½   lb. cooked medium shrimp,
        peeled and deveined

**1.** In a small bowl, combine the cornstarch, soy sauce, ginger and ½ cup cold water; set aside.
**2.** In a large saucepan, combine the broth and remaining water. Bring to a simmer; add the noodles. Cook, uncovered, for 15 minutes. Add the broccoli and carrot; simmer 3-4 minutes longer or until noodles are tender.
**3.** Drizzle beaten egg into hot soup, stirring constantly. Stir cornstarch mixture and add to the pan. Bring to a boil; cook and stir until slightly thickened, about 2 minutes. Add shrimp; heat through.
**1¼ cups:** 241 cal., 4g fat (1g sat. fat), 196mg chol., 1050mg sod., 30g carb. (3g sugars, 2g fiber), 18g pro.

## Carolina Crab Boil

This is a fun way to feed a crowd for a tailgate. You can serve it two ways: Drain the cooking liquid and pour out the pot on a paper-lined table so folks can dig in, or serve it as a stew in its liquid over hot rice.
—Melissa Pelkey Hass, Waleska, GA

**Prep:** 15 min. • **Cook:** 35 min.
**Makes:** 4 servings

    2   tsp. canola oil
    1   pkg. (14 oz.) smoked turkey
        sausage, cut into ½-in. slices
    2   cartons (32 oz. each)
        reduced-sodium
        chicken broth
    4   cups water
    1   bottle (12 oz.) light beer or
        1½ cups additional reduced-
        sodium chicken broth
    ¼   cup seafood seasoning
    5   bay leaves
    4   medium ears sweet corn,
        cut into 2-in. pieces
    1   lb. fingerling potatoes
    1   medium red onion, quartered
    2   lbs. cooked snow crab legs
        Pepper to taste

**1.** In a stockpot, heat the oil over medium-high heat; brown sausage. Stir in broth, water, beer, seafood seasoning and bay leaves. Add the vegetables; bring to a boil. Reduce the heat; simmer, uncovered, for 20-25 minutes or until the potatoes are tender.
**2.** Add crab; heat through. Drain; remove bay leaves. Transfer to a serving bowl; season with pepper.
**1 serving:** 420 cal., 12g fat (3g sat. fat), 143mg chol., 2206mg sod., 37g carb. (7g sugars, 5g fiber), 40g pro.

CAROLINA CRAB BOIL

CURRY
SHRIMP
& RICE

## Curry Shrimp & Rice

My family and I absolutely love curry shrimp and rice. For this recipe, all but two of the ingredients come straight out of the pantry. You can adjust the heat level by using more or less chili paste—or leaving it out altogether.
—*Angela Spengler, Niceville, FL*

**Prep:** 10 min. • **Cook:** 25 min.
**Makes:** 8 servings

- 2  **Tbsp. butter**
- ½  **medium onion, chopped**
- 1  **carton (32 oz.) chicken broth**
- 2  **cans (14½ oz. each) diced potatoes, drained**
- 2  **cans (7 oz. each) white or shoepeg corn, drained**
- 1  **can (13.66 oz.) coconut milk**
- 1  **can (8 oz.) bamboo shoots, drained**
- 1  **Tbsp. curry powder**
- 1  **to 3 tsp. Thai red chili paste, optional**
- ½  **tsp. salt**
- ½  **tsp. pepper**
- 12  **oz. peeled and deveined cooked shrimp (61-70 per lb.)**
- 2  **pkg. (8.8 oz. each) ready-to-serve long grain rice Optional: Lime wedges and fresh basil**

**1.** In a Dutch oven, heat butter over medium-high heat. Add onion; cook and stir until tender, 4-5 minutes. Add the broth, potatoes, corn, coconut milk, bamboo shoots, curry powder, chili paste if desired, salt and pepper. Bring to a boil; reduce heat. Simmer, uncovered, until the flavors have blended, 12-15 minutes, stirring occasionally.
**2.** Add shrimp; heat through. Prepare rice according to package directions; serve with the curry. If desired, serve with lime wedges and basil.
**1 serving:** 354 cal., 13g fat (10g sat. fat), 75mg chol., 1112mg sod., 42g carb. (3g sugars, 3g fiber), 14g pro.

## Chilled Avocado Soup Appetizers with Crab

We have a large avocado tree outside our house, which is very common in Southern California, and I like to put them to good use in recipes. This is a fabulous party dish—I serve it in pretty shot glasses for a perfect appetizer-sized portion.
—*Dori Grasska, Pacific Palisades, CA*

**Prep:** 15 min. + chilling
**Makes:** 28 servings

- 2  **cups chicken or vegetable stock**
- 1  **cup plain yogurt**
- 2  **medium ripe avocados, peeled and pitted**
- 1  **medium apple, peeled and cubed**
- 1  **Tbsp. lime juice**
- ½  **tsp. salt**
- ½  **tsp. crushed red pepper flakes**
- ¼  **tsp. pepper**
- ⅔  **cup creme fraiche or sour cream**
- 8  **oz. lump crabmeat, drained Minced fresh cilantro Lime slices**

**1.** Place the first 8 ingredients in a blender; cover and process until smooth. Transfer to a pitcher; refrigerate 1 hour to allow the flavors to blend.
**2.** To serve, top individual servings with creme fraiche, crab, cilantro and lime slices.
**¼ cup:** 53 cal., 4g fat (2g sat. fat), 14mg chol., 133mg sod., 2g carb. (1g sugars, 1g fiber), 2g pro.

SALMON DILL SOUP

## Salmon Dill Soup

According to my husband, this is the best soup I have ever made! When I get salmon, I try to make this very special dish. It is a treat for both of us.
—*Hidemi Walsh, Plainfield, IN*

**Takes:** 30 min. • **Makes:** 2 servings

- 1   large potato, peeled and cut into 1½-in. pieces
- 1   large carrot, cut into ½-in.-thick slices
- 1½ cups water
- 1   cup reduced-sodium chicken broth
- 5   medium fresh mushrooms, halved
- 1   Tbsp. all-purpose flour
- ¼   cup reduced-fat evaporated milk
- ¼   cup shredded part-skim mozzarella cheese
- ½   lb. salmon fillet, cut into 1½-in. pieces
- ¼   tsp. pepper
- ⅛   tsp. salt
- 1   Tbsp. chopped fresh dill

**1.** Place the first 4 ingredients in a saucepan; bring to a boil. Reduce heat to medium; cook, uncovered, until vegetables are tender, 10-15 minutes.
**2.** Add mushrooms. In a small bowl, mix flour and milk until smooth; stir into soup. Return to a boil; cook and stir until the mushrooms are tender. Reduce heat to medium; stir in the cheese until melted.
**3.** Reduce heat to medium-low. Add salmon; cook, uncovered, until fish just begins to flake easily with a fork, 3-4 minutes. Stir in pepper and salt. Sprinkle with dill.
**2½ cups:** 398 cal., 14g fat (4g sat. fat), 71mg chol., 647mg sod., 37g carb. (7g sugars, 3g fiber), 30g pro. **Diabetic exchanges:** 3 lean meat, 2½ starch.

## Spicy Seafood Stew

The hardest part of this quick and easy recipe is peeling and dicing the potatoes—and you can even do that the night before. Just place the potatoes in water and store them in the refrigerator overnight to speed up assembly the next day.
—*Bonnie Marlow, Ottoville, OH*

**Prep:** 30 min. • **Cook:** 4¾ hours
**Makes:** 9 servings

- 2 lbs. potatoes, peeled and diced
- 1 lb. carrots, sliced
- 1 jar (24 oz.) pasta sauce
- 2 jars (6 oz. each) sliced mushrooms, drained
- 1½ tsp. ground turmeric
- 1½ tsp. minced garlic
- 1 tsp. cayenne pepper
- ¼ tsp. salt
- 1½ cups water
- 1 lb. sea scallops
- 1 lb. uncooked shrimp (31-40 per lb.), peeled and deveined

**1.** In a 5-qt. slow cooker, combine the first 8 ingredients. Cook, covered, on low until potatoes are tender, 4½-5 hours.

**2.** Stir in water, scallops and shrimp. Cook, covered, until the scallops are opaque and the shrimp turn pink, 15-20 minutes longer.

**1 cup:** 229 cal., 2g fat (0 sat. fat), 73mg chol., 803mg sod., 34g carb. (10g sugars, 6g fiber), 19g pro.

SPICY
SEAFOOD
STEW

NEW YEAR'S
OYSTER STEW

## New Year's Oyster Stew

Oyster stew is quite popular along the coast of Ireland, where oysters are served to celebrate many festivals. Immigrants brought the recipe with them to our Atlantic and Gulf coasts.
—*Christa Scott, Santa Fe, NM*

- - - - - - - - - - - - - - - - - - - - - - - - -

**Prep:** 15 min. • **Cook:** 30 min.
**Makes:** 12 servings

- 3 medium leeks
  (white portion only), chopped
- ¼ cup butter, cubed
- 2 medium potatoes,
  peeled and diced
- 2 cups hot water
- 3 tsp. chicken bouillon granules
- 2 cups whole milk
- 2 cups half-and-half cream
- 4 cans (16 oz. each) oysters,
  drained
- ¼ tsp. cayenne pepper
  Salt and pepper to taste
  Minced fresh parsley

**1.** In a Dutch oven, saute the leeks in butter for 10 minutes or until tender. Add the potatoes, water and bouillon; cover and simmer 20 minutes or until potatoes are tender. Cool.
**2.** Transfer to a blender. Cover and process until blended. Return to the pan; stir in the milk, cream, oysters, cayenne, salt and pepper. Cook on low until heated through (do not boil). Garnish with parsley.
**1 cup:** 251 cal., 13g fat (7g sat. fat), 117mg chol., 448mg sod., 17g carb. (5g sugars, 1g fiber), 14g pro.

## Thai Shrimp Soup

This tasty, crowd-pleasing soup comes together in minutes. I love that the once hard-to-find, seemingly exotic ingredients are now available in grocery stores.
—*Jessie Grearson, Falmouth, ME*

- - - - - - - - - - - - - - - - - - - - - - - - -

**Prep:** 20 min. • **Cook:** 20 min.
**Makes:** 8 servings

- 1 medium onion, chopped
- 1 Tbsp. olive oil
- 3 cups reduced-sodium
  chicken broth
- 1 cup water
- 1 Tbsp. brown sugar
- 1 Tbsp. minced fresh gingerroot
- 1 Tbsp. fish sauce or soy sauce
- 1 Tbsp. red curry paste
- 1 lemongrass stalk
- 1 lb. uncooked large shrimp,
  peeled and deveined
- 1½ cups frozen shelled edamame
- 1 can (13.66 oz.) light
  coconut milk
- 1 can (8¾ oz.) whole baby corn,
  drained and cut in half
- ½ cup bamboo shoots
- ¼ cup fresh basil leaves,
  julienned
- ¼ cup minced fresh cilantro
- 2 Tbsp. lime juice
- 1½ tsp. grated lime zest
- 1 tsp. curry powder

**1.** In a Dutch oven, saute the onion in oil until tender. Add the broth, water, brown sugar, ginger, fish sauce, curry paste and lemongrass. Bring to a boil. Reduce heat; carefully stir in shrimp and edamame. Cook, uncovered, for 5-6 minutes or until shrimp turn pink.
**2.** Add coconut milk, corn, bamboo shoots, basil, cilantro, lime juice, lime zest and curry powder; heat through. Discard lemongrass.
**1 cup:** 163 cal., 7g fat (3g sat. fat), 69mg chol., 505mg sod., 9g carb. (5g sugars, 2g fiber), 14g pro.
**Diabetic exchanges:** 2 lean meat, 1 vegetable, 1 fat.

 TIP

When buying lemongrass, choose blemish-free green stalks with white roots. Store fresh lemongrass in the refrigerator, in an airtight container, for up to two weeks.

THAI SHRIMP
SOUP

## German Brat Seafood Boil

Grilled bratwurst and onion add a smoky flavor to corn, potatoes and fish for a hearty meal that's always a hit.
—*Trisha Kruse, Eagle, ID*

**Prep:** 25 min. • **Cook:** 30 min.
**Makes:** 6 servings

SPRING SALMON CHOWDER

- 1 pkg. (19 oz.) uncooked bratwurst links
- 1 medium onion, quartered
- 2 qt. water
- 2 bottles (12 oz. each) beer or 3 cups reduced-sodium chicken broth
- ½ cup seafood seasoning
- 5 medium ears sweet corn, cut into 2-in. pieces
- 2 lbs. small red potatoes
- 1 medium lemon, halved
- 1 lb. cod fillet, cut into 1-in. pieces
  Coarsely ground pepper

**1.** Grill the bratwurst, covered, over medium heat, turning frequently, until the meat is no longer pink, 15-20 minutes. Grill onion, covered, until lightly browned, 3-4 minutes on each side. Cut bratwurst into 2-in. pieces.
**2.** In a stockpot, combine water, beer and seafood seasoning; add corn, potatoes, lemon, bratwurst and onion. Bring to a boil. Reduce heat; simmer, uncovered, until the potatoes are tender, 15-20 minutes.
**3.** Stir in the cod; cook until fish flakes easily with a fork, 4-6 minutes. Drain; transfer to a large serving bowl. Sprinkle with pepper.
**1 serving:** 553 cal., 28g fat (9g sat. fat), 95mg chol., 1620mg sod., 46g carb. (8g sugars, 5g fiber), 30g pro.

## Spring Salmon Chowder

This creamy chowder really hits the spot. Enjoy it with a side salad and fresh bread for a complete meal.
—*Pat Waymire, Yellow Springs, OH*

**Takes:** 30 min.
**Makes:** 8 servings

- 2 cups cauliflowerets
- 1 Tbsp. water
- 2 Tbsp. butter
- 2 celery ribs, thinly sliced
- 8 green onions, thinly sliced
- 2 Tbsp. all-purpose flour
- ½ tsp. salt
- ½ tsp. dill weed
- 4 cups 2% milk
- 1 can (14¾ oz.) salmon, drained, skin and bones remove
- 1 pkg. (9 oz.) frozen peas, thawed
- ½ cup shredded Swiss cheese
- ½ cup shredded cheddar cheese

**1.** In a microwave-safe bowl, combine the cauliflower and water. Microwave, covered, on high for 4-5 minutes or until tender, stirring once.
**2.** In a large saucepan, heat butter over medium-high heat. Add celery and green onions; cook and stir until tender. Stir in flour, salt and dill until blended; gradually whisk in milk. Bring to a boil, stirring constantly; cook and stir for 2 minutes or until thickened.
**3.** Stir in the salmon, peas and cauliflower; heat through. Stir in cheeses until melted. Serve immediately.
**1 cup:** 256 cal., 11g fat (5g sat. fat), 67mg chol., 558mg sod., 15g carb. (9g sugars, 3g fiber), 23g pro.

## Asian Ramen Shrimp Soup

A package of store-bought ramen noodles speeds up assembly of this colorful broth with shrimp and carrots. My mother gave me this recipe because it's delicious and so quick to fix!

—Donna Hellinger, Lorain, OH

------

**Takes:** 15 min. • **Makes:** 4 servings

- 3½ cups water
- 1 pkg. (3 oz.) Oriental ramen noodles
- 1 cup cooked small shrimp, peeled and deveined
- ½ cup chopped green onions
- 1 medium carrot, julienned
- 2 Tbsp. soy sauce

**1.** In a large saucepan, bring water to a boil. Set aside seasoning packet from noodles. Add the noodles to boiling water; cook and stir for 3 minutes.

**2.** Add the shrimp, onions, carrot, soy sauce and the contents of the seasoning packet. Cook until heated through, 3-4 minutes longer.

**1 cup:** 148 cal., 4g fat (2g sat. fat), 83mg chol., 857mg sod., 17g carb. (2g sugars, 1g fiber), 12g pro. **Diabetic exchanges:** 1 starch, 1 lean meat.

## Turkey Shrimp Gumbo

This slimmed-down version of gumbo tastes just as wonderful as the classic.

—Michael Williams, Westfield, NY

------

**Prep:** 10 min. • **Cook:** 2 hours 5 min. **Makes:** 10 servings

- 1 tsp. salt
- 1 tsp. pepper
- 1 tsp. cayenne pepper
- 2 lbs. uncooked skinless turkey breast, cubed
- ½ cup vegetable oil, divided
- ½ cup all-purpose flour
- 1 large onion, chopped
- 1 cup chopped celery
- 1 cup chopped sweet red pepper
- 4 garlic cloves, minced
- 4 cups chicken broth
- 2 cups sliced okra
- 4 green onions, sliced
- 10 oz. uncooked medium shrimp, peeled and deveined
- 5 cups hot cooked rice

**1.** In a small bowl, combine salt and peppers; sprinkle over turkey. In a Dutch oven, brown turkey in 2 Tbsp. oil; remove with a slotted spoon. Add remaining oil and flour, scraping pan bottom to loosen browned bits. Cook over medium-low heat for 25-30 minutes until dark brown in color, stirring occasionally.

**2.** Add the onion, celery, red pepper and garlic. Cook over medium heat until the vegetables are crisp-tender, 4-5 minutes. Gradually stir in broth. Bring to a boil. Reduce heat; cover and simmer for 30 minutes.

**3.** Return turkey to pan; cover and simmer for 30-45 minutes or until turkey is tender.

**4.** Add the okra and green onions; simmer 10 minutes.

**5.** Add the shrimp; simmer until the shrimp turn pink, 4-5 minutes. Serve over rice.

**1 cup with ½ cup rice:** 381 cal., 13g fat (2g sat. fat), 88mg chol., 777mg sod., 33g carb. (3g sugars, 2g fiber), 30g pro.

ASIAN RAMEN SHRIMP SOUP

# Coconut Shrimp Chowder

After trying a coconut soup at a Thai restaurant, I added coconut milk to my fish chowder recipe—and it was perfect! The fresh, simple ingredients allow the seafood to shine.
—*Michalene Baskett, Decatur, GA*

------

**Takes:** 30 min. • **Makes:** 5 servings

- 1  **medium onion, chopped**
- 2  **tsp. canola oil**
- ¼  **tsp. cayenne pepper**
- 2  **cups chicken broth**
- 1  **pkg. (10 oz.) frozen corn**
- ¼  **tsp. salt**
- ¼  **tsp. pepper**
- 1  **can (13.66 oz.) coconut milk**
- 1  **lb. uncooked medium shrimp, peeled and deveined**
- ¼  **cup lime juice**
- 2  **Tbsp. minced fresh cilantro**
- 1  **medium ripe avocado, peeled and cubed**

**1.** In a large saucepan, saute onion in oil until tender. Add cayenne pepper. Stir in broth, corn, salt and pepper. Bring to a boil. Reduce heat; simmer, uncovered, for 5 minutes. Remove from the heat and stir in coconut milk. Cool slightly.

**2.** In a food processor, process soup in batches until blended. Return all to pan. Add shrimp; cook and stir over medium heat for 5-6 minutes or until the shrimp turn pink. Stir in the lime juice and cilantro. Garnish individual servings with avocado.

**1 cup:** 376 cal., 26g fat (16g sat. fat), 112mg chol., 633mg sod., 22g carb. (4g sugars, 5g fiber), 20g pro.

COCONUT SHRIMP
CHOWDER

SPICY FRESH
SEAFOOD CIOPPINO

### Spicy Fresh Seafood Cioppino

Using prepared pasta sauce makes this robust one-pot dinner a cinch.
—*Jeff Mancini, Eagle River, WA*

**Prep:** 25 min. • **Cook:** 25 min.
**Makes:** 8 servings

- 5 garlic cloves, minced
- 2 Tbsp. olive oil
- 1 jar (24 oz.) tomato basil pasta sauce
- 1 bottle (8 oz.) clam juice
- 1 cup dry white wine or chicken broth
- ¼ cup water
- 1 tsp. salt
- 1 tsp. sugar
- 1 tsp. crushed red pepper flakes
- 1 tsp. minced fresh basil
- 1 tsp. minced fresh thyme
- 1 lb. fresh littleneck clams
- 1 lb. fresh mussels, scrubbed and beards removed
- 1 lb. uncooked medium shrimp, peeled and deveined
- 1 lb. bay scallops
- 1 pkg. (6 oz.) fresh baby spinach

**1.** In a Dutch oven, saute garlic in oil until tender. Add pasta sauce, clam juice, wine, water and seasonings. Bring to a boil. Reduce heat; simmer, uncovered, for 10 minutes.

**2.** Add clams, mussels and shrimp. Bring to a boil. Reduce heat; simmer, uncovered, for 10 minutes, stirring occasionally.

**3.** Stir in scallops and spinach; cook 5 to 7 minutes longer or until the clams and the mussels open, the shrimp turn pink and the scallops are opaque. Discard any unopened clams or mussels.

**1½ cups:** 259 cal., 7g fat (1g sat. fat), 108mg chol., 1057mg sod., 15g carb. (7g sugars, 3g fiber), 29g pro.

MARYLAND-STYLE
CRAB SOUP

## Maryland-Style Crab Soup

This filling soup incorporates the best of vegetable soup and flavorful crab. Whole crabs and claws can be broken into pieces and dropped in, which is my personal preference. I serve the soup with saltines and a cold beer.
—*Freelove Knott, Palm Bay, FL*

**Prep:** 20 min. • **Cook:** 6¼ hours
**Makes:** 8 servings

- 2 cans (14½ oz. each) diced tomatoes with green peppers and onions, undrained
- 2 cups water
- 1½ lbs. potatoes, cut into ½-in. cubes (about 5 cups)
- 2 cups cubed peeled rutabaga
- 2 cups chopped cabbage
- 1 medium onion, finely chopped
- 1 medium carrot, sliced
- ½ cup frozen corn, thawed
- ½ cup frozen lima beans, thawed
- ½ cup frozen peas, thawed
- ½ cup cut fresh green beans (1-in. pieces)
- 4 tsp. seafood seasoning
- 1 tsp. celery seed
- 1 vegetable bouillon cube
- ¼ tsp. salt
- ¼ tsp. pepper
- 1 lb. fresh or lump crabmeat, drained

**1.** In a 6-qt. slow cooker, combine the first 16 ingredients. Cook, covered, on low 6-8 hours or until vegetables are tender.
**2.** Stir in the crab. Cook, covered, on low 15 minutes longer or until heated through.
**1½ cups:** 202 cal., 1g fat (0 sat. fat), 55mg chol., 1111mg sod., 34g carb. (11g sugars, 7g fiber), 15g pro.

SHRIMP GAZPACHO

## Shrimp Gazpacho

This refreshing take on classic chilled tomato soup features shrimp, lime and lots of avocado. This recipe is best served the same day it's made.
—*Taste of Home Test Kitchen*

**Prep:** 15 min. + chilling
**Makes:** 12 servings

- 6 cups spicy hot V8 juice
- 2 cups cold water
- ½ cup lime juice
- ½ cup minced fresh cilantro
- ½ tsp. salt
- ¼ to ½ tsp. hot pepper sauce
- 1 lb. peeled and deveined cooked shrimp (31-40 per lb.), tails removed
- 1 medium cucumber, seeded and diced
- 2 medium tomatoes, seeded and chopped
- 2 medium ripe avocados, peeled and chopped

In a large nonreactive bowl, mix the first 6 ingredients. Gently stir in remaining ingredients. Refrigerate, covered, 1 hour before serving.
**1 cup:** 112 cal., 4g fat (1g sat. fat), 57mg chol., 399mg sod., 9g carb. (5g sugars, 3g fiber), 10g pro.
**Diabetic exchanges:** 2 vegetable, 1 lean meat, 1 fat.

## Jazzed-Up Clam Chowder

No one ever guesses that my dressed-up and delicious chowder starts with canned ingredients! It takes only 10 minutes to put together from start to finish.
—*Josephine Piro, Easton, PA*

- - - - - - - - - - - - - - - - - - - - - - - - - - -

**Takes:** 10 min.
**Makes:** 4 servings

- 1  can (19 oz.) chunky New England clam chowder
- 1  can (8¼ oz.) cream-style corn
- ⅔  cup 2% milk
- 2  Tbsp. shredded cheddar cheese
- 2  Tbsp. bacon bits
- 2  Tbsp. minced chives

In a 1½-qt. microwave-safe dish, combine clam chowder, corn and milk. Cover and microwave on high until heated through, 4-6 minutes, stirring every 2 minutes. Sprinkle individual servings with cheese, bacon and chives.
**1 cup:** 211 cal., 10g fat (5g sat. fat), 14mg chol., 780mg sod., 24g carb. (5g sugars, 2g fiber), 8g pro.

## Shrimp & Cod Stew in Tomato-Saffron Broth

This comforting seafood stew is just the thing for a cold day—it's easy to make and so satisfying!
—*Lydia Jensen, Kansas City, MO*

- - - - - - - - - - - - - - - - - - - - - - - - - - -

**Prep:** 20 min. • **Cook:** 25 min.
**Makes:** 8 servings

- 2  Tbsp. olive oil
- 1  large onion, chopped
- 3  garlic cloves, minced
- 1  Tbsp. minced fresh or 1 tsp. dried thyme
- ¼  tsp. saffron threads or 1 tsp. ground turmeric
- 2  bay leaves
- 2  cans (14½ oz. each) no-salt-added diced tomatoes
- 1  lb. cod fillet, cut into 1-in. cubes
- 1  lb. uncooked large shrimp, peeled and deveined
- 2  cups water
- 1  can (14½ oz.) vegetable broth
- 1  cup whole kernel corn
- ¼  tsp. pepper
- 1  pkg. (6 oz.) fresh baby spinach Lemon wedges, optional

**1.** In a 6-qt. stockpot, heat oil over medium heat. Add the onion; cook and stir until tender. Add the garlic, thyme, saffron and bay leaves. Cook and stir 1 minute longer. Add the tomatoes, fish, shrimp, water, broth, corn and pepper.
**2.** Bring to a boil. Reduce heat; simmer, uncovered, 8-10 minutes or until shrimp turn pink and fish flakes easily with a fork. Add the spinach during the last 2-3 minutes of cooking. Discard bay leaves. If desired, serve with lemon wedges.
**1½ cups:** 250 cal., 6g fat (1g sat. fat), 121mg chol., 1005mg sod., 18g carb. (7g sugars, 3g fiber), 27g pro.

SHRIMP & COD STEW IN TOMATO-SAFFRON BROTH

SEAFOOD CHOWDER
WITH SEASONED
OYSTER CRACKERS

1. Preheat oven to 350°. In a small bowl, combine the butter, marinade for chicken, pepper sauce, curry and paprika. Add crackers; toss to coat. Transfer to a greased 15x10x1-in. baking pan. Bake for 8-10 minutes or until golden brown, stirring twice. Set aside.

2. In a stockpot, cook bacon over medium heat until crisp. Using a slotted spoon, remove to paper towels to drain.

3. Saute the potatoes and leeks in the drippings; stir in flour and thyme until blended. Gradually whisk in the broth and clam juice. Bring to a boil, stirring constantly. Cook and stir 1-2 minutes longer. Reduce the heat; cover and simmer for 10 minutes or until the potatoes are tender.

4. Add the corn, zucchini, grouper, shrimp and scallops; cook until fish flakes easily with a fork, 2-4 minutes. Stir in the cream, salt and pepper; heat through. Serve with crackers and bacon.

1½ cups: 295 cal., 12g fat (5g sat. fat), 80mg chol., 885mg sod., 25g carb. (3g sugars, 2g fiber), 22g pro.

Grouper—a member of the sea bass family—has a lean, firm flesh with mild flavor. You can use snapper, mahi mahi or another sea bass in place of the grouper if you like.

## Seafood Chowder with Seasoned Oyster Crackers

With a tantalizing collection of fish, shrimp and scallops, this comforting chowder has been pleasing my family for many years. The seasoned oyster crackers add just a bit of spice.
—Virginia Anthony, Jacksonville, FL

------------------------------------------------

**Prep:** 45 min. • **Cook:** 25 min.
**Makes:** 12 servings

- 1 Tbsp. unsalted butter, melted
- 1 Tbsp. marinade for chicken
- 1 tsp. hot pepper sauce
- ¼ tsp. curry powder
- ¼ tsp. paprika
- 1¼ cups oyster crackers

### CHOWDER

- 8 bacon strips, chopped
- 1½ lbs. red potatoes, cut into ½-in. cubes
- 2 cups thinly sliced leeks (white portion only)
- ¼ cup all-purpose flour
- ¾ tsp. dried thyme
- 1 carton (32 oz.) reduced-sodium chicken broth
- 4 cups clam juice
- 1 pkg. (12 oz.) frozen corn
- 1½ cups diced zucchini
- 1 lb. grouper or tilapia fillets, cut into 1-in. cubes
- ¾ lb. uncooked medium shrimp, peeled and deveined
- ½ lb. bay scallops
- 1 cup half-and-half cream
- 1 tsp. salt
- ¼ tsp. white pepper

CRAB & ASPARAGUS SOUP

## Crab & Asparagus Soup

I get rave reviews from family and friends whenever I make this soup, but the biggest compliment ever was when my son called to ask for the recipe so he could make it for his roommates.
—*Patti Bogetti, Magnolia, DE*

**Prep:** 25 min. • **Cook:** 40 min.
**Makes:** 6 servings

- 1¼ cups chopped sweet onion
- 1 celery rib, chopped
- 2 Tbsp. butter
- 2 Tbsp. all-purpose flour
- ½ tsp. seafood seasoning
- ¼ tsp. salt
- ¼ tsp. pepper
- ⅛ tsp. ground nutmeg
- 1 cup water
- 1½ tsp. chicken bouillon granules
- 2 medium red potatoes, cubed
- 8 oz. fresh asparagus, cut into ¾-in. pieces
- 2 cups half-and-half cream
- 1 can (6½ oz.) lump crabmeat, drained
  Optional: Chopped fresh parsley and cracked pepper

**1.** In a large saucepan, saute onion and celery in butter. Stir in the flour, seafood seasoning, salt, pepper and nutmeg until blended; gradually add water and bouillon. Bring to a boil; cook and stir for 2 minutes or until thickened. Stir in the potatoes. Reduce heat; simmer, uncovered, for 10 minutes.

**2.** Add asparagus; cook 8-12 minutes longer or until vegetables are tender.

**3.** Stir in the cream and crab; heat through. If desired, sprinkle with parsley and pepper.

**¾ cup:** 257 cal., 12g fat (8g sat. fat), 78mg chol., 546mg sod., 22g carb. (6g sugars, 2g fiber), 12g pro.

CREAMY SEAFOOD BISQUE

## Creamy Seafood Bisque

My deceptively simple bisque makes a special first course or even a casual meal with a salad or some bread. I like to top bowlfuls with shredded Parmesan cheese and green onions.
—*Wanda Allende, Orlando, FL*

----------------------------------------

**Prep:** 25 min. • **Cook:** 25 min.
**Makes:** 8 servings

- ½ cup butter, cubed
- 1 medium red onion, chopped
- 1 cup sliced fresh mushrooms
- 2 garlic cloves, minced
- ½ cup all-purpose flour
- 1 tsp. salt
- 1 tsp. coarsely ground pepper
- 2 Tbsp. tomato paste
- 1 carton (32 oz.) chicken broth
- 2 cups whole baby clams, drained
- ½ lb. uncooked medium shrimp, peeled and deveined
- 2 cups lump crabmeat, drained
- 2 cups heavy whipping cream
- ½ cup shredded Parmesan cheese
- 2 green onions, thinly sliced

**1.** In a Dutch oven, heat butter over medium-high heat. Add the red onion and mushrooms; saute for 4-5 minutes or until tender. Add garlic; cook 1 minute longer. Stir in flour, salt and pepper until blended; add tomato paste. Gradually whisk in broth; bring to a boil. Reduce heat; cover and simmer for 5 minutes.
**2.** Add clams and shrimp; return to a boil. Reduce heat; simmer, uncovered, 5-10 minutes longer or until shrimp turn pink, stirring occasionally. Stir in crab and cream; heat through (do not boil). Serve with cheese and green onions.
**1¼ cups:** 453 cal., 36g fat (22g sat. fat), 197mg chol., 1232mg sod., 12g carb. (2g sugars, 1g fiber), 20g pro.

**MEXICAN SHRIMP BISQUE**

½ cup butter, cubed
4 celery ribs, chopped
3 medium carrots, chopped
1 large onion, chopped
½ cup all-purpose flour
¼ tsp. white pepper
2 cups 2% milk
1 can (14½ oz.) chicken broth
¼ cup water
1 Tbsp. chicken base
3 medium potatoes,
    peeled and chopped
1 can (15¼ oz.) whole kernel
    corn, drained
3 bay leaves
2 cups half-and-half cream
2 Tbsp. lemon juice
1 lb. halibut or other whitefish
    fillets, cut into 1-in. pieces
1 cup salad croutons
¾ cup grated Parmesan cheese
½ cup minced chives

## Mexican Shrimp Bisque

I enjoy both Cajun and Mexican cuisine, and this rich, elegant soup combines the best of both. I serve it with a crispy green salad and a glass of white wine.
—Karen Harris, Littleton, CO

- - - - - - - - - - - - - - - - - - - - - - -

**Takes:** 30 min. • **Makes:** 3 servings

1 small onion, chopped
1 Tbsp. olive oil
2 garlic cloves, minced
1 Tbsp. all-purpose flour
1 cup water
½ cup heavy whipping cream
2 tsp. chicken bouillon granules
1 Tbsp. chili powder
½ tsp. ground cumin
½ tsp. ground coriander
½ lb. uncooked medium shrimp,
    peeled and deveined
½ cup sour cream
    Optional: Chopped fresh
    cilantro and sliced avocado

**1.** In a small saucepan, saute onion in oil until tender. Add garlic; cook 1 minute longer. Stir in flour until blended. Stir in the water, cream, bouillon and seasonings; bring to a boil. Reduce heat; cover and simmer for 5 minutes.
**2.** Add the shrimp to soup. Simmer 5-10 minutes longer or until shrimp turn pink.
**3.** Place the sour cream in a small bowl; gradually stir in ½ cup hot soup. Return all to the pan, stirring constantly. Heat through (do not boil). If desired, top with cilantro and avocado.
**1 cup:** 357 cal., 28g fat (15g sat. fat), 173mg chol., 706mg sod., 10g carb. (3g sugars, 2g fiber), 16g pro.

## Halibut & Potato Chowder

I have a passion for cooking and entertaining. Several times a year I invite my retired and current teaching friends to a dinner party— this halibut chowder is a favorite at those parties.
—Teresa Lueck, Onamia, MN

- - - - - - - - - - - - - - - - - - - - - - -

**Prep:** 25 min. • **Cook:** 30 min.
**Makes:** 12 servings

**1.** In a large saucepan, melt butter over medium heat. Add the celery, carrots and onion; cook and stir until tender. Stir in flour and pepper until blended; gradually add milk, broth, water and chicken base. Bring to a boil; cook and stir until thickened, about 2 minutes.
**2.** Add potatoes, corn and bay leaves. Return to a boil. Reduce heat; cover and simmer until potatoes are tender, 15-20 minutes.
**3.** Stir in the cream and lemon juice; return to a boil. Add halibut. Reduce heat; simmer, uncovered, until fish flakes easily with a fork, 7-11 minutes. Discard bay leaves. Serve with the remaining ingredients.
**1 cup:** 316 cal., 16g fat (9g sat. fat), 61mg chol., 671mg sod., 25g carb. (8g sugars, 2g fiber), 16g pro.

HALIBUT &
POTATO
CHOWDER

## Cream of Mussel Soup

Every New England cook has a personal version of mussel soup, depending on the favored regional herbs and cooking customs. Feel free to start with my recipe and then develop your own luscious variation!
—Donna Noel, Gray, ME

**Prep:** 35 min. • **Cook:** 10 min.
**Makes:** 5 servings

- 3 lbs. fresh mussels (about 5 dozen), scrubbed and beards removed
- 2 medium onions, finely chopped
- 2 celery ribs, finely chopped
- 1 cup water
- 1 cup white wine or chicken broth
- 1 bottle (8 oz.) clam juice
- ¼ cup minced fresh parsley
- 2 garlic cloves, minced
- ¼ tsp. salt
- ¼ tsp. pepper
- 1 cup half-and-half cream

**1.** Tap mussels; discard any that do not close. Set aside. In a stockpot, combine the onions, celery, water, wine or broth, clam juice, parsley, garlic, salt and pepper.
**2.** Bring to a boil. Reduce heat; add the mussels. Cover and simmer for 5-6 minutes or until the mussels have opened. Remove the mussels with a slotted spoon, discarding any unopened mussels; set aside opened mussels and keep warm.
**3.** Cool cooking liquid slightly. In a blender, cover and process cooking liquid in batches until blended. Return all to pan. Add cream and reserved mussels; heat through (do not boil).
**1 serving:** 368 cal., 11g fat (4g sat. fat), 102mg chol., 1043mg sod., 20g carb. (6g sugars, 2g fiber), 35g pro.

FROGMORE STEW

## Frogmore Stew

This picnic-style medley of shrimp, smoked kielbasa, corn and spuds is a specialty of South Carolina cuisine. It's commonly dubbed Frogmore or Beaufort stew in recognition of the two low-country communities that lay claim to its origin. No matter what you call it, this one-pot wonder won't disappoint!
—Taste of Home Test Kitchen

**Prep:** 10 min. • **Cook:** 35 min.
**Makes:** 8 servings

- 16 cups water
- 1 large sweet onion, quartered
- 3 Tbsp. seafood seasoning
- 2 medium lemons, halved, optional
- 1 lb. small red potatoes
- 1 lb. smoked kielbasa or fully cooked hot links, cut into 1-in. pieces
- 4 medium ears sweet corn, cut into thirds
- 2 lbs. uncooked medium shrimp, peeled and deveined
  Seafood cocktail sauce
  Melted butter
  Additional seafood seasoning

**1.** In a stockpot, combine water, onion, seafood seasoning and, if desired, lemons; bring to a boil. Add potatoes; cook, uncovered, 10 minutes. Add kielbasa and corn; return to a boil. Reduce heat; simmer, uncovered, 10-12 minutes or until potatoes are tender. Add shrimp; cook 2-3 minutes longer or until shrimp turn pink.
**2.** Drain; transfer to a bowl. Serve with cocktail sauce, butter and additional seasoning.
**1 serving:** 369 cal., 18g fat (6g sat. fat), 175mg chol., 751mg sod., 24g carb. (7g sugars, 2g fiber), 28g pro.

## Chilled Corn & Shrimp Soup

My refreshing, delicately spiced soup is so pretty and unique, guests always remember it. It's hearty, too, unlike other cool soups. Give it a try and see!
—*Mary M. Leverette, Columbia, SC*

**Prep:** 30 min. + chilling
**Makes:** 4 servings

- ½ cup chopped sweet onion
- 3 Tbsp. olive oil
- 1½ lbs. uncooked small shrimp, peeled and deveined
- 2 garlic cloves, minced
- 1 tsp. curry powder
- 2 cups buttermilk
- 1 pkg. (16 oz.) frozen shoepeg corn, thawed, divided
- 1 cup reduced-fat sour cream
- 1 tsp. hot pepper sauce
- 1 tsp. salt
- ½ tsp. coarsely ground pepper
- 2 Tbsp. minced chives

**1.** In a large skillet, saute onion in oil until tender. Add the shrimp, garlic and curry; saute until shrimp turn pink, 4-6 minutes longer. Remove from the heat and set aside.

**2.** In a blender, combine buttermilk, 2 cups corn, sour cream, pepper sauce, salt and pepper. Cover and process until smooth; transfer to a large bowl. Add remaining corn and shrimp mixture. Cover and refrigerate for at least 3 hours. Garnish servings with chives.

**1 cup:** 317 cal., 13g fat (4g sat. fat), 153mg chol., 689mg sod., 23g carb. (10g sugars, 2g fiber), 26g pro.

CHILLED CORN & SHRIMP SOUP

## Spicy Seafood Bisque

Hot pepper sauce and cayenne pepper give this spicy soup some zip. It dresses up any meal and is easy to prepare. Of all the recipes I've borrowed from my mom, I've made this soup the most.
—*Kevin Weeks, North Palm Beach, FL*

**Prep:** 10 min. • **Cook:** 40 min.
**Makes:** 12 servings

- ½ cup chopped onion
- ½ cup chopped celery
- 2 Tbsp. butter
- 4 cups chicken broth
- 3 cups tomato juice
- 1 can (14½ oz.) diced tomatoes, undrained
- 1 Tbsp. Worcestershire sauce
- 1 tsp. seafood seasoning
- 1 tsp. dried oregano
- ½ tsp. garlic powder
- ½ tsp. hot pepper sauce
- ¼ tsp. cayenne pepper
- 1 bay leaf
- ½ cup uncooked small shell pasta or elbow macaroni
- 1 lb. uncooked medium shrimp, peeled and deveined
- 1 can (6 oz.) crabmeat, drained, flaked and cartilage removed

**1.** In a large saucepan, saute onion and celery in butter until tender. Add the broth, tomato juice, tomatoes, Worcestershire sauce and seasonings; bring to a boil. Reduce heat; cover and simmer for 20 minutes.

**2.** Discard bay leaf. Add pasta to the soup; cook, uncovered, until pasta is tender. Add shrimp and crab; simmer 5 minutes longer or until shrimp turn pink.

**1 cup:** 105 cal., 3g fat (1g sat. fat), 65mg chol., 714mg sod., 9g carb. (4g sugars, 1g fiber), 11g pro.

SHERRIED SWEET
POTATO SOUP, P. 162

# Vegetarian & Meatless

Even meat lovers will eat up every last spoonful of these deliciously satisfying soups and stews.

MOROCCAN
VEGETARIAN
STEW, P. 164

SPICY MEATLESS
CHILI

## Spicy Meatless Chili

Before I retired, this recipe was a mainstay in our house. I could prepare the ingredients the night before and then throw everything in the slow cooker on the way out the door in the morning. When I got home later, I just made the toppings and supper was done!

—*Jane Whittaker, Pensacola, FL*

**Prep:** 25 min. • **Cook:** 8 hours
**Makes:** 5 servings

- 2   cans (14½ oz. each) Mexican diced tomatoes, undrained
- 1   can (15 oz.) black beans, rinsed and drained
- 2   cups frozen corn, thawed
- 1   cup salsa
- 1   medium zucchini, cut into ½-in. pieces
- 1   medium green pepper, coarsely chopped
- 1   small onion, coarsely chopped
- 1   celery rib, chopped
- 3   Tbsp. chili powder
- 1   tsp. dried oregano
- 2   garlic cloves, minced
- ¾   tsp. salt
- ¾   tsp. pepper
- ½   tsp. ground cumin
- ¼   tsp. cayenne pepper
      Optional: Sour cream, shredded cheddar cheese and sliced jalapeno pepper

In a 4-qt. slow cooker, combine the first 15 ingredients. Cover and cook on low until vegetables are tender, 8-10 hours. If desired, top with sour cream, cheese and jalapeno pepper.
**1½ cups:** 224 cal., 2g fat (0 sat. fat), 0 chol., 1290mg sod., 48g carb. (15g sugars, 11g fiber), 9g pro.

ROASTED PEPPER POTATO SOUP

## Roasted Pepper Potato Soup

I love potato soup, and this rich, creamy version is different from most I've tried. I enjoy its lemon and cilantro flavors, but you can adjust the ingredients to best suit your family's taste buds.

—*Hollie Powell, St. Louis, MO*

**Prep:** 30 min. • **Cook:** 15 min.
**Makes:** 6 servings

- 2   medium onions, chopped
- 2   Tbsp. canola oil
- 1   jar (7 oz.) roasted sweet red peppers, undrained and chopped
- 1   can (4 oz.) chopped green chiles, drained
- 2   tsp. ground cumin
- 1   tsp. salt
- 1   tsp. ground coriander
- 3   cups diced peeled potatoes
- 3   cups vegetable broth
- 2   Tbsp. minced fresh cilantro
- 1   Tbsp. lemon juice
- ½   cup reduced-fat cream cheese, cubed

**1.** In a large saucepan, saute the onions in oil until tender. Stir in the roasted peppers, chiles, cumin, salt and coriander. Cook and stir 2 minutes. Stir in the potatoes and broth; bring to a boil.
**2.** Reduce heat; cover and simmer for 10-15 minutes or until potatoes are tender. Stir in the cilantro and lemon juice. Cool slightly. In a blender, process the cream cheese and half the soup until smooth. Return all to pan and heat through.
**1 cup:** 204 cal., 9g fat (3g sat. fat), 11mg chol., 1154mg sod., 26g carb. (0 sugars, 4g fiber), 6g pro.

COCONUT
RED CURRY
STEW

## Pico de Gallo Black Bean Soup

Everyone at my table goes for this feel-good soup. It is quick when you're pressed for time and beats fast food, hands down.
—*Darlis Wilfer, West Bend, WI*

**Takes:** 20 min.
**Makes:** 6 servings

- 4 cans (15 oz. each) black beans, rinsed and drained
- 2 cups vegetable broth
- 2 cups pico de gallo
- ½ cup water
- 2 tsp. ground cumin
  Optional: Chopped fresh cilantro and additional pico de gallo

**1.** In a Dutch oven, combine the first 5 ingredients; bring to a boil over medium heat, stirring occasionally. Reduce heat; simmer, uncovered, until the vegetables in pico de gallo are softened, 5-7 minutes, stirring occasionally.
**2.** Puree soup using an immersion blender, or cool soup slightly and puree in batches in a blender. Return to pan and heat through. Serve with toppings as desired.
**Freeze option:** Freeze cooled soup in freezer containers. To use, partially thaw in a refrigerator overnight. Heat through in a saucepan, stirring occasionally; add a little broth or water if necessary. Top as desired.
**1¼ cups:** 241 cal., 0 fat (0 sat. fat), 0 chol., 856mg sod., 44g carb. (4g sugars, 12g fiber), 14g pro.

## Coconut Red Curry Stew

This fragrant and flavorful dish is packed with nutritious goodness. It is delicious with sticky rice.
—*Marly Chaland, Maple, ON*

**Prep:** 20 min. • **Cook:** 50 min.
**Makes:** 4 servings

- 1 Tbsp. canola oil
- 1 medium onion, chopped
- 1 garlic clove, minced
- 3 to 4 Tbsp. red curry paste
- ½ tsp. sugar
- 1 small eggplant, cut into 1-in. pieces (about 4 cups)
- 3 cups cubed peeled butternut squash (1 in.)
- 1 medium sweet red pepper, cut into 1-in. pieces
- 1 medium green pepper, cut into 1-in. pieces
- 1 can (15 oz.) garbanzo beans or chickpeas, rinsed and drained
- 1 carton (32 oz.) vegetable broth, divided
- 1 can (15 oz.) crushed tomatoes
- 1 can (13.66 oz.) coconut milk
  Chopped fresh cilantro
  Optional: Lime wedges and hot cooked rice

**1.** In a 6-qt. stockpot, heat oil over medium-high heat; saute onion until lightly browned, 3-4 minutes. Add garlic; cook and stir 1 minute. Stir in curry paste and sugar.
**2.** Stir in vegetables, beans, 3 cups broth, the tomatoes and coconut milk; bring to a boil. Reduce heat; simmer, covered, until vegetables are tender, 35-40 minutes.
**3.** Stir in the remaining broth; heat through. Serve with cilantro and, if desired, lime wedges and rice.
**1½ cups:** 457 cal., 22g fat (16g sat. fat), 0 chol., 1364mg sod., 59g carb. (20g sugars, 14g fiber), 11g pro.

## Marty's Bean Burger Chili

My husband and I met while working the dinner shift at a homeless shelter, where they served chili made with my recipe. I've since revised the original to use veggie bean burgers.
—*Marty Nickerson, Ellington, CT*

**Prep:** 15 min. • **Cook:** 7 hours
**Makes:** 6 servings

- 2 cans (14½ oz. each) no-salt-added diced tomatoes, drained
- 1 can (14½ oz.) diced tomatoes, drained
- 1 can (16 oz.) kidney beans, undrained
- 1 can (15 oz.) black beans, undrained
- 1 can (15 oz.) garbanzo beans or chickpeas, rinsed and drained
- 4 frozen spicy black bean veggie burgers, thawed and coarsely chopped
- 1 large onion, finely chopped
- 1 large sweet red or green pepper, chopped
- 2 Tbsp. chili powder
- 1 Tbsp. Worcestershire sauce
- 3 tsp. dried basil
- 3 tsp. dried oregano
- 2 tsp. hot pepper sauce
- 2 garlic cloves, minced

Place all ingredients in a 5- or 6-qt. slow cooker; stir to combine. Cook, covered, on low for 7-9 hours to allow the flavors to blend.
**1½ cups:** 348 cal., 6g fat (0 sat. fat), 0 chol., 1151mg sod., 58g carb. (14g sugars, 19g fiber), 21g pro.

## Summer's Bounty Soup

This chunky soup packed with garden-fresh veggies is so versatile. You can add or omit just about any vegetable to make the most of what you have.
—*Victoria Hahn, Northampton, PA*

**Prep:** 20 min. • **Cook:** 7 hours
**Makes:** 14 servings

- 4 medium tomatoes, chopped
- 2 medium potatoes, peeled and cubed
- 2 cups halved fresh green beans
- 2 small zucchini, cubed
- 1 medium yellow summer squash, cubed
- 4 small carrots, thinly sliced
- 2 celery ribs, thinly sliced
- 1 cup cubed peeled eggplant
- 1 cup sliced fresh mushrooms
- 1 small onion, chopped
- 1 Tbsp. minced fresh parsley
- 1 Tbsp. salt-free garlic and herb seasoning
- 4 cups reduced-sodium V8 juice

Combine all ingredients in a 5-qt. slow cooker. Cook, covered, on low for 7-8 hours or until the vegetables are tender.
**1 cup:** 67 cal., 0 fat (0 sat. fat), 0 chol., 62mg sod., 15g carb. (6g sugars, 3g fiber), 2g pro. **Diabetic exchanges:** 2 vegetable.

 **TIP**

Young and tender eggplant can be cooked with the skin on when fried, sauteed or braised, but definitely remove the skin when it is roasted or slow-simmered, as in recipes like this one.

MARTY'S BEAN BURGER CHILI

# Tuscan Portobello Stew

Here's a healthy one-skillet meal that is quick and easy to prepare, yet it is elegant enough for company. I often take this stew to my school's potlucks, where it is devoured by both teachers and students—whether or not they are vegetarians!
—Jane Siemon, Viroqua, WI

**Prep:** 20 min. • **Cook:** 20 min.
**Makes:** 4 servings

- 2 large portobello mushrooms, coarsely chopped
- 1 medium onion, chopped
- 3 garlic cloves, minced
- 2 Tbsp. olive oil
- ½ cup white wine or vegetable broth
- 1 can (28 oz.) diced tomatoes, undrained
- 2 cups chopped fresh kale
- 1 bay leaf
- 1 tsp. dried thyme
- ½ tsp. dried basil
- ½ tsp. dried rosemary, crushed
- ¼ tsp. salt
- ¼ tsp. pepper
- 2 cans (15 oz. each) cannellini beans, rinsed and drained

**1.** In a large skillet, saute mushrooms, onion and garlic in oil until tender. Add the wine. Bring to a boil; cook until liquid is reduced by half.

**2.** Stir in the tomatoes, kale and seasonings. Bring to a boil. Reduce the heat; cover and simmer for 8-10 minutes.

**3.** Add beans; heat through. Discard bay leaf.

**1¼ cups:** 309 cal., 8g fat (1g sat. fat), 0 chol., 672mg sod., 46g carb. (9g sugars, 13g fiber), 12g pro. **Diabetic exchanges:** 2 starch, 2 vegetable, 1½ fat, 1 lean meat.

TUSCAN PORTOBELLO STEW

OVER-THE-RAINBOW MINESTRONE

## Over-the-Rainbow Minestrone

This vegetarian soup features a rainbow of vegetables. You can use any multicolored pasta in place of the spirals.
—*Crystal Schlueter, Northglenn, CO*

**Prep:** 20 min. • **Cook:** 6 hours 20 min.
**Makes:** 10 servings

- 4 large stems Swiss chard (about ½ lb.) or fresh baby spinach
- 2 Tbsp. olive oil
- 1 medium red onion, finely chopped
- 6 cups vegetable broth
- 2 cans (14½ oz. each) fire-roasted diced tomatoes, undrained
- 1 can (16 oz.) kidney beans, rinsed and drained
- 1 can (15 oz.) garbanzo beans or chickpeas, rinsed and drained
- 1 medium yellow summer squash or zucchini, halved and cut into ¼-in. slices
- 1 medium sweet red or yellow pepper, finely chopped
- 1 medium carrot, finely chopped
- 2 garlic cloves, minced
- 1½ cups uncooked spiral pasta or small pasta shells
- ¼ cup prepared pesto
  **Optional: Additional prepared pesto, shredded Parmesan cheese, crushed red pepper flakes and minced fresh basil**

**1.** Cut stems from chard; chop stems and leaves separately. Reserve leaves for adding later. In a large skillet, heat oil over medium heat. Add the onion and the chard stems; cook and stir 3-5 minutes or until tender. Transfer to a 6-qt. slow cooker.

**2.** Stir in broth, tomatoes, kidney beans, garbanzo beans, squash, pepper, carrot and garlic. Cook, covered, on low 6-8 hours or until the vegetables are tender.

**3.** Stir in the pasta and the reserved chard leaves. Cook, covered, on low for 20-25 minutes longer or until the pasta is tender; stir in the pesto. If desired, serve with additional pesto, Parmesan cheese, red pepper flakes and fresh basil.

**1½ cups:** 231 cal., 7g fat (1g sat. fat), 2mg chol., 1015mg sod., 34g carb. (7g sugars, 6g fiber), 9g pro.

SHERRIED SWEET
POTATO SOUP

## Sherried Sweet Potato Soup

I stir up a pot of my smooth, spiced sweet potato soup when I want something out of the ordinary for guests. Using an immersion blender will result in a creamier texture.
—Charlene Chambers, Ormond Beach, FL

- - - - - - - - - - - - - - - - - - - - - - -

**Prep:** 15 min. • **Cook:** 45 min.
**Makes:** 8 servings

- 4   large sweet potatoes, peeled and cubed
- 1   small onion, chopped
- 2   Tbsp. butter
- 2   garlic cloves, minced
- 1   tsp. ground cumin
- ½   tsp. salt
- ½   tsp. minced fresh gingerroot
- ½   tsp. ground coriander
- ¼   tsp. ground cinnamon
- ⅛   tsp. ground cardamom
- 3   cans (14 oz. each) chicken broth
- 1   cup heavy whipping cream
- ⅓   cup sherry
- 1   Tbsp. lime juice
- 2   Tbsp. minced fresh cilantro

**1.** Place the sweet potatoes in a large saucepan and cover with water. Bring to a boil. Reduce heat; cover and cook for 10-15 minutes or just until tender. Drain; set aside.
**2.** In a large saucepan, saute the onion in butter until tender. Add the garlic, cumin, salt, ginger, coriander, cinnamon and cardamom; cook for 2 minutes. Stir in potatoes and broth; bring to a boil. Reduce heat; simmer, uncovered, for 25-30 minutes or until flavors are blended.
**3.** Add the cream and the sherry; bring to a boil. Reduce heat; simmer, uncovered, 5 minutes. Remove from heat; stir in lime juice. Cool slightly. In a blender, process soup in batches until smooth, or use an immersion blender. Garnish with cilantro.
**1 cup:** 337 cal., 14g fat (9g sat. fat), 45mg chol., 903mg sod., 46g carb. (19g sugars, 6g fiber), 5g pro.

## Caribbean Potato Soup

An interesting blend of veggies that includes okra, kale and black-eyed peas goes into this bright and hearty soup. No kale on hand? Use spinach instead.
—Crystal Jo Bruns, Iliff, CO

- - - - - - - - - - - - - - - - - - - - - - -

**Takes:** 30 min. • **Makes:** 6 servings

- 2   medium onions, chopped
- 2   tsp. canola oil
- 3   garlic cloves, minced
- 2   tsp. minced fresh gingerroot
- 2   tsp. ground coriander
- 1   tsp. ground turmeric
- ½   tsp. dried thyme
- ¼   tsp. ground allspice
- 5   cups vegetable broth
- 2   cups cubed peeled sweet potato
- 3   cups chopped fresh kale
- 1   cup frozen sliced okra
- 1   cup coconut milk
- 1   cup canned diced tomatoes, drained
- 1   cup canned black-eyed peas, rinsed and drained
- 2   Tbsp. lime juice

**1.** In a Dutch oven, saute onions in oil until tender. Add the garlic, ginger and spices; cook 1 minute longer.
**2.** Stir in broth and sweet potato. Bring to a boil. Reduce heat; cover and simmer for 5 minutes.
**3.** Stir in kale and okra. Return to a boil; cover and simmer 10 minutes longer or until potato is tender.
**4.** Add the milk, tomatoes, peas and lime juice; heat through.
**1½ cups:** 213 cal., 10g fat (7g sat. fat), 0 chol., 954mg sod., 28g carb. (9g sugars, 6g fiber), 5g pro.

CARIBBEAN
POTATO SOUP

## Spicy Peanut Soup

After enjoying a similar dish at a little cafe, I knew I had to try to duplicate this soup at home. I think my version comes pretty close. It's the best way I know to chase away winter's chill.
—*Lisa Meredith, St. Paul, MN*

**Prep:** 35 min. • **Cook:** 20 min.
**Makes:** 7 servings

- 2   medium carrots, chopped
- 1   small onion, chopped
- 2   Tbsp. olive oil
- 2   garlic cloves, minced
- 1   large sweet potato, peeled and cubed
- ½   cup chunky peanut butter
- 2   Tbsp. red curry paste
- 2   cans (14½ oz. each) vegetable broth
- 1   can (14½ oz.) fire-roasted diced tomatoes, undrained
- 1   bay leaf
- 1   fresh thyme sprig
- ½   tsp. pepper
- ½   cup unsalted peanuts

**1.** In a large saucepan, cook carrots and onion in oil over medium heat for 2 minutes. Add the garlic; cook 1 minute longer.

**2.** Stir in the sweet potato; cook 2 minutes longer. Stir in the peanut butter and curry paste until blended. Add the broth, tomatoes, bay leaf, thyme and pepper.

**3.** Bring to a boil. Reduce heat; cover and simmer for 15-20 minutes or until the sweet potatoes and carrots are tender. (Soup will appear curdled.) Discard bay leaf and thyme sprig. Stir soup until blended.

**4.** Sprinkle with peanuts.

**1 cup:** 276 cal., 18g fat (3g sat. fat), 0 chol., 932mg sod., 22g carb. (9g sugars, 4g fiber), 8g pro.

## Moroccan Vegetarian Stew

This fragrant, spicy garbanzo bean stew can be served over couscous or with warm pita bread. Also, try topping this Moroccan dish with a dollop of yogurt or sour cream to cool it down.
—*Sonya Labbe, West Hollywood, CA*

**Prep:** 20 min. • **Cook:** 30 min.
**Makes:** 8 servings

- 1   Tbsp. olive oil
- 1   large onion, chopped
- 2   tsp. ground cumin
- 2   tsp. ground cinnamon
- 1   tsp. ground coriander
- ½   tsp. ground allspice
- ½   tsp. cayenne pepper
- ¼   tsp. salt
- 1   small butternut squash, peeled and cut into 1-in. cubes (about 4 cups)
- 2   medium potatoes, peeled and cut into 1-in. cubes (about 4 cups)
- 4   medium carrots, sliced
- 3   plum tomatoes, chopped
- 3   cups water
- 2   small zucchini, cut into 1-in. cubes
- 1   can (15 oz.) garbanzo beans or chickpeas, rinsed and drained

**1.** In a 6-qt. stockpot, heat oil over medium-high heat; saute onion until tender. Add seasonings; cook and stir 1 minute.

**2.** Stir in squash, potatoes, carrots, tomatoes and water; bring to a boil. Reduce heat; simmer, uncovered, until squash and potatoes are almost tender, 15-20 minutes.

**3.** Add the zucchini and garbanzo beans; bring to a boil. Reduce heat; simmer, uncovered, until vegetables are tender, 5-8 minutes.

**1½ cups:** 180 cal., 3g fat (0 sat. fat), 0 chol., 174mg sod., 36g carb. (8g sugars, 9g fiber), 5g pro. **Diabetic exchanges:** 2 starch, 1 vegetable.

MOROCCAN VEGETARIAN STEW

MUSHROOM & BROCCOLI SOUP

## Hazelnut Asparagus Soup

My heart is happy when bundles of tender local asparagus start to appear at my grocery store in spring. This restaurant-quality vegetarian soup can be prepared in about 30 minutes.
—*Cindy Beberman, Orland Park, IL*

**Prep:** 20 min. • **Cook:** 15 min.
**Makes:** 4 servings

- 1 Tbsp. olive oil
- ½ cup chopped sweet onion
- 3 garlic cloves, sliced
  Dash crushed red pepper flakes
- 2½ cups cut fresh asparagus (about 1½ lbs.), trimmed
- 2 cups vegetable broth
- ⅓ cup whole hazelnuts, toasted
- 2 Tbsp. chopped fresh basil
- 2 Tbsp. lemon juice
- ½ cup unsweetened almond milk
- 2 tsp. reduced-sodium tamari soy sauce
- ¼ tsp. salt
  Shaved asparagus, optional

**1.** In a large saucepan, heat oil over medium heat. Add onion, garlic and pepper flakes; cook and stir until onion is softened, 4-5 minutes. Add asparagus and broth; bring to a boil. Reduce heat; simmer, covered, until asparagus is tender, 6-8 minutes. Remove from heat; cool slightly.
**2.** Place nuts, basil and lemon juice in a blender. Add asparagus mixture. Process until smooth and creamy. Return to saucepan. Stir in almond milk, tamari sauce and salt. Heat through, taking care not to boil soup. If desired, top with shaved asparagus.
**¾ cup:** 164 cal., 13g fat (1g sat. fat), 0 chol., 623mg sod., 11g carb. (4g sugars, 4g fiber), 5g pro. **Diabetic exchanges:** 2½ fat, ½ starch.

## Mushroom & Broccoli Soup

One of my girls won't eat meat and the other struggles to get enough fiber. This recipe is a fabulous way to give them both what they need in a dish they love. I save my broccoli stems in the freezer until I have about two small bags, and then I make soup.
—*Maria Davis, Flower Mound, TX*

**Prep:** 20 min. • **Cook:** 45 min.
**Makes:** 8 servings

- 1 bunch broccoli (about 1½ lbs.)
- 1 Tbsp. canola oil
- ½ lb. sliced fresh mushrooms
- 1 Tbsp. reduced-sodium soy sauce
- 2 medium carrots, finely chopped
- 2 celery ribs, finely chopped
- ¼ cup finely chopped onion
- 1 garlic clove, minced
- 1 carton (32 oz.) vegetable broth
- 2 cups water
- 2 Tbsp. lemon juice

**1.** Cut broccoli florets into bite-sized pieces. Peel and chop stalks.
**2.** In a large saucepan, heat oil over medium-high heat; saute mushrooms until tender, 4-6 minutes. Stir in soy sauce; remove from pan.
**3.** In the same pan, combine broccoli stalks, carrots, celery, onion, garlic, broth and water; bring to a boil. Reduce heat; simmer, uncovered, until the vegetables are softened, 25-30 minutes.
**4.** Puree soup using an immersion blender. Or cool slightly and, in batches, puree soup in a blender; return to pan. Stir in florets and mushrooms; bring to a boil. Reduce heat to medium; cook until broccoli is tender, 8-10 minutes, stirring occasionally. Stir in lemon juice.
**¾ cup:** 69 cal., 2g fat (0 sat. fat), 0 chol., 574mg sod., 11g carb. (4g sugars, 3g fiber), 4g pro. **Diabetic exchanges:** 2 vegetable, ½ fat.

GOLDEN BEET
& PEACH SOUP
WITH TARRAGON

## Golden Beet & Peach Soup with Tarragon

One year we had a bumper crop of peaches, so I had fun experimenting. I changed up a beet soup recipe to include our homegrown golden beets and sweet peaches.
—*Sue Gronholz, Beaver Dam, WI*

**Prep:** 20 min. • **Bake:** 40 min. + chilling
**Makes:** 6 servings

- 2  lbs. fresh golden beets, peeled and cut into 1-in. cubes
- 1  Tbsp. olive oil
- 2  cups white grape-peach juice
- 2  Tbsp. cider vinegar
- ¼  cup plain Greek yogurt
- ¼  tsp. finely chopped fresh tarragon
- 2  medium fresh peaches, peeled and diced
   Additional fresh tarragon sprigs

**1.** Preheat oven to 400°. Place beets in a 15x10x1-in. baking pan. Drizzle with oil; toss to coat. Roast until tender, 40-45 minutes. Cool slightly.

**2.** Transfer beets to a blender or food processor. Add the juice and the vinegar; process until smooth. Refrigerate for at least 1 hour. In a small bowl, combine Greek yogurt and tarragon; refrigerate.

**3.** To serve, divide the beet mixture among individual bowls; place a spoonful of the yogurt mixture into each bowl. Top with diced peaches and additional tarragon.

**⅔ cup:** 159 cal., 4g fat (1g sat. fat), 3mg chol., 129mg sod., 31g carb. (26g sugars, 4g fiber), 3g pro.
**Diabetic exchanges:** 2 vegetable, 1 fruit, ½ fat.

MARKET BASKET SOUP

## Market Basket Soup

I use kohlrabi in this soothing veggie soup. The veggie has a mellow broccoli-cabbage flavor and can be served raw, but I like it best in a warm bowl of this happiness.
—*Kellie Foglio, Salem, WI*

- - - - - - - - - - - - - - - - - - - - - - - - - -

**Prep:** 25 min. • **Cook:** 40 min.
**Makes:** 11 servings

- 1   Tbsp. olive oil
- 1   large kohlrabi bulb, peeled and chopped
- 4   celery ribs, chopped
- 2   medium onions, chopped
- 2   medium carrots, chopped
- 3   garlic cloves, minced
- 1   tsp. salt
- 1   tsp. coarsely ground pepper
- 6   cups vegetable stock or water
- 2   cans (15½ oz. each) great northern beans, rinsed and drained
- 2   bay leaves
- 2   medium tomatoes, chopped
- 2   Tbsp. minced fresh parsley
- 2   Tbsp. minced fresh tarragon or ¾ tsp. dried tarragon
- 2   Tbsp. minced fresh thyme or ¾ tsp. dried thyme

**1.** In a stockpot, heat the oil over medium-high heat. Stir in kohlrabi, celery, onions and carrots; cook for 5 minutes or until the onions are softened. Add the garlic, salt and pepper; cook and stir 5 minutes.
**2.** Stir in the stock, beans and bay leaves. Bring to a boil over medium-high heat. Reduce heat; simmer, covered, until vegetables are tender, 20-25 minutes. Add the remaining ingredients; simmer 5 minutes more. Discard bay leaves.
**1 cup:** 110 cal., 2g fat (0 sat. fat), 0 chol., 664mg sod., 19g carb. (3g sugars, 6g fiber), 5g pro. **Diabetic exchanges:** 1 starch, 1 vegetable.

SPINACH &
TORTELLINI SOUP

## Spinach & Tortellini Soup

A simple tomato-enhanced broth is perfect for cheese tortellini and fresh spinach. Increase the garlic and add Italian seasoning to suit your taste.
—*Debbie Wilson, Burlington, NC*

-----------------------------------

**Takes:** 20 min.
**Makes:** 6 servings

- 1 tsp. olive oil
- 2 garlic cloves, minced
- 1 can (14½ oz.) no-salt-added diced tomatoes, undrained
- 3 cans (14½ oz. each) vegetable broth
- 2 tsp. Italian seasoning
- 1 pkg. (9 oz.) refrigerated cheese tortellini
- 4 cups fresh baby spinach
  Shredded Parmesan cheese
  Freshly ground pepper

**1.** In a large saucepan, heat oil over medium heat. Add garlic; cook and stir 1 minute. Stir in tomatoes, broth and Italian seasoning; bring to a boil.
**2.** Add tortellini; return to a gentle boil. Cook, uncovered, just until tortellini are tender, 7-9 minutes.
**3.** Stir in spinach. Sprinkle servings with cheese and pepper.
**1⅓ cups:** 164 cal., 5g fat (2g sat. fat), 18mg chol., 799mg sod., 25g carb. (4g sugars, 2g fiber), 7g pro.

**TIP**

You can use whatever flavor of tortellini you like for this recipe or substitute another pasta entirely. Just check the cooking time for the pasta of your choice and adjust the length of time it is added to the soup.

BROCCOLI CHOWDER

## Broccoli Chowder

I serve this comforting soup on chilly stay-at-home evenings. The nutmeg seasons the light, creamy broth that is full of tender broccoli florets and diced potatoes.
—*Sue Call, Beech Grove, IN*

-----------------------------------

**Takes:** 30 min.
**Makes:** 6 servings

- 3 cups fresh broccoli florets
- 2 cups diced peeled potatoes
- 2 cups water
- ⅓ cup sliced green onions
- 1 tsp. salt
- ½ tsp. pepper
- 3 Tbsp. butter
- 3 Tbsp. all-purpose flour
- ⅛ tsp. ground nutmeg
- 2 cups whole milk
- ½ cup shredded cheddar cheese

**1.** In a large saucepan, combine the first 6 ingredients. Bring to a boil. Reduce heat; cover and simmer for 12-14 minutes or until vegetables are tender.
**2.** Meanwhile, in another saucepan, melt the butter. Stir in the flour and nutmeg until smooth. Gradually add the milk. Bring to a boil; cook and stir for 2 minutes or until thickened. Stir into vegetable mixture; heat through. Sprinkle with cheese.
**1 cup:** 200 cal., 11g fat (7g sat. fat), 36mg chol., 561mg sod., 19g carb. (5g sugars, 2g fiber), 7g pro.

## Chilled Cucumber Soup

This is a wonderful way to use all those cucumbers that seem to become ripe at the same time! It's so refreshing on hot summer days.
—*Shirley Kidd, New London, MN*

**Prep:** 10 min. + chilling
**Makes:** 4 servings

- 2   medium cucumbers
- 2   cups buttermilk
- ½   cup reduced-fat sour cream
- 1½  tsp. sugar
- 1   tsp. dill weed
- ½   tsp. salt
- ⅛   tsp. white pepper
- 2   green onions, chopped
      Fresh dill, optional

**1.** Cut 4 thin slices of cucumber; set aside for garnish. Peel and finely chop the remaining cucumbers. In a large bowl, combine the buttermilk, sour cream, sugar, dill, salt, pepper, green onions and chopped cucumbers.
**2.** Refrigerate for 4 hours or overnight. Garnish with cucumber slices and, if desired, fresh dill.
**1 cup:** 110 cal., 4g fat (3g sat. fat), 15mg chol., 445mg sod., 13g carb. (0 sugars, 1g fiber), 7g pro. **Diabetic exchanges:** 1 vegetable, ½ reduced-fat milk.

SUMMER
VEGETABLE SOUP

## Summer Vegetable Soup

This vegetable soup is loaded with garden goodness—zucchini, green beans, celery and potato—but it is the turmeric that gives it a tasty new twist.
—*Edith Ruth Muldoon, Baldwin, NY*

**Takes:** 30 min. • **Makes:** 4 servings

- 1   small onion, quartered and thinly sliced
- 1   Tbsp. olive oil
- 4   cups reduced-sodium chicken or vegetable broth
- 1   cup sliced zucchini
- 1   can (15½ oz.) navy beans, rinsed and drained
- ½   cup diced peeled red potato
- ½   cup cut fresh green beans (2-in. pieces)
- ½   cup chopped peeled tomato
- ¼   tsp. pepper
- ⅛   tsp. ground turmeric
- ¼   cup chopped celery leaves
- 2   Tbsp. tomato paste

**1.** In a large saucepan, saute the onion in oil until tender. Add the next 8 ingredients. Bring to a boil. Reduce heat; cover and simmer 20-30 minutes or until vegetables are tender.
**2.** Stir in celery leaves and tomato paste. Cover and let stand 5 minutes before serving.
**1½ cups:** 210 cal., 4g fat (1g sat. fat), 0 chol., 1128mg sod., 32g carb. (0 sugars, 8g fiber), 13g pro.

# Tomato Basil Tortellini Soup

When my family first tried this soup, they all had to have seconds! Sometimes I include cooked, crumbled bacon and serve it with mozzarella cheese.
—*Christina Addison, Blanchester, OH*

**Prep:** 25 min. • **Cook:** 6¼ hours
**Makes:** 18 servings

2 Tbsp. olive oil
1 medium onion, chopped
3 medium carrots, chopped

5 garlic cloves, minced
3 cans (28 oz. each) crushed tomatoes, undrained
1 carton (32 oz.) vegetable broth
1 Tbsp. sugar
1 tsp. dried basil
1 bay leaf
3 pkg. (9 oz. each) refrigerated cheese tortellini
¾ cup half-and-half cream
  Shredded Parmesan cheese
  Minced fresh basil

**1.** In a large skillet, heat the oil over medium-high heat. Add onion and carrots; cook and stir until crisp-tender, 5-6 minutes. Add garlic; cook 1 minute longer.

**2.** Transfer to a 6- or 7-qt. slow cooker. Add the tomatoes, broth, sugar, basil and bay leaf. Cook, covered, on low until vegetables are tender, 6-7 hours.

**3.** Stir in the tortellini. Cook, covered, on high for 15 minutes. Reduce heat to low; stir in cream until heated through. Discard bay leaf. Serve with Parmesan cheese and basil.

**Freeze option:** Before stirring in half-and-half, cool soup and freeze in freezer containers. To use, partially thaw in a refrigerator overnight. Heat through in a saucepan, stirring occasionally; add the half-and-half as directed.

**1 cup:** 214 cal., 7g fat (3g sat. fat), 23mg chol., 569mg sod., 32g carb. (9g sugars, 4g fiber), 9g pro. **Diabetic exchanges:** 2 starch, 1 fat.

 **TIP**

If you're cooking for a smaller group, make just a third of the recipe in a small slow cooker and decrease the cooking time slightly.

TOMATO BASIL
TORTELLINI SOUP

## Quick Mushroom Barley Soup

I surprised my mother with a visit some years ago, and she was preparing this soup when I walked in. It was so wonderful that I asked for the recipe, and I've been fixing it ever since.
—*Edie Irwin, Cornwall, NY*

------

**Takes:** 30 min. • **Makes:** 6 servings

| | |
|---|---|
| 1 | Tbsp. olive oil |
| 1 | cup sliced fresh mushrooms |
| ½ | cup chopped carrot |
| ⅓ | cup chopped onion |
| 2 | cups water |
| ¾ | cup quick-cooking barley |
| 2 | Tbsp. all-purpose flour |
| 3 | cups whole milk |
| 1½ | tsp. salt |
| ½ | tsp. pepper |

**1.** In a large saucepan, heat oil over medium heat. Add the mushrooms, carrot and onion; cook and stir 5-6 minutes or until tender. Add water and barley. Bring to a boil. Reduce heat; simmer, uncovered, 12-15 minutes or until the barley is tender.

**2.** In a small bowl, mix flour, milk, salt and pepper until smooth; stir into soup. Return to a boil, stirring constantly; cook and stir 1-2 minutes or until thickened.

**1 cup:** 196 cal., 7g fat (3g sat. fat), 12mg chol., 654mg sod., 27g carb. (7g sugars, 5g fiber), 8g pro. **Diabetic exchanges:** 1½ starch, ½ whole milk, ½ fat.

QUICK MUSHROOM
BARLEY SOUP

VEGAN
CABBAGE
SOUP

## Vegan Cabbage Soup

Comforting soups that simmer all day long are staples on cool, busy days. For a heartier version of this vegan soup, stir in canned beans, such as cannellini or navy.
—Taste of Home *Test Kitchen*

- - - - - - - - - - - - - - - - - - - - - - - - - - - -

**Prep:** 15 min. • **Cook:** 6 hours
**Makes:** 10 servings

- 4 **cups vegetable stock**
- 1 **can (14 oz.) Italian diced tomatoes**
- 1 **can (6 oz.) tomato paste**
- 1 **small head cabbage (about 1½ lbs.), shredded**
- 4 **celery ribs, chopped**
- 2 **large carrots, chopped**
- 1 **medium onion, chopped**
- 2 **garlic cloves, minced**
- 2 **tsp. Italian seasoning**
- ½ **tsp. salt**
  **Fresh basil, optional**

In a 5- or 6-qt. slow cooker, whisk together stock, diced tomatoes and tomato paste. Stir in vegetables, garlic and seasonings. Cook, covered, on low until the vegetables are tender, 6-8 hours. If desired, top with fresh basil.

**1 cup:** 110 cal., 0 fat (0 sat. fat), 0 chol., 866mg sod., 24g carb. (13g sugars, 6g fiber), 4g pro.

ASPARAGUS SOUP

## Asparagus Soup

Each spring my husband takes our dogs and searches for wild asparagus. He's been so successful that I finally developed this recipe to use the bounty he finds. We look forward to this special soup every year.
—*Betty Jones, Kohler, WI*

**Prep:** 15 min. • **Cook:** 45 min.
**Makes:** 10 servings

- 1 cup chopped onion
- 6 green onions, sliced
- 3 Tbsp. butter
- 1½ cups sliced fresh mushrooms
- 1 lb. fresh asparagus, trimmed and cut into ½-in. pieces
- 1 can (49½ oz.) chicken or vegetable broth
- ½ cup chopped fresh parsley
- ½ tsp. salt
- ½ tsp. dried thyme
- ¼ tsp. pepper
- ⅛ tsp. cayenne pepper
- 2 cups cooked wild rice
- 3 Tbsp. cornstarch
- ⅓ cup water

**1.** In a 3-qt. saucepan, saute the onions in the butter for 4 minutes. Add the mushrooms and cook until tender. Add the asparagus, broth and seasonings; cover and simmer for 30 minutes.

**2.** Add rice. Combine cornstarch and water until smooth; gradually stir into soup. Bring to a boil; cook and stir for 2 minutes or until thickened.

**1 cup:** 111 cal., 4g fat (2g sat. fat), 10mg chol., 795mg sod., 15g carb. (3g sugars, 2g fiber), 4g pro.

## Taco Twist Soup

Spiral pasta adds a fun twist to this dish. I lightened this soup recipe by substituting black beans for ground beef and by topping it with reduced-fat sour cream and cheese.
—*Colleen Zertler, Menomonie, WI*

**Takes:** 30 min. • **Makes:** 6 servings

- 2 tsp. olive oil
- 1 medium onion, chopped
- 2 garlic cloves, minced
- 3 cups vegetable broth or reduced-sodium beef broth
- 1 can (15 oz.) black beans, rinsed and drained
- 1 can (14½ oz.) diced tomatoes, undrained
- 1½ cups picante sauce
- 1 cup uncooked spiral pasta
- 1 small green pepper, chopped
- 2 tsp. chili powder
- 1 tsp. ground cumin
  Optional: Shredded cheddar cheese, sour cream and fresh cilantro

**1.** In a large saucepan, heat oil over medium-high heat. Add onion and garlic; cook and stir until crisp-tender, 3-4 minutes.

**2.** Stir in broth, beans, tomatoes, picante sauce, pasta, green pepper and seasonings. Bring to a boil, stirring frequently. Reduce heat; cover and simmer until the pasta is tender, 10-12 minutes, stirring occasionally. If desired, serve with shredded cheese, sour cream and fresh cilantro.

**1 cup:** 176 cal., 2g fat (0 sat. fat), 0 chol., 1044mg sod., 32g carb. (7g sugars, 5g fiber), 7g pro.

TACO TWIST SOUP

## Creamed Carrot Soup

Fat-free half-and-half gives velvety flair to this colorful recipe. It is a nice change of pace from tomato soup.
—*Barbara Richard, Houston, OH*

**Prep:** 20 min. • **Cook:** 35 min.
**Makes:** 6 servings

- ¾ cup finely chopped onion
- 3 garlic cloves, minced
- 2 tsp. olive oil
- 3 cans (14½ oz. each) reduced-sodium chicken broth or vegetable broth
- 6 cups sliced carrots (about 2½ lbs.)
- ¾ cup cubed peeled potatoes
- 1 tsp. salt
- 1 tsp. dried thyme
- ¼ tsp. pepper
- 1 bay leaf
- 1 cup fat-free half-and-half cream

**1.** In a large saucepan, saute onion and garlic in oil until tender. Add the broth, carrots, potatoes, salt, thyme, pepper and bay leaf. Bring to a boil. Reduce heat; cover and simmer for 20-30 minutes or until the vegetables are very tender.
**2.** Remove from heat; cool slightly. Discard bay leaf. In a blender, puree carrot mixture in batches. Return to pan. Or use an immersion blender. Stir in half-and-half; heat through (do not boil).

**1⅓ cups:** 133 cal., 2g fat (0 sat. fat), 0 chol., 995mg sod., 24g carb. (13g sugars, 5g fiber), 6g pro. **Diabetic exchanges:** 3 vegetable, ½ starch, ½ fat.

## Kale & Bean Soup

Packed with tasty veggies, this soup soothes both the body and the spirit. The kale is rich in nutrients, including omega-3s, and the beans add natural creaminess.
—*Beth Sollars, Delray Beach, FL*

**Prep:** 20 min. • **Cook:** 70 min.
**Makes:** 8 servings

- 2 medium onions, chopped
- 2 cups cubed peeled potatoes
- 1 Tbsp. olive oil
- 4 garlic cloves, minced
- 1 bunch kale, trimmed and coarsely chopped
- 3½ cups vegetable broth
- 1 can (28 oz.) diced tomatoes, undrained
- 1½ cups water
- 1 tsp. Italian seasoning
- 1 tsp. paprika
- ½ tsp. pepper
- 1 bay leaf
- 1 can (15 oz.) cannellini beans, rinsed and drained

**1.** In a Dutch oven, saute onions and potatoes in oil until tender. Add the garlic; cook 1 minute longer.
**2.** Stir in the kale, broth, tomatoes, water, Italian seasoning, paprika, pepper and bay leaf. Bring to a boil. Reduce heat; cover and simmer for 50-60 minutes or until kale is tender.
**3.** Cool slightly. Discard bay leaf. In a blender, process 3 cups soup until smooth. Return to pan; add beans and heat through.

**1¼ cups:** 152 cal., 2g fat (0 sat. fat), 0 chol., 622mg sod., 29g carb. (7g sugars, 6g fiber), 5g pro. **Diabetic exchanges:** 2 vegetable, 1 starch, 1 lean meat.

KALE & BEAN SOUP

CREAMY CAULIFLOWER PAKORA SOUP

1. In a Dutch oven over medium-high heat, bring the first 14 ingredients to a boil. Cook and stir until vegetables are tender, about 20 minutes.

2. Remove from heat; cool slightly. Process in batches in a blender or food processor until smooth, or use an immersion blender. Adjust consistency as desired with water or additional stock. Sprinkle with fresh cilantro. Serve hot, with lime wedges if desired.

**Freeze option:** Before adding cilantro, freeze cooled soup in freezer containers. To use, partially thaw in refrigerator overnight. Heat in a saucepan, stirring occasionally; add water if needed. Sprinkle with cilantro. If desired, serve with lime wedges.

**1½ cups:** 135 cal., 1g fat (0 sat. fat), 0 chol., 645mg sod., 30g carb. (6g sugars, 5g fiber), 4g pro. **Diabetic exchanges:** 1½ starch, 1 vegetable.

 **TIP**

Garam masala is a versatile aromatic spice blend widely used in Indian cooking. A traditional garam masala may contain cinnamon, mace, peppercorns, coriander seeds, cumin seeds and cardamom pods—all toasted and then ground. In a pinch, allspice can be used instead, but garam masala is worth having in your pantry!

## Creamy Cauliflower Pakora Soup

My husband and I oftentimes crave pakoras, which are deep-fried fritters from India. I wanted to get the same flavors but use a healthier cooking technique, so I made soup using all the classic Indian spices and our favorite veggie, cauliflower!
—*Melody Johnson, Pulaski, WI*

-----

**Prep:** 20 min. • **Cook:** 20 min.
**Makes:** 8 servings

- 1  large head cauliflower, cut into small florets
- 5  medium potatoes, peeled and diced
- 1  large onion, diced
- 4  medium carrots, peeled and diced
- 2  celery ribs, diced
- 1  carton (32 oz.) vegetable stock
- 1  tsp. garam masala
- 1  tsp. garlic powder
- 1  tsp. ground coriander
- 1  tsp. ground turmeric
- 1  tsp. ground cumin
- 1  tsp. pepper
- 1  tsp. salt
- ½  tsp. crushed red pepper flakes
   Water or additional vegetable stock
   Fresh cilantro leaves
   Lime wedges, optional

SPRING ESSENCE SOUP
WITH PISTOU, P. 195

# Healthy & Light

Craveworthy soups and stews can fit into a special diet or eating plan. It's true—here's proof!

LEMON CHICKEN & RICE SOUP, P. 184

CHICKEN
MUSHROOM
STEW

## Chicken Mushroom Stew

The flavors blend beautifully in this pot of chicken, vegetables and herbs as it simmers in a slow cooker. Folks with busy schedules will love this convenient recipe.
—*Kenny Van Rheenen, Mendota, IL*

**Prep:** 20 min. • **Cook:** 4 hours
**Makes:** 6 servings

- 6 boneless skinless chicken breast halves (4 oz. each)
- 2 Tbsp. canola oil, divided
- 8 oz. fresh mushrooms, sliced
- 1 medium onion, diced
- 3 cups diced zucchini
- 1 cup chopped green pepper
- 4 garlic cloves, minced
- 3 medium tomatoes, chopped
- 1 can (6 oz.) tomato paste
- ¾ cup water
- 2 tsp. each dried thyme, oregano, marjoram, and basil
  Chopped fresh thyme, optional

**1.** Cut chicken into 1-in. cubes; brown in 1 Tbsp. oil in a large skillet. Transfer to a 3-qt. slow cooker. In the same skillet, saute mushrooms, onion, zucchini and green pepper in the remaining oil until crisp-tender; add garlic; cook 1 minute longer. Place in slow cooker.

**2.** Add the tomatoes, tomato paste, water and seasonings. Cover and cook on low for 4-5 hours or until the meat is no longer pink and the vegetables are tender. If desired, top with chopped fresh thyme.

**1⅓ cups:** 237 cal., 8g fat (1g sat. fat), 63mg chol., 82mg sod., 15g carb. (7g sugars, 3g fiber), 27g pro. **Diabetic exchanges:** 3 lean meat, 1 starch, 1 fat.

TOMATO GREEN BEAN SOUP

## Tomato Green Bean Soup

This colorful soup is delicious any time of the year. When I can't get homegrown tomatoes and green beans, frozen beans and canned tomatoes (or even stewed tomatoes) work just fine. Served with warm breadsticks, this is a complete meal.
—*Bernice Nolan, Granite City, IL*

**Prep:** 10 min. • **Cook:** 35 min.
**Makes:** 9 servings

- 1 cup chopped onion
- 1 cup chopped carrots
- 2 tsp. butter
- 6 cups reduced-sodium chicken or vegetable broth
- 1 lb. fresh green beans, cut into 1-in. pieces
- 1 garlic clove, minced
- 3 cups diced fresh tomatoes
- ¼ cup minced fresh basil or 1 Tbsp. dried basil
- ½ tsp. salt
- ¼ tsp. pepper

**1.** In a large saucepan, saute onion and carrots in butter for 5 minutes. Stir in the broth, beans and garlic; bring to a boil. Reduce heat; cover and simmer for 20 minutes or until the vegetables are tender.

**2.** Stir in the diced tomatoes, basil, salt and pepper. Cover and simmer 5 minutes longer.

**1 cup:** 58 cal., 1g fat (1g sat. fat), 2mg chol., 535mg sod., 10g carb. (5g sugars, 3g fiber), 4g pro. **Diabetic exchanges:** 2 vegetable.

## Fresh Asparagus Soup

We have a large asparagus patch and are able to freeze a lot for the year. My easy recipe highlights all the flavor of the vegetable. I heat up this soup in a mug for an afternoon snack!

—*Sherri Melotik, Oak Creek, WI*

- - - - - - - - - - - - - - - - - - - - - - - - -

**Prep:** 15 min. • **Cook:** 20 min.
**Makes:** 6 servings

- 1 tsp. canola oil
- 1 small onion, chopped
- 1 garlic clove, minced
- 2 lbs. fresh asparagus, trimmed and cut into 1-in. pieces (about 5 cups)
- 1 can (14½ oz.) reduced-sodium chicken broth
- 4 Tbsp. all-purpose flour, divided
- 2½ cups fat-free milk, divided
- 2 Tbsp. butter
- ¾ tsp. salt
- ⅛ tsp. dried thyme
- ⅛ tsp. pepper
- ½ cup half-and-half cream
- 2 Tbsp. white wine
- 1 Tbsp. lemon juice
  Minced fresh chives, optional

**1.** In a large saucepan, heat oil over medium heat. Add onion; cook and stir 4-6 minutes or until tender. Add garlic; cook 1 minute longer. Add asparagus and broth; bring to a boil. Reduce heat; simmer, uncovered, 8-10 minutes or until asparagus is tender. Remove from heat; cool slightly. Transfer to a blender; cover and process until smooth.

**2.** In a small bowl, mix 2 Tbsp. of flour and ¼ cup milk until smooth; set aside.

**3.** In the same saucepan, heat butter over medium heat. Stir in seasonings and the remaining flour until smooth; cook and stir 45-60 seconds or until light golden brown. Gradually whisk in cream, the remaining milk and reserved flour mixture. Bring to a boil, stirring constantly; cook for 1-2 minutes or until thickened.

**4.** Stir in wine, lemon juice and asparagus mixture; heat through. If desired, top individual servings with chives.

FRESH
ASPARAGUS
SOUP

**1 cup:** 154 cal., 7g fat (4g sat. fat), 22mg chol., 585mg sod., 15g carb. (8g sugars, 2g fiber), 8g pro. **Diabetic exchanges:** 1½ fat, 1 vegetable, ½ fat-free milk.

## Homemade Apple Cider Beef Stew

This recipe is especially nice in fall, when the weather gets crisp and Nebraska's orchards start selling fresh apple cider. This entree's subtle sweetness is a welcome change from other savory stews. We enjoy it with biscuits, apple wedges and sliced cheddar cheese.

—Joyce Glaesemann, Lincoln, NE

**Prep:** 30 min. • **Cook:** 1¾ hours
**Makes:** 8 servings

- 2 lbs. beef stew meat, cut into 1-in. cubes
- 2 Tbsp. canola oil
- 3 cups apple cider or juice
- 1 can (14½ oz.) reduced-sodium beef broth
- 2 Tbsp. cider vinegar
- 1½ tsp. salt
- ¼ to ½ tsp. dried thyme
- ¼ tsp. pepper
- 3 medium potatoes, peeled and cubed
- 4 medium carrots, cut into ¾-in. pieces
- 3 celery ribs, cut into ¾-in. pieces
- 2 medium onions, cut into wedges
- ¼ cup all-purpose flour
- ¼ cup water
  Fresh thyme sprigs, optional

**1.** In a Dutch oven, brown beef on all sides in oil over medium-high heat; drain. Add the cider, broth, vinegar, salt, thyme and pepper; bring to a boil. Reduce heat; cover and simmer for 1¼ hours.

**2.** Add potatoes, carrots, celery and onions; return to a boil. Reduce heat; cover and simmer for 30-35 minutes or until the beef and vegetables are tender.

**3.** Combine flour and water until smooth; stir into the stew. Bring to a boil; cook and stir for 2 minutes or until thickened. If desired, serve with fresh thyme.

**1 cup:** 330 cal., 12g fat (3g sat. fat), 72mg chol., 628mg sod., 31g carb. (14g sugars, 2g fiber), 24g pro.
**Diabetic exchanges:** 3 lean meat, 1½ starch, 1 vegetable.

 **TIP**
If you have the time, try making this recipe the day before to allow the flavors to blend. Refrigerate the stew after the first two steps. Then, the next day, bring it up to a simmer and add the flour and water mixture as directed.

HOMEMADE APPLE CIDER BEEF STEW

## Lemon Chicken & Rice Soup

Years ago, I fell hard for a lemony Greek soup at Panera Bread. It was a seasonal special then, and I created my own version at home so we could eat it whenever a craving hit!
—*Kristin Cherry, Bothell, WA*

- - - - - - - - - - - - - - - - - - - - - - - - -

**Prep:** 35 min. • **Cook:** 4¼ hours
**Makes:** 12 servings

- 2 Tbsp. olive oil
- 2 lbs. boneless skinless chicken breasts, cut into ½-in. pieces
- 5 cans (14½ oz. each) reduced-sodium chicken broth
- 8 cups coarsely chopped Swiss chard, kale or spinach
- 2 large carrots, finely chopped
- 1 small onion, chopped
- 1 medium lemon, halved and thinly sliced
- ¼ cup lemon juice
- 4 tsp. grated lemon zest
- ½ tsp. pepper
- 4 cups cooked brown rice

**1.** In a large skillet, heat 1 Tbsp. oil over medium-high heat. Add half of the chicken; cook and stir until browned. Transfer to a 6-qt. slow cooker. Repeat with remaining oil and chicken.

**2.** Stir broth, vegetables, lemon slices, juice, zest and pepper into chicken. Cook, covered, on low 4-5 hours or until chicken is tender. Stir in rice; heat through.

**1⅓ cups:** 203 cal., 5g fat (1g sat. fat), 42mg chol., 612mg sod., 20g carb. (3g sugars, 2g fiber), 20g pro. **Diabetic exchanges:** 2 lean meat, 1 starch, 1 vegetable, ½ fat.

LEMON CHICKEN & RICE SOUP

ANDOUILLE
SAUSAGE SOUP

## Andouille Sausage Soup

I wanted a vegetable-filled soup with a lot of flavor. Adding andouille sausage made this recipe spicy enough that even my sons enjoy eating it!
—Steven Thurner, Janesville, WI

**Prep:** 20 min. • **Cook:** 35 min.
**Makes:** 10 servings

- 1 Tbsp. canola oil
- 2 large onions, chopped
- 3 medium carrots, chopped
- 1 medium green pepper, chopped
- 2 garlic cloves, minced
- 1 pkg. (12 oz.) fully cooked andouille chicken sausage links, cut into ¼-in. slices
- 1½ lbs. red potatoes (about 5 medium), cut into ½-in. cubes
- 1 can (28 oz.) crushed tomatoes in puree
- 1 tsp. Worcestershire sauce
- ¼ tsp. pepper
- 1 carton (32 oz.) reduced-sodium beef broth
- 2 tsp. liquid smoke, optional
- ¼ tsp. cayenne pepper, optional
  Sour cream, optional

**1.** In a 6-qt. stockpot, heat oil over medium heat. Add onions, carrots and green pepper; cook and stir until tender, 8-10 minutes. Add garlic; cook 1 minute longer. Remove from pot.
**2.** In same pot, brown sausage over medium heat. Add cubed potatoes, tomatoes, Worcestershire sauce, pepper, broth and the onion mixture. If desired, stir in liquid smoke and cayenne. Bring to a boil. Reduce heat; simmer, covered, until potatoes are tender, 15-20 minutes. If desired, top servings with sour cream.

**1⅓ cups:** 168 cal., 5g fat (1g sat. fat), 28mg chol., 540mg sod., 23g carb. (7g sugars, 4g fiber), 10g pro.
**Diabetic exchanges:** 1 starch, 1 lean meat, 1 vegetable.

GOLDEN SUMMER
PEACH GAZPACHO

## Golden Summer Peach Gazpacho

Since peaches and tomatoes are in season together, I like to blend them into a cool, delicious soup. Leftovers keep well in the fridge—but they rarely last long enough to get there.
—*Julie Hession, Las Vegas, NV*

**Prep:** 20 min. + chilling
**Makes:** 8 servings

- 3 cups sliced peeled fresh or frozen peaches, thawed
- 3 medium yellow tomatoes, chopped
- 1 medium sweet yellow pepper, chopped
- 1 medium cucumber, peeled and chopped
- ½ cup chopped sweet onion
- 1 garlic clove, minced
- ⅓ cup lime juice
- 2 Tbsp. rice vinegar
- 1 Tbsp. marinade for chicken
- 1 tsp. salt
- ¼ tsp. hot pepper sauce
- 1 to 3 tsp. sugar, optional
  Chopped peaches, cucumber and tomatoes

**1.** Place the first 6 ingredients in a food processor; process until blended. Add the lime juice, vinegar, marinade for chicken, salt and hot pepper sauce; process until smooth. If desired, stir in sugar.
**2.** Refrigerate, covered, for at least 4 hours. Top individual servings with additional chopped peaches, cucumber and tomatoes.
**⅔ cup:** 56 cal., 0 fat (0 sat. fat), 0 chol., 342mg sod., 13g carb. (8g sugars, 2g fiber), 2g pro. **Diabetic exchanges:** 1 vegetable, ½ fruit.

## Turkey Ginger Noodle Soup

I was looking for a craveworthy soup that's healthy and tasty. Ginger is my favorite spice, so making this recipe was a shoo-in.
—*Adina Monson, Nanaimo, BC*

**Prep:** 20 min. • **Cook:** 4¼ hours
**Makes:** 8 servings

- 2 medium carrots, sliced
- 2 cans (8 oz. each) sliced water chestnuts, drained
- 3 to 4 Tbsp. minced fresh gingerroot
- 2 Tbsp. minced fresh parsley
- 2 tsp. chili powder
- 1 carton (32 oz.) chicken stock
- 1 can (11.8 oz.) coconut water
- 3 Tbsp. lemon juice
- 2 lbs. uncooked skinless turkey breast, cut into 1-in. cubes
- 2 tsp. pepper
- ½ tsp. salt
- 2 Tbsp. canola oil
- 1 cup frozen corn (about 5 oz.), thawed
- 1 cup frozen peas (about 4 oz.), thawed
- 8 oz. rice noodles or thin spaghetti, cooked

**1.** Place the first 8 ingredients in a 4- or 5-qt. slow cooker.
**2.** Toss turkey with pepper and salt. In a large skillet, heat canola oil over medium-high heat; brown turkey in batches. Add to slow cooker.
**3.** Cook, covered, on low 4-5 hours, until carrots are tender. Stir in corn and peas; heat through. Add noodles to soup just before serving.
**1½ cups:** 351 cal., 6g fat (1g sat. fat), 65mg chol., 672mg sod., 41g carb. (5g sugars, 4g fiber), 33g pro.
**Diabetic exchanges:** 3 starch, 3 lean meat.

TURKEY GINGER
NOODLE SOUP

## Miso Soup with Tofu & Enoki

This traditional Japanese soup is soothing and mild, and made with ingredients that are easy to find. Sliced green onions give it a nice presentation at the table.
—*Bridget Klusman, Otsego, MI*

**Takes:** 30 min. • **Makes:** 5 servings

- 2  pkg. (3½ oz. each) fresh enoki mushrooms or ½ lb. sliced fresh mushrooms
- 1  medium onion, chopped
- 2  garlic cloves, minced
- 1  tsp. minced fresh gingerroot
- 1  Tbsp. canola oil
- 4  cups water
- ¼  cup miso paste
- 1  pkg. (16 oz.) firm tofu, drained and cut into ¾-in. cubes
   Thinly sliced green onions

**1.** In a Dutch oven, saute mushrooms, onion, minced garlic and ginger in oil until tender.
**2.** Add the water and miso paste. Bring to a boil. Reduce heat; simmer, uncovered, for 15 minutes.
**3.** Add tofu; heat through. Ladle into bowls; garnish with green onions.
**1 cup:** 147 cal., 8g fat (1g sat. fat), 0 chol., 601mg sod., 10g carb. (4g sugars, 2g fiber), 10g pro. **Diabetic exchanges:** 1½ fat, 1 lean meat, ½ starch.

## Texas Black Bean Soup

This hearty meatless stew made with convenient canned items is perfect for spicing up a family gathering on a cool day. The flavor is rich and layered, yet it requires so little time and attention.
—*Pamela Scott, Garland, TX*

**Prep:** 5 min. • **Cook:** 4 hours
**Makes:** 10 servings

- 2  cans (15 oz. each) black beans, rinsed and drained
- 1  can (14½ oz.) stewed tomatoes or Mexican stewed tomatoes, cut up
- 1  can (14½ oz.) diced tomatoes or diced tomatoes with green chiles
- 1  can (14½ oz.) chicken broth
- 1  can (11 oz.) Mexicorn, drained
- 2  cans (4 oz. each) chopped green chiles
- 4  green onions, thinly sliced
- 2  to 3 Tbsp. chili powder
- 1  tsp. ground cumin
- ½  tsp. dried minced garlic

In a 3-qt. slow cooker, combine all ingredients. Cover and cook on high 4-6 hours or until heated through.
**1 cup:** 91 cal., 0 fat (0 sat. fat), 0 chol., 609mg sod., 19g carb. (6g sugars, 4g fiber), 4g pro.

TEXAS BLACK BEAN SOUP

1. In a large skillet, heat oil over medium-high heat. Add onion and sweet pepper; cook and stir until crisp-tender, 6-8 minutes. Add garlic; cook 1 minute longer. Transfer to a 4- or 5-qt. slow cooker.

2. Add chicken stock, potatoes, chiles, ¼ cup cilantro, serrano pepper and seasonings. Cook, covered, on low for 4-6 hours, until the potatoes are tender.

3. Remove from heat; cool slightly. Process in batches in a blender until smooth. Return to slow cooker. Stir in chorizo and remaining ¼ cup cilantro; heat through. If desired, serve with sour cream and avocado.

**1 cup:** 153 cal., 5g fat (1g sat. fat), 7mg chol., 472mg sod., 23g carb. (3g sugars, 2g fiber), 6g pro. **Diabetic exchanges:** 1½ starch, 1 fat.

 **TIP**

Chorizo is commonly used in both Mexican and Spanish cuisines. Spanish chorizo is made with smoked pork, while Mexican chorizo uses fresh pork. Chorizo is sold in markets both fully cooked and fresh; be sure to use cooked chorizo for this recipe.

SPICY PERUVIAN POTATO SOUP

## Spicy Peruvian Potato Soup

This robust Peruvian soup (known in Peru as *locro de papa*) has the comfort of potatoes and warming spiciness of chiles. Light enough for a simple lunch, it's satisfying as a dinner meal, too.
—Taste of Home *Test Kitchen*

- - - - - - - - - - - - - - - - - - - - - - - - - - - - - -

**Prep:** 35 min. • **Cook:** 4 hours
**Makes:** 8 servings

1  Tbsp. olive oil
1  medium onion, chopped
1  medium sweet red pepper, cut into 1-in. pieces
3  garlic cloves, minced
1  carton (32 oz.) chicken stock
2  large Yukon Gold potatoes, peeled and cut into 1-in. cubes
1  can (4 oz.) chopped green chiles
½  cup minced fresh cilantro, divided
½  to 1 serrano pepper, seeded and finely chopped
2  tsp. ground cumin
1  tsp. dried oregano
¼  tsp. salt
¼  tsp. pepper
1  fully cooked Spanish chorizo link (3 oz.), chopped
   Optional: Sour cream and cubed avocado

APPLE
CHICKEN
STEW

## Apple Chicken Stew

My husband and I enjoy visiting the apple orchards in nearby Nebraska City. We always make sure to buy extra cider to use in this sensational slow-cooked stew.

*—Carol Mathias, Lincoln, NE*

- - - - - - - - - - - - - - - - - - - - - - - - - - - -

**Prep:** 35 min. • **Cook:** 3 hours
**Makes:** 8 servings

- 1½ tsp. salt
- ¾ tsp. dried thyme
- ½ tsp. pepper
- ¼ to ½ tsp. caraway seeds
- 1½ lbs. potatoes (about 4 medium), cut into ¾-in. pieces
- 4 medium carrots, cut into ¼-in. slices
- 1 medium red onion, halved and sliced
- 1 celery rib, thinly sliced
- 2 lbs. boneless skinless chicken breasts, cut into 1-in. pieces
- 2 Tbsp. olive oil
- 1 bay leaf
- 1 large tart apple, peeled and cut into 1-in. cubes
- 1 Tbsp. cider vinegar
- 1¼ cups apple cider or juice
  Minced fresh parsley

**1.** Mix first 4 ingredients. In a 5-qt. slow cooker, layer vegetables; sprinkle with half the salt mixture.
**2.** Toss chicken with oil and remaining salt mixture. In a large skillet over medium-high heat, brown chicken in batches. Add to slow cooker. Top with bay leaf and apple. Add vinegar and cider.
**3.** Cook, covered, on high 3-3½ hours until chicken is no longer pink and vegetables are tender, . Discard bay leaf. Stir before serving. Sprinkle with fresh parsley.

**1 cup:** 284 cal., 6g fat (1g sat. fat), 63mg chol., 533mg sod., 31g carb. (9g sugars, 4g fiber), 26g pro.
**Diabetic exchanges:** 3 lean meat, 2 starch, 1 fat.

AFRICAN PEANUT
SWEET POTATO STEW

## African Peanut Sweet Potato Stew

When I was in college, my mom made an addicting sweet potato stew. I shared it with friends, and now all of us serve it to our own kids. They all love it, of course.
—*Alexis Scatchell, Niles, IL*

**Prep:** 20 min. • **Cook:** 6 hours
**Makes:** 8 servings

- 1 can (28 oz.) diced tomatoes, undrained
- 1 cup fresh cilantro leaves
- ½ cup chunky peanut butter
- 3 garlic cloves, halved
- 2 tsp. ground cumin
- 1 tsp. salt
- ½ tsp. ground cinnamon
- ¼ tsp. smoked paprika
- 3 lbs. sweet potatoes (about 6 medium), peeled and cut into 1-in. pieces
- 1 can (15 oz.) garbanzo beans or chickpeas, rinsed and drained
- 1 cup water
- 8 cups chopped fresh kale
  Optional: Chopped peanuts and additional cilantro leaves

**1.** Place the first 8 ingredients in a food processor; process until pureed. Transfer to a 5-qt. slow cooker.
**2.** Stir in sweet potatoes, beans and water. Cook, covered, on low for 6-8 hours or until the potatoes are tender, adding kale during the last 30 minutes. If desired, top each serving with chopped peanuts and additional cilantro.
**1¼ cups:** 349 cal., 9g fat (1g sat. fat), 0 chol., 624mg sod., 60g carb. (23g sugars, 11g fiber), 10g pro.

CAROLINA
SHRIMP SOUP

## Carolina Shrimp Soup

Fresh shrimp from the Carolina coast is one of our favorite foods. We add kale, garlic, sweet red peppers and black-eyed peas to complete this wholesome, filling soup.
—*Mary M. Leverette, Columbia, SC*

- - - - - - - - - - - - - - - - - - - - - - - - - - - - - -

**Takes:** 25 min. • **Makes:** 6 servings

- 4  tsp. olive oil, divided
- 1  lb. uncooked shrimp (31-40 per lb.), peeled and deveined
- 5  garlic cloves, minced
- 1  bunch kale, trimmed and coarsely chopped (about 16 cups)
- 1  medium sweet red pepper, cut into ¾-in. pieces
- 3  cups reduced-sodium chicken broth
- 1  can (15½ oz.) black-eyed peas, rinsed and drained
- ¼  tsp. salt
- ¼  tsp. pepper
   Minced fresh chives, optional

**1.** In a 6-qt. stockpot, heat 2 tsp. oil over medium-high heat. Add shrimp; cook and stir 2 minutes. Add minced garlic; cook just until shrimp turn pink, 1-2 minutes longer. Remove from pot.
**2.** In same pot, heat remaining oil over medium-high heat. Stir in kale and red pepper; cook, covered, until kale is tender, stirring occasionally, 8-10 minutes.
**3.** Add broth; bring to a boil. Stir in peas, salt, pepper and shrimp; heat through. If desired, sprinkle servings with chives.

**1 cup:** 188 cal., 5g fat (1g sat. fat), 92mg chol., 585mg sod., 18g carb. (2g sugars, 3g fiber), 19g pro.
**Diabetic exchanges:** 2 lean meat, 2 vegetable, ½ starch, ½ fat.

BUTTERNUT GOULASH

## Butternut Goulash

We make this treasured family goulash recipe using squash from our own backyard. The chili powder and cayenne really warm you up!
—*Allison Wilmarth, Forest City, PA*

- - - - - - - - - - - - - - - - - - - - - - - - - - - - - -

**Prep:** 25 min. • **Cook:** 45 min.
**Makes:** 8 servings

- 2  Tbsp. butter
- 1  lb. lean ground beef (90% lean)
- 1  large red pepper, chopped
- 1  cup chopped onion
- 1  can (28 oz.) no-salt-added crushed tomatoes
- 1½  cups peeled butternut squash, cut into ½-in. cubes
- 1  can (8 oz.) no-salt-added tomato sauce
- 1  cup reduced-sodium beef broth
- 1  tsp. salt
- ½  to ¾ tsp. chili powder
- ⅛  to ¼ tsp. cayenne pepper
- ⅛  tsp. dried oregano
- 2  cups chopped zucchini
   Shredded cheddar cheese, optional

**1.** In a Dutch oven, heat butter over medium-high heat. Add beef, red pepper and chopped onion; cook, crumbling beef, until meat is no longer pink and vegetables are tender, 6-8 minutes; drain.
**2.** Add the next 8 ingredients. Bring to a boil; reduce heat to low. Simmer, covered, about 20 minutes.
**3.** Add zucchini. Continue simmering until vegetables are tender, another 20-25 minutes. Just before serving, sprinkle with cheese if desired.

**1¼ cups:** 196 cal., 8g fat (4g sat. fat), 44mg chol., 450mg sod., 17g carb. (7g sugars, 5g fiber), 14g pro. **Diabetic exchanges:** 2 lean meat, 1 starch, 1 fat.

CARROT GINGER SOUP

**5i**

## Cool as a Cucumber Soup

This chilled soup makes a wonderful appetizer or side on a hot summer day. Bright bursts of dill provide a pleasant contrast to the milder flavor of cucumber.

—*Deirdre Cox, Kansas City, MO*

**Prep:** 15 min. + standing
**Makes:** 5 servings

- 1 lb. cucumbers, peeled, seeded and sliced
- ½ tsp. salt
- 1½ cups fat-free plain yogurt
- 1 green onion, coarsely chopped
- 1 garlic clove, minced
- 4½ tsp. snipped fresh dill
  Additional chopped green onion and snipped fresh dill

**1.** In a colander set over a bowl, toss cucumbers with salt. Let stand for 30 minutes. Squeeze and pat dry.
**2.** Place cucumbers, yogurt, onion and garlic in a food processor; cover and process until smooth. Stir in dill. Serve immediately in chilled bowls. Garnish with additional onion and dill.
**⅔ cup:** 40 cal., 0 fat (0 sat. fat), 2mg chol., 279mg sod., 8g carb. (5g sugars, 1g fiber), 3g pro. **Diabetic exchanges:** ½ fat-free milk.

## Carrot Ginger Soup

This light, flavorful carrot ginger soup is vegan! It's made with pantry staples and comes together in a hurry, yet always seems to impress. Fresh ginger makes a big difference—and what isn't used can be wrapped tightly and tossed in the freezer to use later.

—*Jenna Olson, Manchester, MO*

**Prep:** 10 min. • **Cook:** 20 min.
**Makes:** 4 servings

- 1 Tbsp. olive oil
- 1 small onion, chopped
- 1 garlic clove, minced
- 3 tsp. minced fresh gingerroot
- 4 large carrots, peeled and chopped
- 3 cups vegetable broth
- 2 tsp. grated lemon zest
- ½ tsp. salt
- ¼ tsp. ground black pepper
- 2 Tbsp. fresh lemon juice

**1.** In a Dutch oven or stockpot, heat oil over medium heat. Add chopped onion; cook and stir until tender, 4-5 minutes. Add garlic and ginger; cook 1 minute longer. Stir in carrots, broth, zest, salt and pepper; bring to a boil. Reduce heat; simmer, covered, until carrots are tender, 10-12 minutes.
**2.** Pulse mixture in a blender or with an immersion blender to desired consistency; stir in lemon juice. If desired, garnish with additional lemon zest.

**Freeze option:** Cool soup; freeze in freezer containers. To use, partially thaw in refrigerator overnight. Heat in a large saucepan over medium-low heat, stirring occasionally and adding a little broth or water if necessary.
**1¾ cup:** 80 cal., 4g fat (1g sat. fat), 0 chol., 551mg sod., 11g carb. (5g sugars, 2g fiber), 1g pro. **Diabetic exchanges:** 2 vegetable, 1 fat.

## Spring Essence Soup with Pistou

I went outside in the last days of April and picked what I had available in the garden. I found oregano, asparagus, leeks and rhubarb. This became the base for an essence-of-spring recipe. The rhubarb adds a citrus flavor that's balanced by the nutty, earthy pistou. It is truly a layering of flavors.
—*Laurie Bock, Lynden, WA*

- - - - - - - - - - - - - - - - - - - - - - - - - - -

**Prep:** 20 min. • **Cook:** 25 min.
**Makes:** 6 servings

SPRING ESSENCE
SOUP WITH PISTOU

1 medium leek (white portion only), cut into ¼-in. slices
1 large carrot, chopped
1 small sweet red pepper, chopped
1 Tbsp. olive oil
2 garlic cloves, minced
4 cups chicken stock
10 baby red potatoes, quartered
6 fresh asparagus spears, cut into 1-in. pieces
1 cup chopped fresh rhubarb
1 tsp. sugar
½ tsp. salt
¼ tsp. pepper

PISTOU
½ cup loosely packed fresh oregano
2 Tbsp. chopped hazelnuts, toasted
1½ tsp. olive oil
½ tsp. minced garlic
⅛ tsp. salt

**1.** In a large saucepan, saute the leek, carrot and red pepper in oil until crisp-tender. Add minced garlic; cook 1 minute longer. Stir in stock and potatoes. Bring to a boil. Reduce heat; cover and simmer 5 minutes. Stir in the asparagus, rhubarb, sugar, salt and pepper; cover and simmer 4-6 minutes longer or until vegetables are tender.
**2.** Meanwhile, place the oregano, hazelnuts, oil, garlic and salt in a food processor; cover and pulse until blended. Serve with soup.
**1 cup with 1 tsp. pistou:** 147 cal., 5g fat (1g sat. fat), 0 chol., 601mg sod., 21g carb. (4g sugars, 3g fiber), 6g pro. **Diabetic exchanges:** 1 starch, 1 vegetable, 1 fat.

**TIP**

Pistou is the French equivalent of Italian pesto, which is more well-known in the United States. This from-scratch pistou is made with oregano and hazelnuts, so it has a different flavor, but if you need to save time, you can use prepared pesto instead.

# Ground Beef Veggie Stew

This wonderful, hearty stew helps use up all the late-summer veggies in your garden. I like that it's filling enough to make a meal, and it's good for you too!
—*Courtney Stultz, Weir, KS*

**Takes:** 30 min • **Makes:** 6 servings

- 1 lb. lean ground beef (90% lean)
- 1 Tbsp. olive oil
- 1 small yellow summer squash, chopped
- 1 small zucchini, chopped
- 1 small sweet red pepper, chopped
- 2 cans (15 oz. each) diced tomatoes
- 1 cup water
- 1 tsp. salt
- ¼ tsp. pepper
- 3 Tbsp. minced fresh cilantro Reduced-fat sour cream, optional

**1.** In a large saucepan, cook the ground beef over medium-high heat, breaking meat into crumbles, until no longer pink, 5-7 minutes; drain. Remove from pan; set aside.
**2.** In the same saucepan, add oil, squash, zucchini and red pepper; cook and stir until vegetables are crisp-tender, 5-7 minutes.
**3.** Add beef, tomatoes, water, salt and pepper; bring to a boil. Reduce to a simmer; cook, stirring occasionally, until the vegetables are tender, 5-8 minutes. Stir in cilantro to serve. If desired, top with sour cream.

**1¼ cups:** 180 cal., 9g fat (3g sat. fat), 47mg chol., 663mg sod., 9g carb. (6g sugars, 3g fiber), 16g pro. **Diabetic exchanges:** 2 lean meat, 1 vegetable, ½ fat.

GROUND BEEF VEGGIE STEW

MEDITERRANEAN
CHICKEN ORZO SOUP

## Mediterranean Chicken Orzo Soup

My husband is Greek, so I'm always trying new Mediterranean recipes. This soup is his favorite—I'll often sprinkle it with feta or Parmesan.
—*Kristine Kosturos, Olympia, WA*

**Prep:** 20 min. • **Cook:** 25 min.
**Makes:** 6 servings

- 2  Tbsp. olive oil, divided
- ¾  lb. boneless skinless chicken breasts, cubed
- 2  celery ribs, chopped
- 2  medium carrots, chopped
- 1  small onion, chopped
- ½  tsp. salt
- ½  tsp. dried oregano
- ¼  tsp. pepper
- ¼  cup white wine or additional reduced-sodium chicken broth
- 1  carton (32 oz.) reduced-sodium chicken broth
- 1  tsp. minced fresh rosemary
- 1  bay leaf
- 1  cup uncooked whole wheat orzo pasta
- 1  tsp. grated lemon zest
- 1  Tbsp. lemon juice
    Minced fresh parsley, optional

**1.** In a large saucepan, heat 1 Tbsp. oil over medium-high heat. Add chicken; cook and stir 6-8 minutes or until no longer pink. Remove from pan.
**2.** In same pan, heat the remaining oil over medium-high heat. Add the vegetables, salt, oregano and pepper; cook and stir 4-6 minutes or until vegetables are crisp-tender. Add the wine, stirring to loosen browned bits from pan. Stir in broth, rosemary and bay leaf; bring to a boil.
**3.** Add orzo. Reduce heat; simmer, covered, 15-18 minutes or until the orzo is tender, stirring occasionally. Return chicken to pan; heat through. Stir in lemon zest and juice; remove bay leaf. If desired, top each serving with parsley.

**1⅔ cups:** 223 cal., 6g fat (1g sat. fat), 31mg chol., 630mg sod., 23g carb. (2g sugars, 5g fiber), 17g pro.
**Diabetic exchanges:** 2 lean meat, 1 starch, 1 vegetable, 1 fat.

LOADED POTATO-LEEK SOUP

## Veggie Salmon Chowder

I wanted to use up odds and ends in my fridge (waste not, want not!) and came up with this chowder. The recipe began as an experiment but has become a mainstay for me.
—Liv Vors, Peterborough, ON

**Takes:** 30 min. • **Makes:** 2 servings

- 1   medium sweet potato, peeled and cut into ½-in. cubes
- 1   cup reduced-sodium chicken broth
- ½   cup fresh or frozen corn
- ½   small onion, chopped
- 2   garlic cloves, minced
- 1½  cups fresh spinach, torn
- ½   cup flaked smoked salmon fillet
- 1   tsp. pickled jalapeno slices, chopped
- 1   Tbsp. cornstarch
- ½   cup 2% milk
- 1   Tbsp. minced fresh cilantro Dash pepper

**1.** In a large saucepan, combine the first 5 ingredients; bring to a boil. Reduce heat; simmer, covered, until potato is tender, 8-10 minutes.
**2.** Stir in spinach, smoked salmon and jalapeno; cook until the spinach is wilted, 1-2 minutes.
**3.** In a small bowl, mix cornstarch and milk until smooth; stir into the soup. Bring to a boil; cook and stir until thickened, about 2 minutes. Stir in cilantro and pepper.
**1¼ cups:** 202 cal., 3g fat (1g sat. fat), 12mg chol., 645mg sod., 32g carb. (11g sugars, 4g fiber), 13g pro.
**Diabetic exchanges:** 2 starch, 1 lean meat, 1 vegetable.

## Loaded Potato-Leek Soup

When I was growing up, my mother made potato and onion soup because it was affordable and fast. I've since trimmed the calories, but it's still a comforting family favorite.
—Courtney Stultz, Weir, KS

**Prep:** 20 min. • **Cook:** 6 hours
**Makes:** 6 servings

- 1   medium leek
- 1½  lbs. potatoes (about 2 large), peeled and finely chopped
- 2   cups fresh cauliflowerets
- ¾   tsp. rubbed sage
- ½   tsp. salt
- ¼   tsp. pepper
- 4   cups reduced-sodium chicken or vegetable broth
- 2   tsp. olive oil
- 2   tsp. lemon juice Sour cream, optional

**1.** Finely chop white portion of leek. Cut leek greens into thin strips; set aside. In a 3- or 4-qt. slow cooker, combine potatoes, cauliflowerets, seasonings, broth and chopped leek. Cook, covered, on low for 6-8 hours or until vegetables are tender.
**2.** In a small skillet, heat olive oil over medium-high heat. Add the reserved leek greens; cook 3-5 minutes.
**3.** Puree soup using an immersion blender. Or, cool soup slightly and puree in batches in a blender. Stir in lemon juice. Top with leek greens and, if desired, sour cream.
**1 cup:** 108 cal., 2g fat (0 sat. fat), 0 chol., 593mg sod., 20g carb. (3g sugars, 2g fiber), 4g pro.

VEGGIE SALMON
CHOWDER

## Chicken Tortellini Soup

This simple recipe is like an Italian twist on chicken noodle soup. The cheese-filled tortellini and Italian herbs make it special.
—*Jean Atherly, Red Lodge, MT*

- - - - - - - - - - - - - - - - - - - - - - - - - - - -

**Takes:** 30 min. • **Makes:** 8 servings

- 2 cans (14½ oz. each) chicken broth
- 2 cups water
- ¾ lb. boneless skinless chicken breasts, cut into 1-in. cubes
- 1½ cups frozen mixed vegetables
- 1 pkg. (9 oz.) refrigerated cheese tortellini
- 2 celery ribs, thinly sliced
- 1 tsp. dried basil
- ½ tsp. garlic salt
- ½ tsp. dried oregano
- ¼ tsp. pepper

**1.** In a large saucepan, bring broth and water to a boil; add chicken. Reduce heat; cook for 10 minutes.
**2.** Add the remaining ingredients; cook 10-15 minutes longer or until chicken is no longer pink and the vegetables are tender.
**1 cup:** 170 cal., 4g fat (2g sat. fat), 37mg chol., 483mg sod., 20g carb. (2g sugars, 3g fiber), 14g pro. **Diabetic exchanges:** 2 lean meat, 1 starch.

## Dill Chicken Soup

I could eat soup for every meal of the day, all year long. I particularly like dill and spinach—they add a brightness to this light and healthy soup.
—*Robin Haas, Hyde Park, MA*

- - - - - - - - - - - - - - - - - - - - - - - - - - - -

**Takes:** 30 min. • **Makes:** 6 servings

- 1 Tbsp. canola oil
- 2 medium carrots, chopped
- 1 small onion, coarsely chopped
- 2 garlic cloves, minced
- ½ cup uncooked whole wheat orzo pasta
- 1½ cups coarsely shredded rotisserie chicken
- 6 cups reduced-sodium chicken broth
- 1½ cups frozen peas (about 6 oz.)
- 8 oz. fresh baby spinach (about 10 cups)
- 2 Tbsp. chopped fresh dill or 1 Tbsp. dill weed
- 2 Tbsp. lemon juice
  Coarsely ground pepper, optional

**1.** In a 6-qt. stockpot, heat oil over medium heat. Add carrots, onion and garlic; saute until carrots are tender, 4-5 minutes.
**2.** Stir in orzo, chicken and broth; bring to a boil. Reduce heat; simmer, uncovered, 5 minutes. Stir in peas, spinach and dill; return to a boil. Reduce heat; simmer, uncovered, until orzo is tender, 3-4 minutes. Stir in lemon juice. If desired, top each serving with coarsely ground pepper.
**1⅓ cups:** 198 cal., 6g fat (1g sat. fat), 31mg chol., 681mg sod., 20g carb. (4g sugars, 5g fiber), 18g pro. **Diabetic exchanges:** 2 lean meat, 1 starch, 1 vegetable, ½ fat.

DILL CHICKEN SOUP

**LENTIL, BACON & BEAN SOUP**

1. In a Dutch oven, cook bacon over medium heat until crisp, stirring occasionally. Remove with a slotted spoon; drain on paper towels. Reserve drippings in pan.

2. Cook and stir carrots and onions in the bacon drippings until crisp-tender, 3-4 minutes. Add tomato paste, garlic, thyme and pepper; cook 1 minute longer.

3. Add stock and wine; increase heat to medium-high. Cook 2 minutes, stirring to loosen browned bits from pan. Stir in butter beans, lentils and bacon. Bring to a boil. Reduce heat; simmer, covered, 5 minutes. Uncover; continue simmering until vegetables are tender, 15-20 minutes. Garnish with thyme sprigs, if desired.

**1 cup:** 271 cal., 6g fat (2g sat. fat), 9mg chol., 672mg sod., 41g carb. (7g sugars, 13g fiber), 18g pro. **Diabetic exchanges:** 3 starch, 1 medium-fat meat.

 **TIP**

If you have trouble finding butter beans in the store, it might be because of the region you're in. In many parts of the United States, butter beans are known by another name—lima beans!

## Lentil, Bacon & Bean Soup

This quick soup feels extra cozy with lots of lentils and a touch of smoky, bacony goodness. You might want to cook up extra—I think it's even better the next day!
—*Janie Zirbser, Mullica Hill, NJ*

**Prep:** 15 min. • **Cook:** 30 min.
**Makes:** 8 servings

- 4 bacon strips, chopped
- 6 medium carrots, chopped
- 2 small onions, diced
- 2 Tbsp. tomato paste
- 2 garlic cloves, minced
- 1 tsp. minced fresh thyme
- ½ tsp. pepper
- 5 cups chicken stock
- 1 cup dry white wine or additional chicken stock
- 2 cans (15 to 16 oz. each) butter beans, rinsed and drained
- 2 cans (15 oz. each ) lentils, rinsed and drained
  Fresh thyme sprigs, optional

TURKEY
DUMPLING STEW

## Turkey Dumpling Stew

My mom made this stew when I was young, and it was always a hit. Since it's not too time-consuming, I often make it on weekends for our children, who love the tender dumplings.
—*Becky Mohr, Appleton, WI*

**Prep:** 20 min. • **Cook:** 50 min.
**Makes:** 6 servings

- 4   bacon strips, finely chopped
- 1½  lbs. turkey breast tenderloins, cut into 1-in. pieces
- 4   medium carrots, sliced
- 2   small onions, quartered
- 2   celery ribs, sliced
- 1   bay leaf
- ¼   tsp. dried rosemary, crushed
- 2   cups water, divided
- 1   can (14½ oz.) reduced-sodium chicken broth
- 3   Tbsp. all-purpose flour
- ½   tsp. salt
- ⅛   to ¼ tsp. pepper
- 1   cup reduced-fat biscuit/baking mix
- ⅓   cup plus 1 Tbsp. fat-free milk
  Optional: Coarsely ground pepper and chopped fresh parsley

**1.** In a Dutch oven, cook chopped bacon over medium heat until crisp, stirring occasionally. Remove with a slotted spoon; drain on paper towels. Reserve 2 tsp. drippings.

**2.** In drippings, saute turkey breast over medium-high heat until lightly browned. Add vegetables, herbs, 1¾ cups water and broth; bring to a boil. Reduce heat; simmer, covered, until the vegetables are tender, 20-30 minutes.

**3.** Mix flour and the remaining water until smooth; stir into the turkey mixture. Bring to a boil; cook and stir until thickened, about 2 minutes. Discard bay leaf. Stir in salt, pepper and bacon.

**4.** In a small bowl, mix the biscuit mix and milk to form a soft dough; drop in 6 mounds on top of simmering stew. Cover; simmer for 15 minutes or until a toothpick inserted in a dumpling comes out clean. If desired, sprinkle with pepper and parsley before serving.

**1 serving:** 284 cal., 6g fat (1g sat. fat), 52mg chol., 822mg sod., 24g carb. (6g sugars, 2g fiber), 34g pro.
**Diabetic exchanges:** 4 lean meat, 1 starch, 1 vegetable, ½ fat.

CURRIED
VEGETABLE SOUP

## Curried Vegetable Soup

I created this recipe uniting some favorite spices with frozen vegetables to save time. It's an easy recipe to scale up to feed a crowd. I usually prepare enough to make sure there are leftovers. For a buffet, keep this soup warm in a slow cooker, and set yogurt out in a separate dish to let guests serve themselves.
—*Heather Demeritte, Scottsdale, AZ*

**Prep:** 10 min. • **Cook:** 25 min.
**Makes:** 6 servings

- 1 **Tbsp. canola oil**
- 2 **garlic cloves, minced**
- 1 **pkg. (16 oz.) frozen broccoli florets**
- 1 **pkg. (16 oz.) frozen cauliflower**
- 5 **cups vegetable broth**
- 2 **tsp. curry powder**
- ½ **tsp. salt**
- ½ **tsp. pepper**
- ⅛ **tsp. ground nutmeg**
  **Plain Greek yogurt, optional**

**1.** In a 6-qt. stockpot, heat oil over medium heat. Add garlic; cook and stir 1 minute or until fragrant. Add remaining ingredients except yogurt; bring to a boil. Reduce heat; simmer, covered, 8-10 minutes or until the vegetables are tender.
**2.** Remove soup from heat; cool slightly. Process in batches in a blender until smooth; return to pot and heat through. If desired, top individual servings with yogurt.
**1⅓ cups:** 84 cal., 3g fat (0 sat. fat), 0 chol., 793mg sod., 10g carb. (4g sugars, 4g fiber), 4g pro. **Diabetic exchanges:** 2 vegetable, ½ fat.

MEATBALL ALPHABET
SOUP, P. 221

# Pasta & Noodles

Oodles of egg noodles, alphabet pasta, bow ties and more are waiting for you—by the bowlful!

LEMONY CHICKEN
NOODLE SOUP, P. 224

CREAMY CHICKEN
GNOCCHI SOUP

## Creamy Chicken Gnocchi Soup

I tasted a similar soup at Olive Garden and wanted to try making a version myself. Here's the delicious result! It's wonderful on a cool evening.
—*Jaclynn Robinson, Shingletown, CA*

**Prep:** 25 min. • **Cook:** 15 min.
**Makes:** 8 servings

- 1   lb. boneless skinless chicken breasts, cut into ½-in. pieces
- ⅓   cup butter, divided
- 1   small onion, chopped
- 1   medium carrot, shredded
- 1   celery rib, chopped
- 2   garlic cloves, minced
- ⅓   cup all-purpose flour
- 3½  cups 2% milk
- 1½  cups heavy whipping cream
- 1   Tbsp. reduced-sodium chicken bouillon granules
- ¼   tsp. coarsely ground pepper
- 1   pkg. (16 oz.) potato gnocchi
- ½   cup chopped fresh spinach

**1.** In a Dutch oven, brown chicken in 2 Tbsp. butter. Remove and keep warm. In the same pan, saute the onion, carrot, celery and garlic in the remaining butter until tender.
**2.** Whisk in flour until blended; gradually stir in the milk, cream, bouillon and pepper. Bring to a boil. Reduce the heat; cook and stir until thickened, about 2 minutes.
**3.** Add the gnocchi and spinach; cook until spinach is wilted, 3-4 minutes. Add the chicken. Cover and simmer until heated through (do not boil), about 10 minutes.
**1 cup:** 482 cal., 28g fat (17g sat. fat), 125mg chol., 527mg sod., 36g carb. (10g sugars, 2g fiber), 21g pro.

SOUTHWEST-STYLE WEDDING SOUP

## Southwest-Style Wedding Soup

I turned leftover ground chicken into meatballs and dreamed up this cozy Southwestern soup. Now my Italian family asks for it over traditional wedding soup.
—*Teena Petrus, Johnstown, PA*

**Takes:** 30 min.
**Makes:** 6 servings

- 1   Tbsp. canola oil
- 2   medium carrots, chopped
- 2   medium celery ribs, chopped
- ½   cup frozen corn, thawed
- 2   qt. chicken stock
- 1   cup soft bread crumbs
- 1   envelope reduced-sodium taco seasoning
- 1   large egg
- 1   lb. ground chicken
- 1½  cups acini di pepe pasta
- 2   Tbsp. minced fresh cilantro
- ¼   tsp. salt
     Cubed avocado and sour cream

**1.** In a Dutch oven, heat the oil over medium heat. Add carrots, celery and corn; cook until tender. Stir in stock. Increase heat to high; bring to a boil.
**2.** Meanwhile, combine bread crumbs, taco seasoning, egg and chicken; mix lightly. With wet hands, shape into 1½-in. balls.
**3.** Reduce heat to simmer; gently drop meatballs into stock. Cook, covered, until the meatballs are no longer pink, 8-10 minutes. Stir in pasta. Simmer, covered, until pasta is tender, 6-8 minutes. Sprinkle with cilantro and salt. Serve with avocado and sour cream.
**1½ cups:** 455 cal., 10g fat (2g sat. fat), 81mg chol., 1219mg sod., 63g carb. (8g sugars, 3g fiber), 29g pro.

 **TIP**

To make soft bread crumbs, tear bread into pieces and place in a food processor or blender. Cover and pulse until crumbs form. One slice of bread will yield ½-¾ cup of crumbs.

## Creamy Spring Soup

At the end of a long day, there's nothing better than a bowl of this creamy, indulgent soup. It comes together in a flash, and with so many fresh, delicious veggies, you'll know you're filling up on nutrition too!
—*Dora Handy, Alliance, OH*

**Takes:** 25 min. • **Makes:** 2 servings

- 1 can (14½ oz.) reduced-sodium chicken broth
- 4 fresh asparagus spears, trimmed and cut into 2-in. pieces
- 4 baby carrots, julienned
- ½ celery rib, chopped
- 1 green onion, chopped
   Dash garlic powder
   Dash pepper
- ¾ cup cooked elbow macaroni
- 1 can (5½ oz.) evaporated milk
- ¾ cup fresh baby spinach

In a large saucepan, combine the first 7 ingredients. Bring to a boil. Reduce heat; cover and simmer for 5 minutes or until vegetables are tender. Stir in the macaroni, milk and spinach; heat through.

**1⅓ cups:** 207 cal., 6g fat (4g sat. fat), 28mg chol., 677mg sod., 26g carb. (12g sugars, 2g fiber), 12g pro.
**Diabetic exchanges:** 1 starch, 1 vegetable, ½ whole milk.

ONE-POT
SPINACH
BEEF SOUP

## One-Pot Spinach Beef Soup

My idea of a winning weeknight meal is this beefy soup that simmers in one big pot. Grate some Parmesan and pass the saltines.
—*Julie Davis, Jacksonville, FL*

**Takes:** 30 min. • **Makes:** 8 servings

- 1 lb. ground beef
- 3 garlic cloves, minced
- 2 cartons (32 oz. each) reduced-sodium beef broth
- 2 cans (14½ oz. each) diced tomatoes with green pepper, celery and onion, undrained
- 1 tsp. dried basil
- ½ tsp. pepper
- ½ tsp. dried oregano
- ¼ tsp. salt
- 3 cups uncooked bow tie pasta
- 4 cups fresh spinach, coarsely chopped
   Grated Parmesan cheese

**1.** In a 6-qt. stockpot, cook beef and garlic over medium heat until beef is no longer pink, breaking up beef into crumbles, 6-8 minutes; drain.
**2.** Stir in beef broth, tomatoes and seasonings; bring to a boil. Stir in the bow tie pasta; return to a boil. Cook, uncovered, until the pasta is tender, 7-9 minutes.
**3.** Stir in spinach until wilted. Sprinkle servings with cheese.

**1⅓ cups:** 258 cal., 7g fat (3g sat. fat), 40mg chol., 909mg sod., 30g carb. (8g sugars, 3g fiber), 17g pro.

# Red Curry Carrot Soup

With its mix of delicious colors, textures and flavors, this easy soup is something special. The meatballs make it substantial enough to serve as a light entree.

*—Dilnaz Heckman, Buckley, WA*

**Prep:** 20 min. • **Cook:** 15 min.
**Makes:** 8 servings

- 5 pkg. (3 oz. each) ramen noodles
- 3 garlic cloves, minced
- 2 Tbsp. peanut oil
- 1 can (13.66 oz.) coconut milk, divided
- 2 Tbsp. red curry paste
- 1½ tsp. curry powder
- ½ tsp. ground turmeric
- 32 frozen fully cooked homestyle meatballs (½ oz. each)
- 4 cups chicken broth
- 1 medium zucchini, finely chopped
- 1 medium carrot, halved and sliced
- ¼ cup shredded cabbage
- 2 tsp. fish sauce or soy sauce
  Optional: Bean sprouts, chow mein noodles, chopped fresh basil, green onions and micro greens

**1.** Cook ramen noodles according to package directions (discard the seasoning packets or save them for another use).

**2.** Meanwhile, in a Dutch oven, saute the garlic in oil for 1 minute. Spoon ½ cup cream from top of coconut milk and place in the pan. Add curry paste, curry powder and turmeric; cook and stir until the oil separates from the coconut milk mixture, about 5 minutes.

**3.** Stir in the meatballs, chicken broth, zucchini, carrot, cabbage, fish sauce and remaining coconut milk. Bring to a boil. Reduce the heat; simmer, uncovered, until carrots ares tender and meatballs are heated through, 15-20 minutes. Drain noodles; stir into soup.

**4.** Garnish with bean sprouts, chow mein noodles, basil, green onions and micro greens if desired.

**1¼ cups:** 438 cal., 21g fat (11g sat. fat), 52mg chol., 1059mg sod., 42g carb. (3g sugars, 1g fiber), 18g pro.

 **TIP**

Thai curries come in two varieties—red and green. Red curry is made from red chiles; green is made with green chiles, basil, coriander and lime leaf. While we tend to associate the color red with heat, green curry is actually spicier.

RED CURRY
CARROT SOUP

## Creamy Turkey Noodle Soup

I was honored when my fireman son-in-law asked to add this recipe to their firehouse cookbook. You can prepare parts of this soup ahead of time and then assemble it when ready. Serve with crunchy-crusted bread or crackers.
—*Carol Perkins, Washington, MO*

**Takes:** 30 min. • **Makes:** 8 servings

- ⅓  cup butter, cubed
- 1  medium carrot, shredded
- 1  celery rib, finely chopped
- ⅓  cup all-purpose flour
- 1  carton (32 oz.) chicken broth
- ½  cup half-and-half cream
- ½  cup 2% milk
- 1  cup uncooked kluski or other egg noodles
- 2  cups cubed cooked turkey
- 1½  cups shredded cheddar cheese
- ¼  tsp. salt
- ¼  tsp. pepper

**1.** In a large saucepan, heat butter over medium-high heat; saute carrot and celery until tender, 3-5 minutes. Stir in flour until blended; gradually add broth, cream and milk. Bring to a boil, stirring constantly; cook and stir until thickened, 1-2 minutes.
**2.** Stir in egg noodles. Reduce heat; simmer, uncovered, until the noodles are al dente, 7-10 minutes, stirring occasionally. Add the remaining ingredients; cook and stir until the turkey is heated through and cheese is melted.

**1 cup:** 285 cal., 18g fat (11g sat. fat), 92mg chol., 823mg sod., 11g carb. (2g sugars, 1g fiber), 18g pro.

CREAMY TURKEY NOODLE SOUP

ASIAN
LONG NOODLE
SOUP

## Asian Long Noodle Soup

This flavorful soup is perfect when you want something warm and filling in a hurry. If your store doesn't have long noodles, angel hair pasta works well as a substitute.
—*Carol Emerson, Aransas Pass, TX*

**Takes:** 30 min. • **Makes:** 6 servings

- 6 oz. uncooked Asian lo mein noodles
- 1 pork tenderloin (¾ lb.), cut into thin strips
- 2 Tbsp. soy sauce, divided
- ⅛ tsp. pepper
- 2 Tbsp. canola oil, divided
- 1½ tsp. minced fresh gingerroot
- 1 garlic clove, minced
- 1 carton (32 oz.) chicken broth
- 1 celery rib, thinly sliced
- 1 cup fresh snow peas, halved diagonally
- 1 cup coleslaw mix
- 2 green onions, sliced diagonally
  Fresh cilantro leaves, optional

**1.** Cook noodles according to the package directions. Drain and rinse with cold water; drain well.

**2.** Meanwhile, toss pork with 1 Tbsp. soy sauce and the pepper. In a 6-qt. stockpot, heat 1 Tbsp. canola oil over medium-high heat; saute pork until lightly browned, 2-3 minutes. Remove from pot.

**3.** In same pot, heat the remaining oil over medium-high heat; saute ginger and garlic until fragrant, 20-30 seconds. Stir in broth and remaining soy sauce; bring to a boil. Add celery and snow peas; return to a boil. Simmer; uncovered, until crisp-tender, 2-3 minutes. Stir in pork and coleslaw mix; cook just until the cabbage begins to wilt. Add noodles; remove from heat. Top with green onions and, if desired, cilantro.

**1⅓ cups:** 227 cal., 7g fat (1g sat. fat), 35mg chol., 1078mg sod., 23g carb. (2g sugars, 1g fiber), 16g pro.

PEPPERONI
PIZZA SOUP

## Pepperoni Pizza Soup

Once upon a time, my husband and I owned a pizzeria, where this dish was always popular. We've since sold the restaurant, but I still make the soup for potlucks and other gatherings.
—*Estella Peterson, Madras, OR*

**Prep:** 20 min. • **Cook:** 8¼ hours
**Makes:** 6 servings

- 2 cans (14½ oz. each) Italian stewed tomatoes, undrained
- 2 cans (14½ oz. each) reduced-sodium beef broth
- 1 small onion, chopped
- 1 small green pepper, chopped
- ½ cup sliced fresh mushrooms
- ½ cup sliced pepperoni, halved
- 1½ tsp. dried oregano
- ⅛ tsp. pepper
- 1 pkg. (9 oz.) refrigerated cheese ravioli
  Shredded part-skim mozzarella cheese and sliced ripe olives

**1.** In a 4-qt. slow cooker, combine the first 8 ingredients. Cook, covered, on low 8-9 hours.

**2.** Stir in ravioli; cook, covered, on low 15-30 minutes or until the pasta is tender. Top servings with cheese and olives.

**1½ cups:** 203 cal., 6g fat (3g sat. fat), 26mg chol., 1008mg sod., 28g carb. (8g sugars, 4g fiber), 10g pro.

## Spaghetti & Meatball Soup

Our family ends up eating in shifts a couple of nights a week because everyone is going every which way, all at the same time. Having a hearty soup simmering in the slow cooker is an easy way to make sure everyone gets a warm meal.
—*Susan Stetzel, Gainesville, NY*

**Prep:** 45 min. • **Cook:** 6¼ hours
**Makes:** 8 servings

- 1 cup soft bread crumbs
- ¾ cup 2% milk
- 2 large eggs, lightly beaten
- ½ cup freshly grated Parmesan cheese
- ¾ tsp. salt
- ½ tsp. garlic powder
- ½ tsp. pepper
- 2 lbs. bulk mild Italian sausage
SOUP
- 4 cups beef stock
- 1 jar (24 oz.) marinara sauce
- 3 cups water
- 1 tsp. dried basil
  Parmesan rind, optional
- 8 oz. angel hair pasta, broken into 1½-in. pieces
  Additional freshly grated Parmesan cheese, optional

**1.** Preheat oven to 400°. In a large bowl, mix bread crumbs and milk. Let stand 5 minutes; drain. Stir in eggs, cheese and seasonings. Add sausage; mix lightly but thoroughly. Shape into 1-in. balls. Place the meatballs on a greased rack in a 15x10x1-in. baking pan. Bake until cooked through, 12-15 minutes.

**2.** Transfer meatballs to a 6-qt. slow cooker. Add stock, marinara sauce, water, basil and, if desired, Parmesan rind. Cook, covered, on low 6-8 hours to allow flavors to blend.

**3.** Discard the Parmesan rind. Stir in pasta; cook, covered, on high until pasta is tender, 15-20 minutes longer. If desired, serve with additional Parmesan cheese.

**1½ cups:** 394 cal., 26g fat (9g sat. fat), 95mg chol., 1452mg sod., 23g carb. (9g sugars, 2g fiber), 17g pro.

SPAGHETTI
& MEATBALL
SOUP

# Ramen Corn Chowder

This chowder tastes as good as if it simmered for hours, but it's ready in 15 minutes. I thought the recipe I had was lacking in flavor, so I jazzed it up with extra corn and bacon bits.
—*Darlene Brenden, Salem, OR*

- - - - - - - - - - - - - - - - - - - - - - - - - -

**Takes:** 15 min. • **Makes:** 4 servings

- 2 cups water
- 1 pkg. (3 oz.) chicken ramen noodles
- 1 can (15¼ oz.) whole kernel corn, drained
- 1 can (14¾ oz.) cream-style corn
- 1 cup 2% milk
- 1 tsp. dried minced onion
- ¼ tsp. curry powder
- ¾ cup shredded cheddar cheese
- 1 Tbsp. crumbled cooked bacon
- 1 Tbsp. minced fresh parsley

**1.** In a small saucepan, bring water to a boil. Break ramen noodles into large pieces. Add the noodles and contents of seasoning packet to water. Reduce heat to medium. Cook, uncovered, for 2-3 minutes or until noodles are tender.

**2.** Stir in the corn, cream-style corn, milk, onion and curry; heat through. Stir in the cheese, bacon and parsley until blended.

**1 cup:** 333 cal., 9g fat (5g sat. fat), 17mg chol., 1209mg sod., 49g carb. (13g sugars, 4g fiber), 13g pro.

# Pork & Rice Noodle Soup

My husband and I are crazy for the Korean noodle bowls at our favorite restaurant. I created this recipe to enjoy the same flavors in an easy make-at-home meal. You can find rice noodles in the Asian section of the grocery store.
—*Lisa Renshaw, Kansas City, MO*

- - - - - - - - - - - - - - - - - - - - - - - - - -

**Prep:** 15 min. • **Cook:** 6½ hours
**Makes:** 8 servings

- 1½ lbs. boneless country-style pork ribs, cut into 1-in. cubes
- 6 garlic cloves, minced
- 2 Tbsp. minced fresh gingerroot
- 2 cans (14½ oz. each) reduced-sodium chicken broth
- 2 cans (13.66 oz. each) coconut milk
- ¼ cup reduced-sodium soy sauce
- 4 oz. uncooked thin rice noodles
- 2 cups frozen pepper strips, thawed
- 1 can (8 oz.) sliced water chestnuts, drained
- ¼ cup minced fresh cilantro
- 2 Tbsp. lime juice

**1.** In a 5-qt. slow cooker, combine the first 6 ingredients. Cook, covered, on low for 6-8 hours or until the meat is tender.

**2.** Add rice noodles, pepper strips and water chestnuts; cook 30-35 minutes longer or until the noodles are tender. If desired, skim soup. Just before serving, stir in cilantro and lime juice.

**1½ cups:** 380 cal., 23g fat (18g sat. fat), 49mg chol., 677mg sod., 21g carb. (4g sugars, 1g fiber), 20g pro.

PORK & RICE
NOODLE SOUP

ASIAN CHICKEN
NOODLE SOUP

## Winter Country Soup

My soup will warm your family up on the chilliest of winter nights. Featuring smoked sausage, beans and plenty of vegetables, it can be a hearty way to start a meal, or a satisfying dinner all by itself!
—*Jeannette Sabo, Lexington Park, MD*

**Prep:** 15 min. • **Cook:** 40 min.
**Makes:** 12 servings

1 Tbsp. butter
1 pkg. (14 oz.) smoked sausage, cut into ¼-in. slices
1 large sweet red pepper, cut into ½-in. pieces
8 shallots, chopped
8 cups chopped fresh kale
3 cups frozen corn (about 15 oz.)
1 can (15½ oz.) great northern beans, rinsed and drained
½ tsp. cayenne pepper
¼ tsp. pepper
8 cups vegetable broth
¾ cup uncooked orzo pasta

**1.** In a Dutch oven, heat butter over medium-high heat; saute sausage with red pepper slices and shallots until browned.
**2.** Add kale; cook, covered, until kale is wilted, 2-3 minutes. Stir in all the remaining ingredients except orzo; bring to a boil. Reduce heat; simmer, uncovered, 20 minutes.
**3.** Return to a boil. Stir in orzo. Cook until pasta is tender, 8-10 minutes, stirring occasionally.
**1 cup:** 258 cal., 11g fat (4g sat. fat), 25mg chol., 1067mg sod., 32g carb. (5g sugars, 4g fiber), 10g pro.

## Asian Chicken Noodle Soup

One night I realized I didn't have any noodles for my chicken soup, so I improvised and used some wonton wrappers. It was great! Don't skip the celery leaves; they bring great flavor to this soup.
—*Noelle Myers, Grand Forks, ND*

**Prep:** 15 min. • **Cook:** 40 min.
**Makes:** 10 servings

1½ lbs. boneless skinless chicken breasts, cut into 1-in. cubes
1 Tbsp. sesame oil
3 medium carrots, sliced
2 celery ribs, chopped
1 medium onion, chopped
6 cups chicken broth
⅓ cup teriyaki sauce
¼ cup chili garlic sauce
1 pkg. (14 oz.) wonton wrappers, cut into ¼-in. strips

2 cups sliced fresh shiitake mushrooms
⅓ cup chopped celery leaves
¼ cup minced fresh basil
2 Tbsp. minced fresh cilantro
2 green onions, sliced

**1.** In a Dutch oven, cook chicken in oil over medium heat until no longer pink. Remove and keep warm.
**2.** In the same pot, saute the carrots, celery and onion until tender. Stir in the broth, teriyaki sauce, garlic sauce and chicken. Bring to a boil. Reduce heat; simmer, uncovered, for 20 minutes.
**3.** Add wonton strips, mushrooms, celery leaves, basil and cilantro. Cook and stir for 4-5 minutes or until the wonton strips and mushrooms are tender. Sprinkle with green onions.
**1 cup:** 227 cal., 4g fat (1g sat. fat), 44mg chol., 1344mg sod., 27g carb. (5g sugars, 2g fiber), 19g pro.

SHRIMP PAD
THAI SOUP

## Shrimp Pad Thai Soup

Pad thai is one of my favorite dishes, but it's loaded with extra calories. This version is a healthier option but still packs all the flavor of traditional pad thai.

—*Julie Merriman, Seattle, WA*

**Prep:** 15 min. • **Cook:** 30 min.
**Makes:** 8 servings

- 1 Tbsp. sesame oil
- 2 shallots, thinly sliced
- 1 Thai chili pepper or serrano pepper, seeded and finely chopped
- 1 can (28 oz.) no-salt-added crushed tomatoes
- ¼ cup creamy peanut butter
- 2 Tbsp. reduced-sodium soy sauce or fish sauce
- 6 cups reduced-sodium chicken broth
- 1 lb. uncooked shrimp (31-40 per lb.), peeled and deveined
- 6 oz. uncooked thick rice noodles
- 1 cup bean sprouts
- 4 green onions, sliced
  Chopped peanuts, optional
  Lime wedges

**1.** In a 6-qt. stockpot, heat oil over medium heat. Add shallots and chili pepper; cook and stir 4-6 minutes or until tender. Stir in crushed tomatoes, peanut butter and soy sauce until blended; add broth. Bring to a boil; cook, uncovered, 15 minutes to allow flavors to blend.

**2.** Add shrimp and noodles; cook 4-6 minutes longer or until shrimp turn pink and the noodles are tender. Top each serving with bean sprouts, green onions and, if desired, chopped peanuts and additional chopped chili pepper. Serve with lime wedges.

**1⅓ cups:** 252 cal., 7g fat (1g sat. fat), 69mg chol., 755mg sod., 31g carb. (5g sugars, 4g fiber), 17g pro.
**Diabetic exchanges:** 2 lean meat, 1½ starch, 1 vegetable, 1 fat.

VERMICELLI
BEEF STEW

## Vermicelli Beef Stew

I love to try out new recipes for my husband and me, and also when we entertain friends and relatives. Using pasta makes this stew a little lighter than one made with potatoes, yet still heartier than a typical soup.
—*Sharon Delaney-Chronis,*
*South Milwaukee, WI*

- - - - - - - - - - - - - - - - - - - - - - - - - - -

**Prep:** 20 min. • **Cook:** 8½ hours
**Makes:** 8 servings

1½ lbs. beef stew meat, cut into
     1-in. cubes
1   medium onion, chopped
2   Tbsp. canola oil
3   cups water
1   can (14½ oz.) diced tomatoes
1   pkg. (16 oz.) frozen mixed
     vegetables, thawed
1   Tbsp. dried basil
1   tsp. salt
1   tsp. dried oregano
6   oz. uncooked vermicelli,
     broken into 2-in. pieces
¼   cup grated Parmesan cheese

**1.** In a large skillet, brown stew meat and onion in oil; drain. Transfer to a 5-qt. slow cooker. Stir in the water, tomatoes, vegetables, basil, salt and oregano. Cover and cook on low for 8-10 hours or until the meat and vegetables are tender.
**2.** Stir in vermicelli. Cover and cook for 30 minutes or until the pasta is tender. Sprinkle with cheese.
**1 cup:** 294 cal., 10g fat (3g sat. fat), 55mg chol., 455mg sod., 28g carb. (5g sugars, 5g fiber), 22g pro.
**Diabetic exchanges:** 2 lean meat, 2 vegetable, 1 starch, 1 fat.

COUSCOUS
MEATBALL SOUP

## Couscous Meatball Soup

This soup will warm you up and is really easy to pull together, making it a perfect winter weeknight meal.
—*Jonathan Pace, San Francisco, CA*

**Prep:** 25 min. • **Cook:** 40 min.
**Makes:** 10 servings

- 1 lb. lean ground beef (90% lean)
- 2 tsp. dried basil
- 2 tsp. dried oregano
- ½ tsp. salt
- 1 large onion, finely chopped
- 2 tsp. canola oil
- 1 bunch collard greens, chopped (8 cups)
- 1 bunch kale, chopped (8 cups)
- 2 cartons (32 oz. each) vegetable stock
- 1 Tbsp. white wine vinegar
- ½ tsp. crushed red pepper flakes
- ¼ tsp. pepper
- 1 pkg. (8.8 oz.) pearl (Israeli) couscous

**1.** In a small bowl, combine the beef, basil, oregano and salt. Shape into ½-in. balls. In a large skillet coated with cooking spray, brown meatballs; drain. Remove meatballs and set aside.
**2.** In the same skillet, brown onion in oil. Add collard greens and kale; cook 6-7 minutes longer or until wilted.
**3.** In a Dutch oven, combine the greens mixture, meatballs, stock, vinegar, pepper flakes and pepper. Bring to a boil. Reduce heat; cover and simmer for 10 minutes. Return to a boil. Stir in couscous. Reduce heat; cover and simmer, stirring once, until couscous is tender, 10-15 minutes.
**1 cup:** 202 cal., 5g fat (2g sat. fat), 28mg chol., 583mg sod., 26g carb. (1g sugars, 2g fiber), 13g pro.
**Diabetic exchanges:** 1½ starch, 1 lean meat, 1 vegetable.

SAUSAGE PASTA STEW

## Sausage Pasta Stew

If you like chili, I think you'll enjoy my slow-cooker specialty packed with turkey sausage, pasta and vegetables. My family gobbles it up! It's not only tasty, but loaded with protein and low in fat. Win-win!
—*Sara Bowen, Upland, CA*

**Prep:** 20 min. • **Cook:** 7¼ hours
**Makes:** 8 servings

- 1 lb. turkey Italian sausage links, casings removed
- 4 cups water
- 1 jar (24 oz.) meatless spaghetti sauce
- 1 can (16 oz.) kidney beans, rinsed and drained
- 1 medium yellow summer squash, halved lengthwise and cut into 1-in. pieces
- 2 medium carrots, sliced
- 1 medium sweet red or green pepper, diced
- ⅓ cup chopped onion
- 1½ cups uncooked spiral pasta
- 1 cup frozen peas
- 1 tsp. sugar
- ¼ tsp. salt
- ¼ tsp. pepper

**1.** In a nonstick skillet, cook sausage over medium heat until no longer pink; drain and place in a 5-qt. slow cooker. Stir in the water, spaghetti sauce, kidney beans, summer squash, carrots, red pepper and onion. Cover and cook on low for 7-9 hours or until vegetables are tender.
**2.** Stir in the pasta, peas, sugar, salt and pepper. Cover and cook on high for 15-20 minutes or until the pasta is tender.
**1⅓ cups:** 276 cal., 6g fat (2g sat. fat), 30mg chol., 1111mg sod., 38g carb. (0 sugars, 6g fiber), 18g pro.

## Spicy Couscous & Tomato Soup

This vegetarian soup has a wonderful Middle Eastern flavor. It's also low in calories and fat, so it's an appealing option when you're looking for a healthy meal.

—Rita Combs, Valdosta, GA

- - - - - - - - - - - - - - - - - - - - - - - - - -

**Prep:** 15 min. • **Cook:** 40 min.
**Makes:** 7 servings

- 2 medium sweet yellow peppers, chopped
- 1 medium red onion, chopped
- 2½ tsp. olive oil
- 3 garlic cloves, minced
- 6 cups vegetable broth
- 6 plum tomatoes, chopped
- 1½ tsp. ground cumin
- 1½ tsp. ground coriander
- ½ tsp. ground cinnamon
- ½ tsp. cayenne pepper
- ¼ tsp. pepper
- ½ cup uncooked couscous

**1.** In a Dutch oven, saute peppers and onion in oil until tender. Add garlic; cook 1 minute longer. Stir in the broth, tomatoes and spices. Bring to a boil. Reduce heat; cover and simmer for 20-25 minutes or until the flavors are blended.
**2.** Stir in couscous; cover and cook 4-6 minutes longer or until couscous is tender.
**Freeze option:** Freeze cooled soup in freezer containers. To use, partially thaw in refrigerator overnight. Heat soup through in a saucepan, stirring occasionally and adding a little broth or water if necessary.
**1 cup:** 106 cal., 2g fat (0 sat. fat), 0 chol., 812mg sod., 19g carb. (5g sugars, 2g fiber), 3g pro.
**Diabetic exchanges:** 1 starch.

PORK & BOK CHOY UDON SOUP

## Pork & Bok Choy Udon Soup

While traveling in Thailand, my husband ate a local version of this tasty soup from street vendors. We have tried many variations on this dish, and this recipe comes closest to replicating the flavors he remembers. We always double the recipe so we'll have lots of leftovers.

—Donna Noecker, Tulalip, WA

- - - - - - - - - - - - - - - - - - - - - - - - - -

**Takes:** 25 min. • **Makes:** 6 servings

- 6 oz. dried Japanese udon noodles or fettuccine
- 1 small bunch bok choy, coarsely chopped
- 1 pork tenderloin (1 lb.), cut into ¼-in. slices
- 6 cups reduced-sodium chicken broth
- 3 Tbsp. reduced-sodium soy sauce
- 4 tsp. minced fresh gingerroot
- 3 garlic cloves, minced
  Optional: Thinly sliced green onions and Sriracha chili sauce

**1.** Cook udon noodles according to package directions; drain and rinse with water. Meanwhile, in a Dutch oven, combine bok choy, pork, broth, soy sauce, ginger and garlic; bring just to a boil. Reduce heat; gently simmer, uncovered, 5-7 minutes or just until bok choy and pork are tender.
**2.** Add udon noodles to soup. Serve immediately. If desired, sprinkle with green onions and serve with Sriracha chili sauce.
**1½ cups:** 225 cal., 4g fat (1g sat. fat), 42mg chol., 1309mg sod., 24g carb. (5g sugars, 3g fiber), 25g pro.

## Meatball Alphabet Soup

Bite-sized ground turkey meatballs perk up this fun alphabet soup. A variety of vegetables mix in a rich tomato broth seasoned with herbs.
—Taste of Home *Test Kitchen*

**Prep:** 20 min. • **Cook:** 35 min.
**Makes:** 9 servings

- 1 large egg, lightly beaten
- 2 Tbsp. quick-cooking oats
- 2 Tbsp. grated Parmesan cheese
- ¼ tsp. garlic powder
- ¼ tsp. Italian seasoning
- ½ lb. lean ground turkey
- 1 cup chopped onion
- 1 cup chopped celery
- 1 cup chopped carrots
- 1 cup diced peeled potatoes
- 1 Tbsp. olive oil
- 2 garlic cloves, minced
- 4 cans (14½ oz. each) reduced-sodium chicken broth
- 1 can (28 oz.) diced tomatoes, undrained
- 1 can (6 oz.) tomato paste
- ¼ cup minced fresh parsley
- 1 tsp. dried basil
- 1 tsp. dried thyme
- ¾ cup uncooked alphabet pasta

MEATBALL
ALPHABET SOUP

**1.** In a bowl, combine the first 5 ingredients. Crumble turkey over mixture and mix well. Shape into ½-in. balls. In a nonstick skillet, brown the meatballs in small batches over medium heat until no longer pink. Remove from the heat; set aside.

**2.** In a large saucepan or Dutch oven, saute the onion, celery, carrots and potatoes in oil for 5 minutes or until crisp-tender. Add garlic; saute for 1 minute longer. Add the broth, tomatoes, tomato paste, parsley, basil and thyme; bring to a boil.

**3.** Add pasta; cook for 5-6 minutes. Reduce heat; add meatballs. Simmer, uncovered, for 15-20 minutes or until vegetables are tender.

**1½ cups:** 192 cal., 5g fat (1g sat. fat), 39mg chol., 742mg sod., 26g carb. (8g sugars, 4g fiber), 13g pro.

 **TIP**

Consider preparing meatballs in bulk to save time. You can make several batches of meatballs, cook them, and then freeze until needed. Simply thaw the frozen meatballs in the refrigerator overnight and you'll be ready to go.

## Coconut Curry Chicken Soup

Similar to a Vietnamese pho rice noodle soup, my coconut curry chicken soup packs big flavor and a bit of heat. The crisp raw vegetables help cool things down.
—*Monnie Norasing, Mansfield, TX*

**Prep:** 20 min. • **Cook:** 35 min.
**Makes:** 6 servings

- 2 cans (13.66 oz. each) coconut milk
- ⅓ to ½ cup red curry paste
- 1 pkg. (8.8 oz.) thin rice noodles
- 2 cans (14½ oz. each) chicken broth
- ¼ cup packed brown sugar
- 2 Tbsp. fish sauce or soy sauce
- ¾ tsp. garlic salt
- 3 cups shredded rotisserie chicken
- 1½ cups shredded cabbage
- 1½ cups shredded carrots
- ¾ cup bean sprouts
   Fresh basil and cilantro leaves

**1.** In a Dutch oven, bring coconut milk to a boil. Cook, uncovered, for 10-12 minutes or until the liquid is reduced to 3 cups. Stir in curry paste until completely dissolved.

**2.** Prepare rice noodles according to package directions.

**3.** Add broth, brown sugar, fish sauce and garlic salt to the curry mixture; return to a boil. Reduce heat; simmer, uncovered, 10 minutes, stirring occasionally. Stir in shredded chicken; heat through.

**4.** Drain the noodles; divide among 6 large soup bowls. Ladle the soup over noodles; top servings with vegetables, basil and cilantro.

**1 serving:** 601 cal., 34g fat (26g sat. fat), 65mg chol., 1722mg sod., 50g carb. (12g sugars, 4g fiber), 27g pro.

COCONUT CURRY
CHICKEN SOUP

LENTIL &
PASTA STEW

# Lentil & Pasta Stew

Warm up with a big bowl of this
stick-to-your-ribs stew. Loaded with
chopped smoked sausage, hearty
veggies and tender lentils, it's terrific
with bread fresh from the oven.
—*Geraldine Saucier,*
*Albuquerque, NM*

- - - - - - - - - - - - - - - - - - - - - - - - - - - - -

**Prep:** 25 min. • **Cook:** 8 hours
**Makes:** 8 servings

½  lb. smoked kielbasa or Polish
    sausage, chopped
3   Tbsp. olive oil
3   Tbsp. butter
1   cup cubed peeled potatoes
¾   cup sliced fresh carrots
1   celery rib, sliced
1   small onion, finely chopped
5   cups beef broth
1   cup dried lentils, rinsed
1   cup canned diced tomatoes
1   bay leaf
1   tsp. coarsely ground
    pepper
¼   tsp. salt
1   cup uncooked ditalini or
    other small pasta
    Shredded Romano cheese

**1.** In a large skillet, brown the kielbasa
in olive oil and butter. Add potatoes,
carrots, celery and onion. Cook and
stir for 3 minutes over medium heat.
Transfer to a 4- or 5-qt. slow cooker.
**2.** Stir in the broth, lentils, tomatoes,
bay leaf, pepper and salt. Cover and
cook on low for 8-10 hours or until
lentils are tender.
**3.** Cook pasta according to package
directions; drain. Stir pasta into the
slow cooker. Discard bay leaf. Sprinkle
individual servings with cheese.
**1 cup:** 364 cal., 18g fat (6g sat. fat),
30mg chol., 1021mg sod., 36g carb.
(3g sugars, 9g fiber), 15g pro.

VEGGIE THAI CURRY SOUP

## Lemony Chicken Noodle Soup

This isn't your grandma's chicken soup, but it is comforting. Lemon juice gives this easy and updated soup enough zip to make it interesting.
—*Bill Hilbrich, St. Cloud, MN*

**Takes:** 30 min. • **Makes:** 2 servings

- 1 small onion, chopped
- 2 Tbsp. olive oil
- 1 Tbsp. butter
- ¼ lb. boneless skinless chicken breast, cubed
- 1 garlic clove, minced
- 2 cans (14½ oz. each) chicken broth
- 1 medium carrot, cut into ¼-in. slices
- ¼ cup fresh or frozen peas
- ½ tsp. dried basil
- 2 cups uncooked medium egg noodles
- 1 to 2 Tbsp. lemon juice

**1.** In a small saucepan, saute onion in oil and butter until tender. Add chicken; cook and stir until chicken is lightly browned and the meat is no longer pink. Add garlic; cook 1 minute longer.
**2.** Stir in the broth, carrot, peas and basil. Bring to a boil. Reduce heat; cover and simmer for 5 minutes.
**3.** Add the noodles. Cover and simmer until noodles are tender, 8-10 minutes. Stir in lemon juice.
**1 cup:** 435 cal., 23g fat (6g sat. fat), 83mg chol., 949mg sod., 38g carb. (7g sugars, 4g fiber), 21g pro.

## Veggie Thai Curry Soup

My go-to Thai restaurant inspired this curry soup. Shiitake mushrooms are my favorite, but any fresh mushroom will work. Fresh basil and lime add a burst of bright flavors.
—*Tre Balchowsky, Sausalito, CA*

**Takes:** 30 min. • **Makes:** 6 servings

- 1 pkg. (8.8 oz.) thin rice noodles or uncooked angel hair pasta
- 1 Tbsp. sesame oil
- 2 Tbsp. red curry paste
- 1 cup light coconut milk
- 1 carton (32 oz.) reduced-sodium chicken broth or vegetable broth
- 1 Tbsp. reduced-sodium soy sauce or fish sauce
- 1 pkg. (14 oz.) firm tofu, drained and cubed
- 1 can (8¾ oz.) whole baby corn, drained and cut in half
- 1 can (5 oz.) bamboo shoots, drained
- 1½ cups sliced fresh shiitake mushrooms
- ½ medium sweet red pepper, cut into thin strips
  Torn fresh basil leaves and lime wedges

**1.** Prepare rice noodles according to package directions.
**2.** In a 6-qt. stockpot, heat oil over medium heat. Add curry paste; cook until aromatic, about 30 seconds. Gradually whisk in coconut milk until blended. Stir in broth and soy sauce; bring to a boil.
**3.** Add the tofu and vegetables to stockpot; cook until vegetables are crisp-tender, 3-5 minutes. Drain noodles; add to soup. Top servings with basil; serve with lime wedges.
**1⅔ cups:** 289 cal., 9g fat (3g sat. fat), 0 chol., 772mg sod., 41g carb. (3g sugars, 2g fiber), 11g pro. **Diabetic exchanges:** 2½ starch, 1 medium-fat meat, ½ fat.

LEMONY CHICKEN
NOODLE SOUP

## Vegetable Orzo Soup

This inviting soup is a perfect way to enjoy a rustic-style dish that's heavy on the veggies but light on the prep work. Hearty broth, protein-rich beans and a handful of orzo help fortify against the cold.
—Taste of Home *Test Kitchen*

**Prep:** 15 min. • **Cook:** 25 min.
**Makes:** 6 servings

- 1 medium sweet yellow pepper, chopped
- 1 medium onion, chopped
- 2 tsp. olive oil
- 3 garlic cloves, minced
- 1 jar (24 oz.) garden-style spaghetti sauce
- 1 pkg. (16 oz.) frozen Italian vegetables
- 1 can (15 oz.) cannellini beans, rinsed and drained
- 1 can (14½ oz.) chicken broth
- ½ lb. small red potatoes, quartered
- 1 cup water
- ⅓ cup uncooked orzo pasta
- ½ tsp. dried marjoram
- ½ tsp. dried thyme

Saute pepper and onion in oil in a Dutch oven until tender. Add garlic; cook 1 minute longer. Stir in the remaining ingredients. Bring to a boil. Reduce heat; cover and simmer for 15-20 minutes or until potatoes and pasta are tender.

**1⅓ cups:** 254 cal., 4g fat (0 sat. fat), 2mg chol., 841mg sod., 45g carb. (12g sugars, 8g fiber), 8g pro.

## Garlic Tortellini Soup

I like to top bowls of this tasty soup with a little grated Parmesan cheese, and serve it with slices of crusty bread to round out the meal.
—*Donna Morgan, Hendersonville, TN*

**Takes:** 25 min. • **Makes:** 6 servings

- 1 Tbsp. butter
- 2 garlic cloves, minced
- 3 cans (14½ oz. each) reduced-sodium chicken broth or vegetable broth
- 1 pkg. (9 oz.) refrigerated cheese tortellini
- 1 can (14½ oz.) diced tomatoes with green chiles, undrained
- 1 pkg. (10 oz.) frozen chopped spinach, thawed and squeezed dry

In a large saucepan, heat butter over medium heat; saute minced garlic until tender, about 1 minute. Stir in chicken broth; bring to a boil. Add tortellini; cook, uncovered, until tender, 7-9 minutes. Stir in tomatoes and spinach; heat through.

**1 cup:** 189 cal., 6g fat (3g sat. fat), 23mg chol., 1074mg sod., 25g carb. (2g sugars, 3g fiber), 11g pro.

 **TIP**

Even though the chicken broth is reduced-sodium, it still adds nearly 600 milligrams of sodium per serving. If you want to cut that back, substitute 5½ cups water plus 3 tsp. reduced-sodium chicken bouillon granules for the broth. That will bring the total sodium to just 636 milligrams per serving.

GARLIC TORTELLINI SOUP

SLOW-COOKED LASAGNA SOUP

**3.** Add noodles; cook 1 hour longer or until tender. Stir in the spinach. Remove insert; let stand 10 minutes. Divide mozzarella cheese among serving bowls; ladle soup over cheese. If desired, sprinkle with Parmesan cheese and basil.

**1⅓ cups:** 266 cal., 8g fat (3g sat. fat), 36mg chol., 725mg sod., 30g carb. (11g sugars, 5g fiber), 18g pro. **Diabetic exchanges:** 2 lean meat, 2 vegetable, 1½ starch.

## Slow-Cooked Lasagna Soup

I modified one of my favorite soup recipes so I can prep it the night before and put it in the slow cooker in the morning. It makes a welcome contribution to work parties. My colleagues love it!
—*Sharon Gerst, North Liberty, IA*

**Prep:** 35 min.
**Cook:** 5 hours + standing
**Makes:** 8 servings

- 1 pkg. (19½ oz.) Italian turkey sausage links, casings removed
- 1 large onion, chopped
- 2 medium carrots, chopped
- 2 cups sliced fresh mushrooms
- 3 garlic cloves, minced
- 1 carton (32 oz.) reduced-sodium chicken broth
- 2 cans (14½ oz. each ) no-salt-added stewed tomatoes
- 2 cans (8 oz. each ) no-salt-added tomato sauce
- 2 tsp. Italian seasoning
- 6 lasagna noodles, broken into 1-in. pieces
- 2 cups coarsely chopped fresh spinach
- 1 cup cubed or shredded part-skim mozzarella cheese
  Optional: Shredded Parmesan cheese and minced fresh basil

**1.** In a large skillet, cook sausage over medium-high heat, breaking into crumbles, until no longer pink, 8-10 minutes; drain. Transfer to a 5- or 6-qt. slow cooker.
**2.** Add onion and carrots to the same skillet; cook and stir until softened, 2-4 minutes. Stir in mushrooms and garlic; cook and stir until mushrooms are softened, 2-4 minutes. Transfer to slow cooker. Stir in chicken broth, tomatoes, tomato sauce and Italian seasoning. Cook, covered, on low 4-6 hours, until vegetables are tender.

## Kielbasa Spinach Soup

When it comes to meal-in-a-bowl soups, this is one of the best. Collard greens or chopped kale can be used instead of spinach. The hot pepper sauce adds real kick, but it's fine to leave it out and let each person flavor their own serving.
—*Antoinette Pisicchio, Easton, PA*

**Takes:** 20 min. • **Makes:** 4 servings

- 1 carton (32 oz.) chicken broth
- 1 pkg. (10 oz.) frozen chopped spinach
- ½ lb. smoked kielbasa or Polish sausage, halved and sliced
- 1 can (15 oz.) cannellini beans, rinsed and drained
- ⅔ cup uncooked elbow macaroni
- 8 to 10 drops hot pepper sauce

Combine the broth, spinach and kielbasa in a large saucepan. Bring to a boil. Add beans and macaroni. Reduce heat; simmer, uncovered, for 7-9 minutes or until the macaroni is tender. Stir in pepper sauce.

**1½ cups:** 334 cal., 17g fat (6g sat. fat), 43mg chol., 1777mg sod., 29g carb. (1g sugars, 7g fiber), 16g pro.

TERIYAKI BEEF
STEW, P. 248

# Heartiest Stews

Brimming with chunks of meat, vegetables and more, these meal-in-one dishes always satisfy.

CASABLANCA
CHUTNEY
CHICKEN, P. 236

BRAISED
PORK STEW

## Braised Pork Stew

Pork tenderloin becomes an amazing treat in this hearty braised stew. It's a fantastic meal for a cold winter night.
—*Nella Parker, Jersey, MI*

- - - - - - - - - - - - - - - - - - - - -

**Takes:** 30 min. • **Makes:** 4 servings

- 1 **lb. pork tenderloin, cut into 1-in. cubes**
- ½ **tsp. salt**
- ½ **tsp. pepper**
- 5 **Tbsp. all-purpose flour, divided**
- 1 **Tbsp. olive oil**
- 16 **oz. assorted frozen vegetables**
- 1½ **cups reduced-sodium chicken broth**
- 2 **garlic cloves, minced**
- 2 **tsp. stone-ground mustard**
- 1 **tsp. dried thyme**
- 2 **Tbsp. water**

**1.** Sprinkle pork with salt and pepper; add 3 Tbsp. flour and toss to coat. In a large skillet, heat oil over medium heat. Brown pork. Drain if necessary.
**2.** Stir in vegetables, broth, garlic, mustard and thyme. Bring to a boil. Reduce heat; simmer, covered, until pork and vegetables are tender, 10-15 minutes.
**3.** In a small bowl, mix the remaining flour and water until smooth; stir into stew. Return to a boil, stirring constantly; cook and stir until thickened, 1-2 minutes.
**1 cup:** 250 cal., 8g fat (2g sat. fat), 64mg chol., 646mg sod., 16g carb. (3g sugars, 3g fiber), 26g pro.
**Diabetic exchanges:** 3 lean meat, 1 starch, ½ fat.

SLOPPY JOE STEW

## Sloppy Joe Stew

This old-fashioned stew has a slightly sweet taste from the addition of canned corn. You can make the stew ahead of time and reheat it for a quick meal later on.
—*Clair Long, Destrehan, LA*

- - - - - - - - - - - - - - - - - - - - -

**Ptrep:** 10 min. • **Cook:** 1¼ hours
**Makes:** 6 servings

- 2 **lbs. ground beef**
- 1 **medium onion, chopped**
- 1 **small green pepper, chopped**
- 2½ **cups water**
- 1 **can (11 oz.) whole kernel corn, drained**
- 2 **cans (10¾ oz. each) condensed tomato soup, undiluted**
- 1 **to 2 Tbsp. sugar**
- 1 **Tbsp. Worcestershire sauce**
- 1 **tsp. hot pepper sauce**
  **Salt and pepper to taste**

**1.** In a large saucepan, cook the beef, onion and green pepper over medium heat until meat is no longer pink; drain.
**2.** Stir in the remaining ingredients; bring to a boil. Reduce heat; cover and simmer for 1 hour or until vegetables are tender.
**1½ cups:** 353 cal., 15g fat (6g sat. fat), 74mg chol., 666mg sod., 25g carb. (15g sugars, 3g fiber), 29g pro.

## Sausage Sauerkraut Supper

With big, tender chunks of sausage, potatoes and carrots, this old-fashioned dinner will satisfy even the biggest appetites. It always disappears in a hurry at family gatherings or office potlucks.
—*Joalyce Graham, St. Petersburg, FL*

- - - - - - - - - - - - - - - - - - - - - - - - - - -

**Prep:** 25 min. • **Cook:** 8 hours
**Makes:** 10 servings

| | |
|---|---|
| 4 | cups carrot chunks (2-in. pieces) |
| 4 | cups red potato chunks |
| 2 | cans (14 oz. each) sauerkraut, rinsed and drained |
| 2½ | lbs. fresh Polish sausage links |
| 1 | medium onion, thinly sliced |
| 3 | garlic cloves, minced |
| 1½ | cups dry white wine or chicken broth |
| 1 | tsp. pepper |
| ½ | tsp. caraway seeds |

**1.** In a 5-qt. slow cooker, layer the carrots, potatoes and sauerkraut.
**2.** In a large skillet, brown sausages. When cool enough to handle, cut into 3-in. pieces; transfer to slow cooker (slow cooker will be full). Reserve 1 Tbsp. drippings.
**3.** Saute onion and garlic in reserved drippings until tender. Gradually add wine. Bring to a boil; stir to loosen browned bits. Stir in pepper and caraway seeds.
**4.** Pour onion mixture over sausage. Cover and cook on low for 8-10 hours or until a thermometer inserted in the sausage reads 160°.
**1 cup:** 517 cal., 37g fat (12g sat. fat), 72mg chol., 1442mg sod., 24g carb. (6g sugars, 5g fiber), 16g pro.

GROUNDNUT STEW

## Groundnut Stew

My Aunt Linda was a missionary in Africa for more than 40 years and gave me the recipe for this cozy stew with a hint of peanut butter.
—*Heather Ewald, Bothell, WA*

- - - - - - - - - - - - - - - - - - - - - - - - - - -

**Takes:** 30 min. • **Makes:** 7 servings

| | |
|---|---|
| 6 | oz. lamb stew meat, cut into ½-in. pieces |
| 6 | oz. pork stew meat, cut into ½-in. pieces |
| 2 | Tbsp. peanut oil |
| 1 | large onion, cut into wedges |
| 1 | large green pepper, cut into wedges |
| 1 | cup chopped tomatoes |
| 4 | cups cubed eggplant |
| 2 | cups water |
| ½ | cup fresh or frozen sliced okra |
| ½ | cup creamy peanut butter |
| 1 | tsp. salt |
| ½ | tsp. pepper |
| | Hot cooked rice |
| | Chopped green onions, optional |

**1.** In a large skillet, brown meat in oil; set aside. In a food processor, combine the onion, green pepper and tomatoes; cover and process until blended.
**2.** In a large saucepan, combine the eggplant, water, okra and onion mixture. Bring to a boil. Reduce heat; cook, uncovered, until the vegetables are tender, 7-9 minutes.
**3.** Stir in the peanut butter, salt, pepper and browned meat. Cook, uncovered, until heated through, about 10 minutes. Serve with rice. If desired, top with chopped green onions.
**Freeze option:** Freeze cooled stew in freezer containers. To use, partially thaw in refrigerator overnight. Heat stew through in a saucepan, stirring occasionally and adding a little broth or water if necessary.
**1 cup:** 230 cal., 13g fat (3g sat. fat), 31mg chol., 470mg sod., 14g carb. (7g sugars, 4g fiber), 16g pro.
**Diabetic exchanges:** 2 lean meat, 1 starch, 1 fat.

## Mainly Mushroom Beef Carbonnade

This is the ultimate comfort food, an earth-and-turf combo that smells delicious while cooking and tastes like home. The mushrooms taste so meaty, you can decrease the amount of beef and add more portabellos if you like.
—*Susan Asanovic, Wilton, CT*

- - - - - - - - - - - - - - - - - - - - - - - - -

**Prep:** 45 min. • **Bake:** 2 hours
**Makes:** 6 servings

MAINLY MUSHROOM
BEEF CARBONNADE

2 Tbsp. plus 1½ tsp. canola oil, divided
1½ lbs. beef stew meat, cut into 1-in. cubes
¾ tsp. salt
¼ tsp. plus ⅛ tsp. pepper
3 medium onions, chopped
1¼ lbs. portobello mushrooms, stems removed, cut into ¾-in. dice
4 garlic cloves, minced
2 Tbsp. tomato paste
½ lb. fresh baby carrots
1 thick slice day-old rye bread, crumbled (about 1½ cups)
3 bay leaves
1½ tsp. dried thyme
1 tsp. beef bouillon granules
1 bottle (12 oz.) light beer or beef broth
1 cup water
1 oz. bittersweet chocolate, grated

**1.** Preheat oven to 325°. In an ovenproof Dutch oven, heat 2 Tbsp. oil over medium-high heat. Sprinkle beef with salt and pepper; brown in batches in oil. Remove with a slotted spoon, reserving the drippings.

**2.** Reduce heat to medium. Add the onions to drippings; cook, stirring frequently, until dark golden brown, about 8 minutes. Stir in the remaining oil; add mushrooms and garlic. Saute until the mushrooms begin to brown and release their liquid. Stir in the tomato paste.

**3.** Add carrots, bread, bay leaves, thyme and bouillon. Add beer and water, stirring to loosen any browned bits from pot. Bring to a boil; return beef to pot.

**4.** Bake, covered, until meat is tender, 2-2¼ hours. Remove from the oven; discard bay leaves. Stir in chocolate until melted.

**1 cup:** 333 cal., 16g fat (4g sat. fat), 71mg chol., 547mg sod., 18g carb. (7g sugars, 4g fiber), 26g pro.

 **TIP**

A light-bodied beer can be replaced with dark beer or red wine. Serve on top of mashed potatoes, egg noodles or seasoned rice.

## One-Pot Salsa Chicken

This stovetop recipe is a colorful and healthy main dish that can be on the table in just over an hour. The subtle, sweet-spicy flavor is a nice surprise.
—*Ann R. Sheehy, Lawrence, MA*

**Prep:** 20 min. • **Cook:** 45 min.
**Makes:** 6 servings

- 2 Tbsp. canola oil
- 2 lbs. boneless skinless chicken thighs, cut into 1-in. pieces
- 1 tsp. pepper
- ½ tsp. salt
- 2 medium sweet potatoes, peeled and chopped
- 1 jar (16 oz.) medium salsa
- 2 medium nectarines, peeled and chopped
- 2 Tbsp. Tajin seasoning
- 1 cup uncooked instant brown rice
- 1 cup water
- ¼ cup minced fresh parsley
  Minced fresh chives

**1.** In a Dutch oven, heat oil over medium-high heat. Sprinkle chicken with pepper and salt. Brown chicken in batches; return to pot.

**2.** Add the sweet potatoes, salsa, nectarines and seasoning. Bring to a boil; reduce heat. Cover and simmer until potatoes are almost tender, about 15 minutes.

**3.** Stir in rice and water; bring to a boil. Reduce heat. Cover and simmer until the sweet potatoes are tender, about 10 minutes. Stir in parsley. Serve in bowls; sprinkle with chives.

**1⅔ cups:** 432 cal., 16g fat (3g sat. fat), 101mg chol., 1254mg sod., 39g carb. (13g sugars, 4g fiber), 31g pro.

 **TIP**

Tajin seasoning is a blend of lime, chile peppers and sea salt. Look for it in the spice aisle.

ONE-POT
SALSA CHICKEN

HEARTY
BRUNSWICK
STEW

## Hearty Brunswick Stew

This thick stew is filled to the brim with a bounty of potatoes, lima beans, sweet corn and tomatoes. Authentic versions of the stew call for rabbit or squirrel, but I think you'll love the tender chunks of chicken.
—*Mildred Sherrer, Fort Worth, TX*

- - - - - - - - - - - - - - - - - - - - - - - - - - - - -

**Prep:** 1 hour + cooling
**Cook:** 45 min. • **Makes:** 6 servings

1   broiler/fryer chicken (3½ to 4 lbs.), cut up
2   cups water
4   medium potatoes, peeled and cubed
2   medium onions, sliced
1   can (15¼ oz.) lima beans, rinsed and drained
1   tsp. salt
½   tsp. pepper
    Dash cayenne pepper
1   can (15¼ oz.) corn, drained
1   can (14½ oz.) diced tomatoes, undrained
¼   cup butter
½   cup dry bread crumbs

**1.** In a Dutch oven, slowly bring the chicken and water to a boil. Cover and simmer for 45-60 minutes or until chicken is tender, skimming the surface as foam rises.

**2.** Remove chicken and set aside until cool enough to handle. Remove and discard skin and bones. Cube chicken and return to broth.

**3.** Add the potatoes, onions, beans and seasonings. Bring to a boil. Reduce heat; simmer, uncovered, for 30 minutes or until potatoes are tender. Stir in remaining ingredients. Simmer, uncovered, for 10 minutes or until slightly thickened.

**1 cup:** 589 cal., 25g fat (9g sat. fat), 123mg chol., 1147mg sod., 47g carb. (9g sugars, 7g fiber), 40g pro.

SPICED LAMB STEW
WITH APRICOTS

## Casablanca Chutney Chicken

If you enjoy Indian food, you'll love this dish. An array of spices and dried fruit slowly simmer with boneless chicken thighs for an aromatic and satisfying meal. To make it complete, serve over jasmine or basmati rice.
—*Roxanne Chan, Albany, CA*

**Prep:** 25 min. • **Cook:** 4 hours
**Makes:** 4 servings

- 1 **lb. boneless skinless chicken thighs, cut into ¾-in. pieces**
- 1 **can (14½ oz.) chicken broth**
- ⅓ **cup finely chopped onion**
- ⅓ **cup chopped sweet red pepper**
- ⅓ **cup chopped carrot**
- ⅓ **cup chopped dried apricots**
- ⅓ **cup chopped dried figs**
- ⅓ **cup golden raisins**
- 2 **Tbsp. orange marmalade**
- 1 **Tbsp. mustard seed**
- 2 **garlic cloves, minced**
- ½ **tsp. curry powder**
- ¼ **tsp. crushed red pepper flakes**
- ¼ **tsp. ground cumin**
- ¼ **tsp. ground cinnamon**
- ¼ **tsp. ground cloves**
- 2 **Tbsp. minced fresh parsley**
- 2 **Tbsp. minced fresh mint**
- 1 **Tbsp. lemon juice**
- 4 **Tbsp. chopped pistachios
  Cooked pearl (Israeli) couscous, optional**

**1.** In a 3-qt. slow cooker, combine the first 16 ingredients. Cover and cook on low for 4 hours or until chicken is tender.
**2.** Stir in the parsley, mint and lemon juice; heat through. Sprinkle each serving with pistachios; if desired, serve with cooked Israeli couscous.
**1 cup:** 389 cal., 13g fat (3g sat. fat), 78mg chol., 567mg sod., 44g carb. (31g sugars, 6g fiber), 26g pro.

## Spiced Lamb Stew with Apricots

My family loves lamb, especially my son. Once when he came home during his first year of college, I had a pot of my lamb stew simmering in the kitchen. When my husband and I were ready to eat dinner, there were only a few shreds of meat left floating in the gravy—and my son confessed he was the culprit!
—*Arlene Erlbach, Morton Grove, IL*

**Prep:** 30 min. • **Cook:** 5 hours
**Makes:** 5 servings

- 2 **lbs. lamb stew meat, cut into ¾-in. cubes**
- 3 **Tbsp. butter**
- 1½ **cups chopped sweet onion**
- ¾ **cup dried apricots**
- ½ **cup orange juice**
- ½ **cup chicken broth**
- 2 **tsp. paprika**
- 2 **tsp. ground allspice**
- 2 **tsp. ground cinnamon**
- 1½ **tsp. salt**
- 1 **tsp. ground cardamom
  Hot cooked couscous
  Chopped dried apricots, optional**

**1.** In a large skillet, brown lamb in butter in batches. With a slotted spoon, transfer to a 3-qt. slow cooker.
**2.** In the same skillet, saute onion in drippings until tender. Stir in the apricots, orange juice, broth and seasonings; pour over lamb.
**3.** Cover and cook on high for 5-6 hours or until meat is tender. Serve with couscous. Sprinkle with chopped apricots if desired.
**1 cup:** 404 cal., 17g fat (8g sat. fat), 136mg chol., 975mg sod., 24g carb. (15g sugars, 5g fiber), 38g pro.

CASABLANCA
CHUTNEY CHICKEN

## Hearty Cabbage Patch Stew

I like to serve hot helpings of this stew with thick slices of homemade bread. For a quicker prep, substitute a bag of prepared coleslaw mix for the chopped cabbage.
—Karen Ann Bland, Gove, KS

**Prep:** 20 min. • **Cook:** 6 hours
**Makes:** 8 servings

- 1 lb. lean ground beef (90% lean)
- 1 cup chopped onions
- 2 celery ribs, chopped
- 11 cups coarsely chopped cabbage (about 2 lbs.)
- 2 cans (14½ oz. each) stewed tomatoes, undrained
- 1 can (15 oz.) pinto beans, rinsed and drained
- 1 can (10 oz.) diced tomatoes with green chiles, undrained
- ½ cup ketchup
- 1 to 1½ tsp. chili powder
- ½ tsp. dried oregano
- ½ tsp. pepper
- ¼ tsp. salt
  Optional: Sour cream and shredded cheddar cheese

**1.** In a large skillet, cook beef, onions and celery over medium heat until the meat is no longer pink; drain.
**2.** Transfer to a 5-qt. slow cooker. Stir in the cabbage, stewed tomatoes, beans, diced tomatoes, ketchup, chili powder, oregano, pepper and salt. Cover and cook on low for 6-8 hours or until cabbage is tender.
**3.** Serve with sour cream and cheese if desired.
**1½ cups:** 214 cal., 5g fat (2g sat. fat), 28mg chol., 642mg sod., 29g carb. (11g sugars, 6g fiber), 16g pro.
**Diabetic exchanges:** 2 lean meat, 2 vegetable, 1 starch.

## Turkey Biscuit Stew

This chunky stew makes a satisfying supper, especially in the fall and winter. It's also a great way to use extra turkey during the holidays.
—Lori Schlecht, Wimbledon, ND

**Prep:** 15 min. • **Bake:** 20 min.
**Makes:** 8 servings

- ⅓ cup chopped onion
- ¼ cup butter, cubed
- ⅓ cup all-purpose flour
- ½ tsp. salt
- ⅛ tsp. pepper
- 1 can (10½ oz.) condensed chicken broth, undiluted
- ¾ cup 2% milk
- 2 cups cubed cooked turkey
- 1 cup cooked peas
- 1 cup cooked whole baby carrots
- 1 tube (10 oz.) refrigerated buttermilk biscuits

**1.** Preheat oven to 375°. In a 10-in. ovenproof skillet, saute chopped onion in butter until tender. Stir in the flour, salt and pepper until blended. Gradually add broth and milk. Bring to a boil. Cook and stir until thickened and bubbly, about 2 minutes. Add the turkey, peas and carrots; heat through.
**2.** Separate the biscuits and arrange over the stew. Bake until biscuits are golden brown, 20-25 minutes.
**1 serving:** 263 cal., 10g fat (5g sat. fat), 45mg chol., 792mg sod., 27g carb. (4g sugars, 2g fiber), 17g pro.

TURKEY BISCUIT STEW

JAMAICAN-STYLE
BEEF STEW

⅛ tsp. hot pepper sauce
1 Tbsp. cornstarch
2 Tbsp. cold water
  Hot cooked rice or mashed
  potatoes, optional

1. In a Dutch oven, heat canola oil over medium-high heat. Add sugar; cook and stir until lightly browned, 1 minute. Add beef and brown on all sides.
2. Stir in the tomatoes, vegetables, broth, barbecue sauce, soy sauce, steak sauce and seasonings. Bring to a boil. Reduce heat; cover and simmer until the meat and vegetables are tender, 1-1¼ hours.
3. Combine cornstarch and water until smooth; stir into stew. Bring to a boil; cook and stir until thickened, about 2 minutes. If desired, serve with rice or potatoes.

**Freeze option:** Freeze cooled stew in freezer containers. To use, partially thaw in refrigerator overnight. Heat stew through in a saucepan, stirring occasionally and adding a little water if necessary.

**1 cup:** 285 cal., 9g fat (2g sat. fat), 56mg chol., 892mg sod., 18g carb. (10g sugars, 3g fiber), 32g pro.

**TIP**

Cornstarch needs just a few minutes of boiling to thicken gravy or sauce. If it cooks too long, the cornstarch will begin to lose its thickening power. Follow the recipe carefully for the best results.

❄

## Jamaican-Style Beef Stew

This delicious stew makes a filling supper with a lighter touch. It's so flavorful, you won't want to stop at just one bowlful!
—*James Hayes, Ridgecrest, CA*

- - - - - - - - - - - - - - - - - - - - -

**Prep:** 25 min. • **Cook:** 1¼ hours
**Makes:** 5 servings

1 Tbsp. canola oil
1 Tbsp. sugar
1½ lbs. beef top sirloin steak, cut into ¾-in. cubes
5 plum tomatoes, finely chopped
3 large carrots, cut into ½-in. slices
3 celery ribs, cut into ½-in. slices
4 green onions, chopped
¾ cup reduced-sodium beef broth
¼ cup barbecue sauce
¼ cup reduced-sodium soy sauce
2 Tbsp. steak sauce
1 Tbsp. garlic powder
1 tsp. dried thyme
¼ tsp. ground allspice
¼ tsp. pepper

CREAMY BRATWURST STEW

## Creamy Bratwurst Stew

I adapted a baked stew recipe from the newspaper to create a simple slow-cooked version. Rich and creamy, it is the best comfort food for cold winter nights.
—*Susan Holmes, Germantown, WI*

- - - - - - - - - - - - - - - - - - - - - - - - - - - - - -

**Prep:** 20 min. • **Cook:** 6½ hours
**Makes:** 8 servings

- 1¾ lbs. potatoes (about 4 medium), peeled and cubed
- 2 medium carrots, chopped
- 2 celery ribs, chopped
- 1 medium onion, chopped
- 1 medium green pepper, chopped
- 2 lbs. uncooked bratwurst links
- ½ cup chicken broth
- 1 tsp. salt
- 1 tsp. dried basil
- ½ tsp. pepper
- 2 cups half-and-half cream
- 1 Tbsp. cornstarch
- 3 Tbsp. cold water

**1.** Place the first 5 ingredients in a 5-qt. slow cooker; toss to combine. Top with bratwurst. Mix broth and seasonings; pour over top.

**2.** Cook, covered, on low 6-7 hours, until sausage is cooked through and vegetables are tender. Remove the sausages from slow cooker; cut into 1-in. slices. Return sausages to potato mixture; stir in cream.

**3.** Mix cornstarch and water until smooth; stir into the stew. Cook, covered, on high until thickened, about 30 minutes.

**1 cup:** 544 cal., 39g fat (15g sat. fat), 114mg chol., 1367mg sod., 25g carb. (5g sugars, 2g fiber), 19g pro.

## Slow-Cooker Meatball Stew

This recipe was a real lifesaver when I worked full time and needed a dinner the kids would enjoy when we got home. It is perfect to let your young ones help prepare. They can chop, peel, mix and pour. It doesn't matter if the veggies are all different sizes— your children will still devour this fun and tasty stew.
—*Kallee Krong-McCreery, Escondido, CA*

**Prep:** 20 min. • **Cook:** 6 hours
**Makes:** 8 servings

| | |
|---|---|
| 4 | peeled medium potatoes, cut into ½-in. cubes |
| 4 | medium carrots, cut into ½-in. cubes |
| 2 | celery ribs, cut into ½-in. cubes |
| 1 | medium onion, diced |
| ¼ | cup frozen corn |
| 1 | pkg. (28 to 32 oz.) frozen fully cooked home-style meatballs |
| 1½ | cups ketchup |
| 1½ | cups water |
| 1 | Tbsp. white vinegar |
| 1 | tsp. dried basil |
| | Biscuits or dinner rolls, optional |

**1.** In a 5-qt. slow cooker, combine potatoes, carrots, celery, onion and corn. Add meatballs.
**2.** In a bowl, mix ketchup, water, white vinegar and basil; pour over meatballs. Cook, covered, on low for 6-8 hours, until meatballs are cooked through. If desired, serve stew with biscuits or dinner rolls.
**1 cup:** 449 cal., 26g fat (12g sat. fat), 41mg chol., 1322mg sod., 40g carb. (17g sugars, 4g fiber), 16g pro.

SLOW-COOKER
MEATBALL STEW

ANCIENT GRAIN
BEEF STEW

## Ancient Grain Beef Stew

My version of beef stew is comfort food with a healthy twist. I use lentils and red quinoa rather than potatoes. If leftover stew seems too thick, add more beef stock when reheating.
—*Margaret M. Roscoe, Keystone Heights, FL*

- - - - - - - - - - - - - - - - - - - - - - -

**Prep:** 25 min. • **Cook:** 6 hours
**Makes:** 10 servings

- 2 Tbsp. olive oil
- 1 lb. beef stew meat, cut into 1-in. cubes
- 4 celery ribs with leaves, chopped
- 2 medium carrots, peeled, chopped
- 1 large onion, chopped
- 1½ cups dried lentils, rinsed
- ½ cup red quinoa, rinsed
- 5 large bay leaves
- 2 tsp. ground cumin
- 1½ tsp. salt
- 1 tsp. dried tarragon
- ½ tsp. pepper
- 2 cartons (32 oz. each) beef stock

**1.** Heat oil in a large skillet over medium heat. Add beef; brown on all sides. Transfer meat and drippings to a 5- or 6-qt. slow cooker.
**2.** Stir in the remaining ingredients. Cook, covered, on low 6-8 hours, until the meat is tender. Discard the bay leaves.

**1⅓ cups:** 261 cal., 7g fat (2g sat. fat), 28mg chol., 797mg sod., 29g carb. (5g sugars, 5g fiber), 21g pro.
**Diabetic exchanges:** 2 starch, 2 lean meat, ½ fat.

MOROCCAN APPLE BEEF STEW

## Moroccan Apple Beef Stew

I love the mix of sweet and savory flavors in this stew. It's the ideal blend of adventurous and comforting, and makes a fun and unexpected dish to share with guests.
—*Trisha Kruse, Eagle, ID*

- - - - - - - - - - - - - - - - - - - - - - -

**Prep:** 20 min. • **Cook:** 2 hours
**Makes:** 8 servings

- 1¼ tsp. salt
- ½ tsp. ground cinnamon
- ½ tsp. pepper
- ¼ tsp. ground allspice
- 2½ lbs. beef stew meat, cut into 1-in. pieces
- 2 to 3 Tbsp. olive oil
- 1 large onion, chopped (about 2 cups)
- 3 garlic cloves, minced
- 1 can (15 oz.) tomato sauce
- 1 can (14½ oz.) beef broth
- 1 cup pitted dried plums, coarsely chopped
- 1 Tbsp. honey
- 2 medium Fuji or Gala apples, peeled and cut into 1½-in. pieces

Hot cooked rice or couscous, optional

**1.** Mix salt, cinnamon, pepper and allspice; sprinkle over beef and toss to coat. In a Dutch oven, heat 2 Tbsp. oil over medium heat.
**2.** Brown beef in batches, adding more oil as necessary. Remove beef with a slotted spoon.
**3.** Add onion to same pot; cook and stir until tender, 6-8 minutes. Add garlic; cook 1 minute longer. Stir in tomato sauce, broth, dried plums and honey. Return beef to pot; bring to a boil. Reduce heat; simmer, covered, 1½ hours.
**4.** Add apples; cook, covered, until beef and apples are tender, 30-45 minutes longer. Skim fat. If desired, serve stew with rice.

**Freeze option:** Freeze cooled stew in freezer containers. To use, partially thaw in refrigerator overnight. Heat through in a saucepan, stirring stew occasionally and adding a little broth if necessary.

**1 cup:** 339 cal., 13g fat (4g sat. fat), 88mg chol., 905mg sod., 24g carb. (14g sugars, 2g fiber), 29g pro.

## Red Flannel Stew

When I was child, every Saturday night was "red flannel night." Grandpa and I wore our red flannel underwear to supper and Grandma, the cook, dressed in a long calico dress and sunbonnet. We'd eat this stew spooned over fluffy Southern-style biscuits. Grandma learned to make the stew from earlier generations.
—*Kathy Padgett, Diamond City, AR*

- - - - - - - - - - - - - - - - - - - - - - - - - -

**Prep:** 25 min. • **Cook:** 1½ hours
**Makes:** 5 servings

- 2 whole fresh beets, washed, trimmed and halved
- 6 cups water, divided
- 1 lb. corned beef brisket, trimmed and cut into 1-in. pieces
- 4 small carrots, sliced
- 1 large potato, cubed
- 1 small turnip, peeled and cubed
- 1 small onion, chopped
- 1 tsp. each dried parsley flakes, basil and thyme
- ¼ tsp. salt
- ⅛ tsp. pepper

**1.** In a large saucepan, bring beets and 4 cups water to a boil. Reduce the heat; simmer, uncovered, until tender, 20-25 minutes. Drain beets, reserving 2 cups cooking liquid. Peel and dice beets; set aside.
**2.** In the same pan, combine the corned beef, carrots, potato, turnip, onion, seasonings, remaining water and reserved cooking liquid. Bring to a boil. Reduce heat; cover and simmer until meat and vegetables are tender, 1¼-1½ hours. Stir in the diced beets; heat through.
**1⅓ cups:** 209 cal., 9g fat (3g sat. fat), 31mg chol., 881mg sod., 22g carb. (6g sugars, 3g fiber), 11g pro.

TACO STEW

## Taco Stew

The ingredients may be simple, but together, they make an awesome stew with a bit more body than a tortilla soup. Crush a few tortilla chips over each bowl for crunch.
—*Suzanne Francis, Marysville, WA*

- - - - - - - - - - - - - - - - - - - - - - - - - -

**Takes:** 30 min. • **Makes:** 6 servings

- 1 lb. ground beef
- 2 cans (15 oz. each) black beans, rinsed and drained
- 2 cans (10 oz. each) diced tomatoes and green chiles
- 1 can (15 oz.) tomato sauce
- 1½ cups frozen corn (about 7 oz.)
- 2 tsp. chili powder
- ½ tsp. ground cumin
  Crushed tortilla chips, optional

**1.** In a large saucepan, cook ground beef over medium heat until no longer pink, breaking into crumbles, 6-8 minutes; drain.
**2.** Stir in beans, tomatoes, tomato sauce, corn, chili powder and cumin. Bring to a boil. Reduce heat; simmer 5-10 minutes to allow flavors to blend. If desired, top each serving with tortilla chips.
**Freeze option:** Freeze cooled stew in freezer containers. To use, partially thaw in refrigerator overnight. Heat through in a saucepan, stirring stew occasionally and adding a little water if necessary.
**1⅓ cups:** 313 cal., 10g fat (3g sat. fat), 47mg chol., 1041mg sod., 35g carb. (3g sugars, 9g fiber), 23g pro.

## Barley Risotto & Beef Stroganoff

I miss my Russian grandmother's barley porridge and beef Stroganoff, so I combined the two dishes. I cook the barley using the same method as risotto to keep the grains whole and irresistibly chewy.
—*Tatiana Kireeva, New York, NY*

**Prep:** 25 min. + marinating
**Cook:** 45 min. • **Makes:** 4 servings

- 1 **beef top sirloin steak (1 lb.), cut into 1-in. cubes**
- 3 **Tbsp. Cognac or brandy**
- 3 **Tbsp. butter, divided**
- 1 **Tbsp. all-purpose flour**
- 2 **cups chicken stock**
- 1 **tsp. Dijon mustard**
- 1 **medium beefsteak tomato**
- 1 **tsp. coarsely ground pepper**
- ¼ **tsp. salt**
- 2 **Tbsp. sour cream**
- 1 **medium onion, sliced**

### BARLEY RISOTTO
- 5 **cups water**
- 1 **medium onion, finely chopped**
- ½ **tsp. salt**
- 1 **Tbsp. white wine, optional**
- 1 **cup medium pearl barley**
- 2 **Tbsp. minced fresh parsley**

**1.** In a shallow dish, toss beef with Cognac. Refrigerate, covered, for 2 hours.

**2.** In a small saucepan, melt 1 Tbsp. butter over medium heat. Stir in flour until smooth; gradually whisk in the chicken stock and mustard. Bring to a boil, stirring constantly; cook and stir until thickened, 3-5 minutes. Reduce heat; simmer, uncovered, 5 minutes.

**3.** Meanwhile, cut tomato into thick strips. In a large skillet over medium-low heat, cook tomato until softened, 3-5 minutes. Stir into the mustard sauce; add coarsely ground pepper and salt. Stir in sour cream.

**4.** In the same skillet, melt 1 Tbsp. butter over medium-high heat. Drain beef, discarding marinade, and pat dry. Add sliced onion and beef to pan; cook and stir until the onions are softened and meat is no longer pink, 6-8 minutes. Add the mustard sauce; reduce the heat to low and simmer, uncovered, until thickened, about 15 minutes. Keep warm until serving.

**5.** For risotto, bring water to a boil in a large saucepan. Reduce heat to maintain simmer. In another large saucepan, melt the remaining butter over medium heat. Add chopped onion, salt and, if desired, white wine. Cook and stir until liquid evaporates. Add barley; toast in pan.

**6.** Stir hot water into barley 1 cup at a time, waiting until the liquid has almost absorbed before adding more. Cook until barley is softened but still slightly chewy, 15-20 minutes; stir in parsley. Serve immediately with the beef.

**4 oz. cooked steak with 1 cup barley:** 463 cal., 15g fat (8g sat. fat), 74mg chol., 859mg sod., 48g carb. (4g sugars, 9g fiber), 33g pro.

BARLEY RISOTTO & BEEF STROGANOFF

## Hearty Baked Beef Stew

This is such an easy way to make a wonderful beef stew. You don't need to brown the meat first—just combine it with chunks of carrots, potatoes and celery...and let it all cook together in a flavorful gravy. My daughter Karen came up with this recipe to satisfy her busy family.
—*Doris Sleeth, Naples, FL*

-----------------------------------

**Prep:** 15 min. • **Bake:** 1¾ hours
**Makes:** 8 servings

- 1 can (14½ oz.) diced tomatoes, undrained
- 1 cup water
- 3 Tbsp. quick-cooking tapioca
- 2 tsp. sugar
- 1½ tsp. salt
- ½ tsp. pepper
- 2 lbs. beef stew meat, cut into 1-in. cubes
- 4 medium carrots, cut into 1-in. chunks
- 3 medium potatoes, peeled and quartered
- 2 celery ribs, cut into ¾-in. chunks
- 1 medium onion, cut into chunks
- 1 slice bread, cubed

**1.** Preheat oven to 375°. In a large bowl, combine the tomatoes, water, tapioca, sugar, salt and pepper. Stir in the remaining ingredients.
**2.** Pour into a greased 13x9-in. or 3-qt. baking dish. Cover and bake for 1¾-2 hours or until the meat and vegetables are tender. Serve in bowls.
**1 cup:** 300 cal., 8g fat (3g sat. fat), 70mg chol., 628mg sod., 31g carb. (7g sugars, 4g fiber), 25g pro.
**Diabetic exchanges:** 3 lean meat, 2 starch.

MY BRAZILIAN
FEIJOADA

HEARTY BAKED
BEEF STEW

## My Brazilian Feijoada

A co-worker's mom used to make this dish for him and it was his favorite. So I made him my own version. It's an adaptable recipe—instead of sausage you can use ham hocks, or substitute lean white meat for the red meat.
—*Christiane Counts, Webster, TX*

**Prep:** 20 min. + soaking
**Cook:** 7 hours • **Makes:** 10 servings

- 8 **oz. dried black beans (about 1 cup)**
- 2 **lbs. boneless pork shoulder butt roast, trimmed and cut into 1-in. cubes**
- 3 **bone-in beef short ribs (about 1½ lbs.)**
- 4 **bacon strips, cooked and crumbled**
- 1¼ **cups diced onion**
- 3 **garlic cloves, minced**
- 1 **bay leaf**
- ¾ **tsp. salt**
- ¾ **tsp. pepper**
- 1½ **cups chicken broth**
- 1 **cup water**
- ½ **cup beef broth**
- 8 **oz. smoked sausage, cut into ½-in. slices**
  **Orange sections**
  **Hot cooked rice, optional**

**1.** Rinse and sort black beans; soak according to package directions. Meanwhile, place pork roast, short ribs and bacon in a 6-qt. slow cooker. Add diced onion, garlic, bay leaf and seasonings; pour chicken broth, water and beef broth over meat. Cook, covered, on high 2 hours.
**2.** Stir in beans and sausage. Cook, covered, on low 5-6 hours, until meat and beans are tender.
**3.** Discard bay leaf. Remove short ribs. When cool enough to handle, remove meat from bones; discard bones. Shred the meat with 2 forks; return to slow cooker. Top servings with orange sections. If desired, serve with hot cooked rice.
**1 serving:** 481 cal., 27g fat (11g sat. fat), 123mg chol., 772mg sod., 17g carb. (2g sugars, 4g fiber), 41g pro.

**TERIYAKI BEEF STEW**

## Caribbean Chicken Stew

I lived with a West Indian family for a while and enjoyed watching them cook. I lightened up this recipe by leaving out the cooking oil and sugar, removing the skin from the chicken and using chicken sausage.
—*Joanne Lovino, Kings Park, NY*

**Prep:** 25 min. + marinating
**Cook:** 6 hours • **Makes:** 8 servings

- ¼ cup ketchup
- 3 garlic cloves, minced
- 1 Tbsp. sugar
- 1 Tbsp. hot pepper sauce
- 1 tsp. browning sauce, optional
- 1 tsp. dried basil
- 1 tsp. dried thyme
- 1 tsp. paprika
- ½ tsp. salt
- ½ tsp. dried oregano
- ½ tsp. ground allspice
- ½ tsp. pepper
- 8 bone-in chicken thighs (about 3 lbs.), skin removed
- 1 lb. fully cooked andouille chicken sausage links, sliced
- 1 medium onion, finely chopped
- 2 medium carrots, finely chopped
- 2 celery ribs, finely chopped

**1.** In a bowl, combine ketchup, garlic, sugar, pepper sauce and, if desired, browning sauce; stir in seasonings. Add chicken thighs, sausage and vegetables. Cover; refrigerate for 8 hours or overnight.
**2.** Transfer chicken mixture to a 4- or 5-qt. slow cooker. Cook, covered, on low 6-8 hours, until chicken is tender.

**1 serving:** 309 cal., 14g fat (4g sat. fat), 131mg chol., 666mg sod., 9g carb. (6g sugars, 1g fiber), 35g pro.
**Diabetic exchanges:** 5 lean meat, ½ starch.

## Teriyaki Beef Stew

In the spirit of the saying "necessity is the mother of invention," I created this sweet-tangy beef recipe because I had a package of stew meat that needed to be used. After I spotted ginger beer in the fridge, the rest was history! It's nice to have a new way to serve an affordable cut of meat.
—*Leslie Simms, Sherman Oaks, CA*

**Prep:** 20 min. • **Cook:** 6½ hours
**Makes:** 8 servings

- 2 lbs. beef stew meat
- 1 bottle (12 oz.) ginger beer or ginger ale
- ¼ cup teriyaki sauce
- 2 garlic cloves, minced
- 2 Tbsp. sesame seeds
- 2 Tbsp. cornstarch
- 2 Tbsp. cold water
- 2 cups frozen peas, thawed
  Hot cooked rice, optional

**1.** In a large nonstick skillet, brown beef in batches. Transfer to a 3-qt. slow cooker.
**2.** In a small bowl, combine ginger beer, teriyaki sauce, minced garlic and sesame seeds; pour over the beef. Cover and cook on low for 6-8 hours or until meat is tender.
**3.** Combine cornstarch and cold water until smooth; gradually stir into the stew. Stir in peas. Cover and cook on high for 30 minutes or until thickened. Serve with rice if desired.

**1 cup stew:** 310 cal., 12g fat (4g sat. fat), 94mg chol., 528mg sod., 17g carb. (9g sugars, 2g fiber), 33g pro.
**Diabetic exchanges:** 4 lean meat, 1 starch.

CARIBBEAN
CHICKEN STEW

## Shipwreck Stew

I got this recipe from a minister's wife, and I imagine she used it many times at church meetings and gatherings. It is an inexpensive, stick-to-the-ribs dinner, and is even better the next day! It's also extremely easy to make.
—Estelle Bates, Fallbrook, CA

**Prep:** 20 min. • **Bake:** 1 hour
**Makes:** 10 servings

- 1  lb. ground beef
- 1  cup chopped onion
- 3  cups cubed peeled potatoes
- 3  medium carrots, peeled and sliced
- 1  cup chopped celery
- ¼  cup minced fresh parsley
- 1  pkg. (9 oz.) frozen cut green beans, thawed
- 1  can (16 oz.) kidney beans, rinsed and drained
- 1  can (8 oz.) tomato sauce
- ¼  cup uncooked long-grain rice
- 1  tsp. salt
- 1  tsp. Worcestershire sauce
- ½  to 1 tsp. chili powder
- ¼  tsp. ground pepper
- 1  cup water

**1.** Preheat oven to 350°. In a large skillet, cook beef and onion over medium heat until the meat is no longer pink; drain.
**2.** In a 3-qt. baking dish, combine the beef mixture with the remaining ingredients. Cover and bake for about 1 hour or until the rice and potatoes are tender.
**1 cup:** 204 cal., 4g fat, 32mg chol., 390mg sod., 28g carb., 15g pro.
**Diabetic exchanges:** 1½ starch, 1½ lean meat, 1 vegetable.

## Squash & Lentil Lamb Stew

My family lived in New Zealand many years ago. Every Sunday my mother made a lamb stew—it was Dad's favorite! I changed the recipe to suit my family's more modern palates, but it seems just as exotic and delicious.
—Nancy Heishman, Las Vegas, NV

**Prep:** 30 min. • **Cook:** 6 hours
**Makes:** 8 servings

- 1  can (13.66 oz.) coconut milk
- ½  cup creamy peanut butter
- 2  Tbsp. red curry paste
- 1  Tbsp. hoisin sauce
- 1  tsp. salt
- ½  tsp. pepper
- 1  can (14½ oz.) chicken broth
- 3  tsp. olive oil, divided
- 1  lb. lamb or beef stew meat (1½ in. pieces)
- 2  small onions, chopped
- 1  Tbsp. minced fresh gingerroot
- 3  garlic cloves, minced
- 1  cup dried brown lentils, rinsed
- 4  cups cubed peeled butternut squash (about 1 lb.)
- 2  cups chopped fresh spinach
- ¼  cup minced fresh cilantro
- ¼  cup lime juice

**1.** In a 5- or 6-qt. slow cooker, whisk together the first 7 ingredients.
**2.** In a large skillet, heat 2 tsp. oil over medium heat; brown lamb in batches. Add to slow cooker.
**3.** In same skillet, saute onions in the remaining oil over medium heat until tender, 4-5 minutes. Add ginger and garlic; cook and stir 1 minute. Add to slow cooker. Stir in lentils and squash.
**4.** Cook, covered, on low 6-8 hours, until meat and lentils are tender. Stir in spinach until wilted. Stir in cilantro and lime juice.
**1¼ cups:** 411 cal., 21g fat (11g sat. fat), 38mg chol., 777mg sod., 34g carb. (7g sugars, 6g fiber), 23g pro.

SQUASH & LENTIL LAMB STEW

STOVETOP
ROOT VEGETABLE
BEEF STEW

## Hearty Hunter's Stew

Tender meat and thick, rich gravy are the hallmarks of my rustic stew. This is winter comfort at its finest.
—*Joyce Worsech, Catawba, WI*

**Prep:** 25 min. • **Cook:** 2 hours 50 min.
**Makes:** 8 servings

- 2   lbs. boneless venison or beef chuck roast, cut in 1-in. cubes
- 2   Tbsp. canola oil
- 4¼  cups water, divided
- ½   cup tomato juice
- 2   medium onions, cut in wedges
- 2   celery ribs, sliced
- 1   tsp. Worcestershire sauce
- 2   bay leaves
- 2   to 3 tsp. salt
- ½   tsp. pepper
- 6   medium carrots, quartered
- 1   large rutabaga, peeled and cubed
- 6   medium potatoes, peeled and quartered
- 1   cup frozen peas
- 1   Tbsp. cornstarch

**1.** In a Dutch oven, brown meat in oil over medium heat. Add 4 cups water and scrape to loosen any browned drippings from pan.
**2.** Add the tomato juice, onions, celery, Worcestershire sauce, bay leaves, salt and pepper. Bring to a boil. Reduce heat; cover and cook for 2 hours, stirring occasionally.
**3.** Discard bay leaves; add the carrots, rutabaga and potatoes. Cover and cook for 40-60 minutes.
**4.** Stir in the peas; cook 10 minutes. Combine cornstarch and remaining water until smooth; stir into stew. Bring to a boil. Cook and stir for 2 minutes or until thickened.
**1 cup:** 351 cal., 7g fat (2g sat. fat), 96mg chol., 778mg sod., 42g carb. (14g sugars, 7g fiber), 31g pro.

## Stovetop Root Vegetable Beef Stew

To me, the definition of cozy is a pot of tender beef simmering with sweet potatoes and parsnips. It doesn't get better than that.
—*Beth Rossos, Estacada, OR*

**Prep:** 30 min. • **Cook:** 1¾ hours
**Makes:** 8 servings

- ⅔   cup all-purpose flour
- 1½  tsp. salt, divided
- 1¼  tsp. pepper, divided
- 2   lbs. beef stew meat
- 2-4 Tbsp. olive oil, divided
- ⅔   cup Burgundy wine
- 3   cups water
- 1   can (14½ oz.) stewed tomatoes
- 2   garlic cloves, minced
- 2   tsp. beef base
- ¼   tsp. dried thyme
- ¼   tsp. ground cinnamon
- ¼   tsp. crushed red pepper flakes
- 1   large sweet potato (about 1 lb.), peeled and coarsely chopped
- 2   medium carrots, coarsely chopped
- 1   medium onion, chopped
- 1   medium parsnip, peeled and coarsely chopped
     Sliced green onions, optional

**1.** In a shallow bowl, mix flour and 1 tsp. each salt and pepper. Add beef, a few pieces at a time, and toss to coat; shake off excess.
**2.** In a Dutch oven, heat 2 Tbsp. oil over medium heat. Brown beef in batches, adding additional oil as necessary. Remove the beef with a slotted spoon. Add wine, stirring to loosen browned bits from pan.
**3.** Return beef to pan. Add water, tomatoes, garlic, beef base, thyme, cinnamon, pepper flakes and the remaining salt and pepper; bring to a boil. Reduce heat; simmer, covered, 1¼ hours, stirring halfway through cooking time.
**4.** Stir in sweet potato, carrots, onion and parsnip. Cook, covered, 30-45 minutes longer or until beef and vegetables are tender. If desired, sprinkle with green onions.
**1 cup:** 344 cal., 15g fat (4g sat. fat), 71mg chol., 696mg sod., 27g carb. (9g sugars, 3g fiber), 25g pro.

WINTERTIME
BRAISED
BEEF STEW

HAM & BEAN
STEW

## Wintertime Braised Beef Stew

This wonderful beef stew makes an easy Sunday meal. It's even better a day or two later, so we always make a double batch for leftovers.
—*Michaela Rosenthal, Woodland Hills, CA*

**Prep:** 40 min. • **Bake:** 2 hours
**Makes:** 8 servings

- 2 lbs. boneless beef sirloin steak or chuck roast, cut into 1-in. pieces
- 2 Tbsp. all-purpose flour
- 2 tsp. Montreal steak seasoning
- 2 Tbsp. olive oil, divided
- 1 large onion, chopped
- 2 celery ribs, chopped
- 2 medium parsnips, peeled and cut into 1½-in. pieces
- 2 medium carrots, peeled and cut into 1½-in. pieces
- 2 garlic cloves, minced
- 1 can (14½ oz.) diced tomatoes, undrained
- 1 cup dry red wine or reduced-sodium beef broth
- 2 Tbsp. red currant jelly
- 2 bay leaves
- 2 fresh oregano sprigs
- 1 can (15 oz.) cannellini beans, rinsed and drained
  Minced fresh parsley, optional

**1.** Preheat oven to 350°. Toss beef with flour and steak seasoning.
**2.** In an ovenproof Dutch oven, heat 1 Tbsp. oil over medium heat. Brown the beef in batches; remove with a slotted spoon.
**3.** In same pot, heat the remaining oil over medium heat. Add onion, celery, parsnips and carrots; cook and stir until onion is tender. Add minced garlic; cook 1 minute longer. Stir in tomatoes, wine, jelly, bay leaves, oregano and beef; bring to a boil.
**4.** Bake, covered, 1½ hours. Stir in beans; bake, covered, 30-40 minutes longer or until beef and vegetables are tender. Remove bay leaves and oregano sprigs. If desired, sprinkle with parsley.
**1 cup:** 310 cal., 9g fat (3g sat. fat), 64mg chol., 373mg sod., 26g carb. (8g sugars, 5g fiber), 25g pro.
**Diabetic exchanges:** 3 lean meat, 1 starch, 1 vegetable, 1 fat.

## Ham & Bean Stew

You only need five ingredients to fix this thick and flavorful stew. It's so easy to make and always a favorite with my family. I top bowls with a sprinkling of shredded cheese.
—*Teresa D'Amato, East Granby, CT*

- - - - - - - - - - - - - - - - - - - - - - - - - - - - - - -

**Prep:** 5 min. • **Cook:** 7 hours
**Makes:** 6 servings

- 2 cans (16 oz. each) baked beans
- 2 medium potatoes, peeled and cubed
- 2 cups cubed fully cooked ham
- 1 celery rib, chopped
- ½ cup water

In a 3-qt. slow cooker, combine all ingredients; mix well. Cover and cook on low for 7 hours or until potatoes are tender.

**1 cup:** 213 cal., 5g fat (2g sat. fat), 30mg chol., 919mg sod., 29g carb. (6g sugars, 5g fiber), 14g pro.

 **TIP**

Feel free to experiment with this stew—try a smoked pork chop instead of ham, different flavors of baked beans, or a sprinkling of cheese on top.

# Recipe Index